LESSONS IN GRATITUDE

CAMPUS VOICES

STORIES OF EXCELLENCE FROM THE UNIVERSITY OF MICHIGAN

Books in the Series

Lessons in Gratitude: A Memoir on Race, the Arts, and Mental Health
  by Aaron P. Dworkin

A Passion for Cooperation: Adventures of a Wide-Ranging Scientist
  by Robert Axelrod

LESSONS IN
GRATITUDE

A Memoir on Race, the Arts, and Mental Health

by Aaron P. Dworkin

University of Michigan Press
Ann Arbor

For questions or permissions, please contact um.press.perms@umich.edu

Published in the United States of America by the
University of Michigan Press
Manufactured in the United States of America
Printed on acid-free paper
First published August 2024

A CIP catalog record for this book is available from the British Library.

Library of Congress Cataloging-in-Publication data has been applied for.

ISBN 978-0-472-07699-4 (hardcover : alk. paper)
ISBN 978-0-472-05699-6 (paper : alk. paper)
ISBN 978-0-472-90476-1 (open access ebook)
ISBN 978-0-472-00576-5 (audiobook)

DOI: https://doi.org/10.3998/mpub.12819261

The University of Michigan Press's open access publishing program is made possible
thanks to additional funding from the University of Michigan Office of the Provost and
the generous support of contributing libraries.

For Amani, Noah and Afa

There is no destination
For the leisurely words
I have to offer
Without the love
I have of you
Enveloping them
With meaning.

CONTENTS

PROLOGUE

You can't know me until you know my story. I am the outcome of multiple circumstances and events, significant and not so significant. Decisions and non-decisions made by others as well as by me, influenced the person I am today and the person I am becoming. Being a biracial adopted child, I have experienced the heartache and pride of difference. I know the frustrations and anger of being judged not for my own accomplishments and failures but for the color of my skin. I have battled the depths of depression and loneliness, struggling to understand "Why me?"

Through a combination of talent, persistence, and good fortune, including the intervention by good people—White and Black—I have achieved a moderate degree of success and happiness. More importantly, I've grown comfortable in my own skin; I am proud to be different without having to belittle or malign others to feel valued.

My struggles are not uncommon. Each year, more than 100,000 children are adopted in the United States. Approximately 40% of adoptions are transracial, meaning the child is of a different race than its adoptive parents. The number of multiracial children has grown steadily since miscegenation laws were ruled unconstitutional by the Supreme Court in 1967. According to 2020 Census figures, the multiracial population in the United States now exceeds 33 million. We share the sin of being different and the yearning that people will look past the obvious to the values of our character and heart.

I write my story for those still caught in the deep, dark chasms between cultures, being part of each side and rejected by each. Despite the seemingly insurmountable obstacles, there is a time coming with blue skies and green fields, in which the person in the mirror smiles back. I know because I've traveled that path.

PART I

PART I

CHAPTER 1

THE BEGINNING

"'Tis education forms the common mind, Just as the twig is bent the tree's inclined."

    —ALEXANDER POPE, *EPISTLES TO SEVERAL PERSONS*

I was born during the most beautiful time of year, the fall—a time of marvelous contradictions. Just as the foliage in the northern mountains of New York reaches their brilliant peak, they begin their colorful yet silent descent to the ground. Likewise, my birth mother brought me into this world, only to give me away. With this relationship ending the moment it began, I was thus placed on a path filled with duality and caprice that took decades of introspection to understand. This path would ultimately lead to forgiveness, redemption, and a role in society for me beyond imagination.

September 11, 1970, was an exciting day and year on which I was born. Unlike people who proudly recite their genealogy when asked about their backgrounds, I must sample from my source: a one-and-a-quarter-page letter from my adoption agency stating:

> Birth mother was 20 years old, single, and Catholic. She is of Irish, English, and Scotch background. She was a high school graduate who was attending college. Birth father was a 21-year-old dark-skinned black man. He was a high school graduate who worked as a supervisor at a training school. They met in high school and dated sporadically against the wishes of their maternal grandparents.

The agency's freewheeling use of the past tense in their description—
she was 20, is Irish, etc.—and their intentional vagueness frustrated me
for years as I searched for an understanding of myself. Who were the people described in the report? Were they real or simply a composite of stereotypes to explain babies of mixed heritage? I did not know.

Despite the progress of civil rights leaders—Black and White—to break
down historical barriers of legal racism during the 1960s, vast portions
of the country remained racist, a combination of ignorance and apathy.
Consequently, Black male babies, whether of two Black parents or mixed
race, are the least likely to be chosen by adoptive parents, more likely to
be consigned to a revolving set of custodial and foster homes until aging
out of the system. So, there I was, a definably biracial baby born into the
transient world of 1970, with a life of foster care and identity crisis laid
out in front of me: an endless, barren landscape.

What transpired from that point was a repeating pattern of unique
occurrences that have affixed my life to an unpredictable roller coaster
ride from which I fear to stray even to this day. At the age of two weeks, I
was adopted by a White Jewish couple and their three-year-old son in a
process not unlike choosing a puppy from the local animal shelter. Barry
and Susan Dworkin, with their three-year-old son, Jonathan, visited a
small New Jersey clinic to look me over. After spending a short time playing with me, they said, "He seems great. We'll take him." Then, like an
item purchased from a shopping network that looks great on TV until
you get it home . . . I was off to a new life.

Adoptions peaked in 1970 at 175,000, though approximately half
occurred within family members. According to data collected by the Boys
& Girls Aid Society of Oregon, 6,474 Black children were adopted across
the United States that year, one-third by White families. The same source
suggests I was one of the 79 Black children adopted by a White family
that year in New Jersey.

I wondered for years later about the motives that led the Dworkins
to adopt a child, especially one who differed so much from them. What
did they expect from me? Those questions were never wholly answered.

Were their actions due to White guilt? Did they want to be rescuing
a minority child from a future of poverty, ignorance, and crime? Maybe,
both. Young people in the 1960s rebelled against the establishment in

their choice of lifestyles, music, dress, and other social norms previously considered sacrosanct. Few acts were accorded the cachet in an increasingly liberal nation as the presence of a Black child in a White family.

Was their motive scientific curiosity, a personal experiment to test George Bernard Shaw's theme in *Pygmalion*? Would they someday paraphrase Higgins's bet "You see this creature with her curbstone English . . . In three months, I could pass that girl off as a duchess at an ambassador's garden party."? As behavioral scientists, what would be better to prove the dominant influence of nature versus nurture than the ability to control a test subject every waking hour.

Did they want a loving brother for their three-year-old son? This answer presupposes that they were unable to conceive a second time or discovered that their natural child had inherited a genetic disorder that might also appear in a second birth. In my adoptive parents' case, I am unaware of either possibility. My adoptive parents had brothers and sisters; my adopted brother has two children of his own today.

I may never learn the reasons for my adoption. However, I know I was blessed to be part of a family that provided a future I might not have otherwise discovered. Most people, I suspect, adopt for the right reasons. They feel a hole in their heart and life that can only be filled with a child. I believe that my mother chose me with the best intentions, persuading my father to accept me, even if just to please his wife. I doubt my brother, then aged three years, had any impact on their decision. At best, I was his new plaything.

Nevertheless, the stage was set for an adolescence of confusion and schism as a biracial child with White parents and a White brother, though at the time, each surely believed the future would be bright. And so, the Dworkins drove their new son home across the George Washington Bridge, down Riverside Drive, past Grant's Tomb, and through Central Park, its ticker-tape parade of maple, sweetgum, and ash trees standing at attention, their red, purple, and yellow leaves floating brightly on the macadam byways, a last gesture of goodwill as the season came to an end.

The Dworkins lived right in the heart of Manhattan, 66th Street and York Avenue, in the section of the city called Lenox Hill. My father, Barry, worked as a behavioral scientist at Rockefeller University, one of the nation's premier graduate schools and research centers. The successor to the prestigious Rockefeller Institute, the sixteen-acre tree-lined campus with broad walkways and bike paths borders the East River and abuts the Memorial Sloan Kettering Cancer Center on its north end.

When I was older, my best friend Leslie and I (sometimes, with my brother) hopped across York Avenue to the Rockefeller University grounds. Leslie's dad ran a classical music recital series at the University. The concerts were held at the blue dome structure, immediately visible anywhere on campus. Its lower level contained a strange exhibit, which I often visited, exploring the sculptures and visual art, then hearing the recitals. As I understood, her dad ran various special events in that building. The guards, all of whom knew us, would let us in, and we would play basketball on one of the outdoor courts.

Our home was a combination of two small apartments on the fourth floor of one of the century-old five- and six-storied buildings on East 66th Street, most of which did not have elevators or central air conditioning. Despite their limited income, my parents were able to afford to rent the adjoining apartment and knocked down the wall between them to provide more space. Apartment 5H disappeared, Apartment 4G led to 6F, the residence of Leslie and her family. They had a "normal" apartment, unlike ours. With a couple of conventional bedrooms and a small general area.

My parents were behavioral scientists at their core, consummate academics who believed explicitly in dispassionate observation and the link between cause and effect. My father and mother suffered from the arrogance of education, certain that their superior knowledge gave them a unique authority to judge the people and culture around us. Perhaps that sense of preeminence limited their need for social connection; I can remember few times in my early years that my parents invited guests to our home or visited other people, with rare exceptions for family. Even those occasions seemed impassive, without a memorable sense of personal connection.

Aside from an occasional gesture from my mother—a smile, a pat on the head, a nod that showed me she was listening—my adopted family was generally aloof from each other and other people around them. A stranger, if kind, might think them reserved. A harsher description would be "cold." Whether my parents' demeanor was hereditary or adopted in the pursuit of their careers, I don't know. I suppose that the study and practice of science promotes detachment and stoicism, qualities that are esteemed in a laboratory but problematic for an adopted biracial child trying to find his place.

While Jewish, neither of my parents were religious. We never attended Temple or regularly observed religious holidays, whether Jewish or otherwise. I cannot recall a single birthday party for any member of the family, and the idea of a gift being anything other than a reward for meeting their expectations was unthinkable. In those early years, I did not consider the lack of ritualistic celebration unusual.

Their parenting reflected their belief that one should not spend time in life doing things that do not further one's knowledge, awareness, or proficiency in a skill. The idea of play for pleasure was nonsensical. In their minds, idle time was wasteful and something certainly not to be condoned. A corollary of Barry and Susan Dworkin's clinical approach to life was reflected in their practice of conditional love, valuing a child for what they do, not who they are.

I have few memories of my early years. One of my first had a life-long effect on my nature and emotional development. Around the age of three, my adoptive mother, Susan, started playing the violin. She said that spark was ignited within her when she heard a recording of Nathan Milstein performing Bach's Sonatas and Partitas for Solo Violin. However, she didn't really "get into it" until I began playing.

In many ways, my mother was not only my angel in that she pushed for my adoption, but she was a physical angel, as well. Susan Dworkin was tall and strikingly beautiful, extraordinarily fit and thin, with long hair flowing down to her waist (she would later wear it cropped, à la Grace Jones). As I watched her draw the hairs of her bow across the strings . . . there were no words to express the full sense of what happened to me at that moment. I can share, however, how the cascading chord progressions of Milstein's interpretation of Bach brought about a sense of dance within my young body.

I yearned to be able to speak in the voice of the violin. The music resonated deep within my soul, stirring a sense of beauty and connection with my adoptive mother and the world. I cried when I heard her play, loving how the violin made me feel. Hearing her made me want the power to affect my own feelings—as well as the feelings of others—made possible by the mastery of that strange combination of burnished wood, magical strings, and flying bow.

At age five, I began to study, discovering a voracious appetite for mastery of this difficult instrument. As I look back, strangely enough, I do not recall a time when I was uncomfortable with the violin. It was truly molded into my being before I was even aware of my whole physical self, particularly my gender and race. I think for this reason, I have always been comfortable telling people that my identity as the adopted Aaron carries certain philosophical perspectives, moral guidance, and personal passions, foremost amongst them the love of the violin. Beyond Aaron, I am Black, and that suggests certain definitions whose origins should become clearer along the varied paths of this book. I am also male, which also carries its own unique definition. Beyond that, I am American, human, and a host of other labels through which each of us chooses to define ourselves to others as much as to ourselves.

My plunge into the world of classical music shaped a key aspect of my identity. It was the focus of my first decade of life. My first teacher was Vladimir Graffman, a Russian Jewish immigrant, who was an incredible pedagogue. His roster of students included Josef Gingold, along with a host of other notable icons in the classical music world. I was completely unaware of the prestige of these individuals and their contributions, for I was too young to understand. Nevertheless, I progressed quickly with the violin, exhibiting what some referred to as a "unique" talent.

Mr. Graffman was in his 70s, the oldest person I knew at that time. He had a wrinkled face and kept hard candy in a dish on a side table, my prize for a great lesson. His stature and physical height were not much greater than mine; however, even when he was seated, I felt like I was looking up to him. I saw him as a master who could impart greatness upon me.

One day a week, I would take a long walk up to the 92nd Street Young Men's Hebrew Association or to Mr. Graffman's apartment on East 85th for my lessons. My mother usually accompanied me, waited while I learned, and returned with me home. Sometime between the ages of seven and eight, I began to make the trip alone.

Mr. Graffman's lessons were quite fun. I loved playing the violin for him and I liked his strictness. "You no talk, you play" was what he said when I offered excuses for my delivery of a piece that was insufficiently prepared, or when I asked too many questions. Like many inquisitive children, I asked "Why?" all the time.

One of the most notable times during my childhood was when Mr. Graffman died, though my studies continued under the tutelage of several other teachers. One might find my use of the word "notable" to be odd, in place of a more conventional "sad," "terrible" or "frightening." His death was the first one I encountered, and I was unable to fully comprehend the finality of the process. When I came to realize what had really happened months later, the space separating me from the event seemed like several lifetimes, inhibiting my feelings to feel true "sorrow." To this day, I wish I could have grieved better; it was what he deserved.

I missed him intensely, especially the musical impact that he had upon me. To this day, I have never quite felt the same energy and passion from any of my subsequent teachers. Possibly due to my young age, I could feel Mr. Graffman's love for the violin, infusing me with his passion for the music. With his loss, I had to find that passion from within. While some might consider the latter core to a musician, sharing that rich, vibrant energy with someone else intensified one's own pleasure. Without Mr. Graffman, my feelings of loneliness and loss seemed to escalate in the monotony and rigidity of my home.

My only friend before starting school was my neighbor Leslie, literally "the girl next door." She was the only human being I'd call a true friend back then. Leslie had a doll house, and I have clear memories of playing together in her room. She had the Russian oval-shaped Matryoshka dolls, a series of sizes so that each doll rested in the next largest one. I remember the bright colors of those dolls, stacking them together endlessly, and I loved playing with her doll house.

Leslie had a big collection of original Tintin and Asterix comics purchased by her parents in France. Tintin was a detective with a couple of sidekick policemen in bowler hats who followed him around as he solved mysteries around the world. Asterix was a little guy who had a big friend named Obelix. The two of them tackled various Roman Generals and the like. I remember sitting and reading Tintin and Asterix, and sometimes I would even get to borrow them. Until recent years, I kept some in my closet and read them from time to time.

Since playing was a waste of potentially productive time, I had few toys to occupy my imagination. My collection amounted to a single drawer of red, white, and blue Legos and five Matchbox cars. My pleas for different colored Legos such as black ones were met with, "Why do you need those? You already have white, blue and red ones." When I asked for more cars, I was told, "You don't need that many cars, you've got the Legos. You should build houses and other different things with your Legos. You have a couple of cars to drive through them, but you just don't need that many."

They never considered why I needed more cars. At least ten or twenty, maybe even thirty. One cannot build and operate a small Lego town with five cars. Five cars just didn't cut it for a whole town. For a kid with my imagination being limited in such a way while building a minor civilization was completely unacceptable. I needed the cars to build tomorrow's world in my little playroom, but my wishes were ignored "for my own good."

Between the ages of six and when we moved to Hershey, Pennsylvania, weekdays were a series of scheduled events, each day identical to the day before. They began with waking up, having breakfast, going to school at PS 183 across the street, leaving school for a quick lunch and practice at home, returning to school, and rushing home to avoid being caught by the chasing bullies. I suppose I was an irresistible target, a violin player with a huge Afro. It was as if I went up to them and said, "Hey, bully, take my lunch"—if I had one.

Arriving home out of breath, I turned to my music, practicing a series of scales, arpeggios, and trills before turning to the piece Mr. Graffman had assigned. Then I would have dinner—often chopped liver or lentil soup, presumably, for their nutritional value—before doing homework and going to bed.

My dread of Saturdays exceeded my weariness of the weekday routine. Growing up in a big city for most kids should mean looking forward to the weekend; no school meant having time to play or do nothing. Ironically, Saturdays before I started school were my favorites. It was the one time in the week that my father Barry spent time with me and seemed to enjoy it.

Each Saturday morning until the age of six, I rushed to curl up in my father's bed while he read *Tom Swift, Boy Adventurer* to me, and my mother jogged through the neighborhood, my brother in tow. I suppose the deliberate laziness became an indulgence that conflicted with their need for self-improvement. They became obsessed with walking. These were far from a normal leisurely fifteen-minute stroll around the neighborhood, perhaps accompanied by the family dog.

We had no dog, and our treks were epic journeys, mirroring Lewis and Clark's discovery of the West. We marched in all directions, to explore the different parts of the city—the Bowery, the Bronx, or Brooklyn. An excursion to Harlem meant walking from 66th Street up to 125th and far beyond. The walks were certainly among the most miserable, excruciating, depressing activities in my memories of childhood. I dreaded the walks so much that I tried everything to avoid them, including the feigning of deathly illness and dislocated limbs. Yet my attempts were to no avail; the forced marches were imposed despite my protests.

In the beginning, my parents tried positive reinforcement, coaxing me with an M&M for every successfully completed couple of blocks. However, as the walks became longer, their patience grew thinner, and the bribery discontinued. Commands replaced the M&Ms. One Olympic trial was the crossing of the Verrazano Bridge, when we nearly walked the New York Marathon route, so, three or four or more hours every Saturday were spent aimlessly wandering the New York metropolis, my parents ignoring my petulant distress. Years later, I would hesitate every time my wife suggested that we take a nice stroll, fearing it would end up in a lengthy sojourn in the neighboring town or state.

At about the same time, I joined my older brother Jonathan Emmanuel (Jon) for our weekly laundry chore. The two of us, pulling a wagon with baskets of dirty clothes, would trudge across York Street to the laundromat at Rockefeller University. In addition to the commercial, coin-operated washers and dryers, we discovered our first television set. At the time, we did not have a set in our apartment, our parents agreeing with the elitist view that the screen was a "vast wasteland" filled with "game shows, formula comedies about totally unbelievable families, blood and thunder, mayhem, violence, sadism, murder, western bad men, western good men, private eyes, gangsters, more violence, and cartoons. And endlessly, commercials—many screaming, cajoling, and offending."

The laundry's TV set was our secret. We quickly fell into a routine of putting the first load of clothes in the washer, rushing to Peppermint Park (the incredible ice cream store up on the corner at 66th Street) to get very special sundaes and hurrying back to eat the sundaes and watch The Little Rascals on the secondhand, scarified, yet very large color television set as our laundry continued to churn. As I recall, I didn't think about race viewing The Little Rascals; I didn't really think much about race until I moved to Hershey at age ten. I do remember Buckwheat and wondering why he talked like he did. At the time, I assumed that the poor grammar and exaggerated mispronunciations were meant to be comical, not a stereotype of a Black child. That was also the only explanation I had. All in all, doing laundry was something that I looked forward to every Saturday even as I anticipated the afternoon marathons.

The lack of toys and media access led to an insatiable appetite for books of all kinds. I read everything from Tom Swift and The Hardy Boys to Philip Roth and Roald Dahl's *Charlie and the Chocolate Factory*, *The Great Glass Elevator* and *James and the Giant Peach*, along with other fascinating stories which enraptured me when I was a child. I was also fascinated by Dahl's adult book series. I was able to run the entire gambit with love and passion for all books.

Aside from our weekly laundry trips, my brother and I shared little in common and infrequently spent time together voluntarily. Jon was three years older, very smart and expected by our parents to excel scholastically as they expected me to be a musical prodigy. When we lived in New York, he attended Hunter College Elementary School, a highly competitive, tuition-free school for the intellectually gifted. With different interests and ages, each of us preferred our own world. The absence of parental encouragement to form brotherly bonds and identify as a family unit aggravated our sense of separateness.

Regarding my violin playing, things seemed to be shaping up. I was working on a fair amount of relatively advanced repertoire for someone my age and practicing a minimum of three or four hours every day. Quickly advancing in my skill by the tutelage of Mr. Graffman and others, I was getting noticed. A brochure of the 92nd Street Y (where I would later give several recitals) featured me. When I performed under Mr. Graffman's tutelage, whether in a public concert or in his studio on 72nd Street for my parents or others, he pulled no punches. There were no hasty promotions and no sense of importance of building up my ego. His focus was similar to my parents—Did I play well or not? If I didn't, then Number 1: *No candy*. Number 2: I had to endure a critique—What did I do wrong? How did I prepare incorrectly or insufficiently? How could I do better next time? Literally, nothing else mattered. Even at that young age, when I thought I had a good explanation for a poor performance, he would interrupt me, shaking his head with the same curt instruction: "You no talk. You play."

Those words were probably the most important lesson Mr. Graffman ever taught me. One of my personal tenets is that "It's not what you say, but rather what you do." I cannot begin to count the stories of students, mentees, colleagues and even teachers of mine who talked a great game and wasted great spans of my time before I learned to look beyond empty promises and disappointing effort. Even now, I occasionally realize the truth too late to avoid a significant price of time, resource or belief in someone.

In certain ways, I think music and the way in which I experienced it through my violin was a minor detriment to the development of my technique. When I played, I inevitably found myself thinking of or imagining something specific. I rarely focused on the music alone. I did strive to learn the notes as quickly as possible to get past the "logistics" and reach the phase of exploring the feelings and emotions that I wanted to create in my mind. I suspect that this relationship with music in the early years developed my love for it. While I did not want to practice learning the notes, I always wanted to play as a means to escape. I closed my eyes and let the music take me on a journey to the wonderful, magical places that I created in my mind. I *loved* the violin.

Easily, one of the greatest moments of my years in New York City was the arrival of Nigel. Nigel was a beautiful black cat, a gift from my parents. Nigel became my best friend, keeping me company and listening not only to my endless hours of practicing, but also my woes, fears, and wild expectations of life. He soon began acting like a dog, coming when I called him and following me around. Without his comfort, I have no doubt that I might not have made it through some of the rough times that awaited me as adolescence approached. He was my best friend aside from Leslie.

Leslie . . . Where do I begin? Leslie was the most beautiful person I had known up to that point. She had incredibly long blonde hair that gently tumbled around her. Her hair was an extension of herself, integrated with her perfect body, almost as if it were a lioness's mane. I felt a sheer and simple joy every time I was in her presence. Leslie played the cello. She was the first person with whom I made music—we would play duets in the evenings and on the weekends.

When she played, her hair would come alive with her music; it seemed to strut and bow around her face, as if each strand had a role to play in the delicate melodies emanating from her instrument. Despite the many years that have since passed, I still have vivid recollections of sitting and looking up, either ready to give her a cue to come in or just connect with her through the music. I felt almost enveloped by her hair. I was not quite ten years old, so those feelings were not romantic. The best way that I can describe them now would simply be awe. Even more poignantly, I was eager to count her as a friend because I had few other friends at PS 183, my school across the street. As if her beauty was not enough, the dear friendship she offered was something I did not enjoy with others at the time and was not to find again for years to come.

One day, as we played on the Rockefeller basketball court, the rain began as mist, then a shower, and finally a torrent. We got utterly soaked. Realizing that we were soaked, we returned to her apartment on the sixth floor to dry off. My clothes dripped water, impervious to my efforts to wipe and blot the wet away. Leslie let me borrow some clothes, authoring a moment that, to this day, seems frozen in time.

My mind was blank, overwhelmed by a series of questions. Where *would* I change? Would we change in the same room? What does that mean? Where *should* I change? Was she going to change? It was one of the most frightening, yet exhilarating moments in my early years, where time suddenly became still. I got a feeling similar to the one I would get right before walking out on stage. Electricity shot through my body, and things seemed beyond my control. Such moments can shift time and etch an indelible imprint on one's mind and experiences, never to be forgotten. That was one of those moments.

Afterwards, there came clear memories of thinking about changing in her room with her while not really looking, turning away, yet imagining what she had looked like as she changed. Oddly, I have no real recollection as to whether we truly changed in the same room.

I suspect that I had such a vivid imagination in childhood because of my lack of access to television, movies, and other media outlets. I read all the time. I created detailed scenes in my mind that I can envision even to this day. I could go on infinitely in my mind, sitting for hours, entertaining myself, imagining. So, after I went back to my apartment to sit with Nigel and go over what had happened that day, I imagined that I was in the same room with Leslie. In the vision, I did turn ever so briefly to see her hair, a cocoon around her perfect body . . . Those observations were certainly strange, given my age. Yet it was somehow fulfilling. I was convinced that moment was the first time that I experienced romance.

One benefit of Saturday's mandatory patrols was the knowledge I gained of the city's avenues and streets. Manhattan is the most densely populated of the five New York City boroughs and probably the most diverse. Numbered streets run east and west, bisected by wide avenues. Irregularly shaped neighborhoods reflected the majority race and ethnicity of the residents, the whole blending into a kaleidoscope of color, language, and music unlike any other place in the world. I loved Manhattan.

Around the age of eight, my parents allowed me to visit places around the city on my own. Often during the summer, I made my way to the library and various music festivals in the local parks and nearby neighborhoods. I ventured as far as Lincoln Center, that magnificent complex of concert halls with musicians making beautiful music. I enjoyed the Mostly Mozart Festivals that took place, but what I really loved were the outdoor fairs, the booths with different foods and art. The fire-eaters, special plays and shows out on the courtyard were incredibly exciting to a young boy. A vivid memory of fire-eaters with their open shirts, as if one could see through their chests as they consumed fire, pops into my mind.

During those great days at the summer festivals, I often met adults and kids on my various adventures around the city. One time, I met several slightly older kids, also on their own. We walked around together, marveling at what we saw. After a while, one boy asked me, "Hey, man, have you ever seen the world's largest paper airplane? Do you want to see it?"

"Ain't no such thing, man," I said.

"Yea, we've all seen it! They keep it down in this empty subway tun-nel," he replied.

"No way!" I said again. "Why would anyone build a giant paper airplane?"

Laughing, the boy ignored my question. Others in the group, listen-ing to our conversation, began yelling, "Come on, it won't take long. You gotta see it. It's so cool!"

I gave in and followed them to a nearby subway station. I was still skeptical and a little worried as I followed them down the steps. We began to run. The one nearest me shouted, "Alright. Now, we gotta jump the turnstiles, and then we'll head down the tunnel."

I had never tried to sneak on the subway, even though I knew the guard sitting in the small cubicle at the end of the turnstiles was unlikely to chase an offender for a minor infraction that probably occurred hun-dreds of times each day. (For non-New Yorkers, jumping the turnstiles is an easy way to avoid paying to ride the subway.) The group made its way to the bottom of the steps and began to leap over the turnstiles, laughing and yelling, "Come on, come on! It's down here."

I thought I was ready when my heart leapt to my throat and terror struck every nerve of my body. I stopped and bolted back up the stairs out of the subway station, running home as fast as I could. I never told my parents, though they must have noticed my panting and wild eyes. For days afterward, my imagination took me back to that tunnel. What would have happened if I had jumped the turnstiles? Did they have ill will towards me? Would something terrible have happened to me down that tunnel? Was the world's largest paper airplane really there? I don't know to this day, but I've never seen any news about its existence.

Refusing to sanction purely recreational activities and making me practice hours on end every day, my parents also believed that one should not eat sweets, as they possessed little to no nutritional value. It would have been nice to have an occasional treat. Was that too much for a kid to ask? The lunches of the other kids in my class always had a dessert, a Swiss Roll or a Nutty Bar from Little Debbie. Why couldn't mine?

I had no money and never received an allowance, but I wanted candy in my lunch like the other kids. I wanted to add to my Matchbox car collection. I was too young to find a job and I had no time to work with my violin practice. The dilemma plagued me. Despite what I knew to be right, it drove me to do what, in retrospect, is one of the worst things I ever did in my childhood, the one I regret more than just about anything else.

My dad was the primary breadwinner of the family. Although I do not know what he earned, I suspect money was quite tight for the young professor and his family living in Manhattan. Perhaps to ensure we lived within our means, my mother paid cash for the necessities of life, such as the liver and the other "wonderful" things that I hated to eat.

Unlike most women, she did not carry a purse. She carried a backpack that included a removable section that functioned as a purse. It was connected to her backpack with a chain, so she could slide it in and out when needed.

Each week she gave my brother and me the money for laundry and ice cream treats. Every couple of weeks after cashing my father's paycheck, a huge wad of twenty-dollar bills filled the purse, more twenty-dollar bills than one could possibly imagine. Certainly, I thought, too many for anyone to count or even know what they had.

One day, my mom left her backpack on our dining room table, its wooden surface of etched car models scratched from wear. The little table sat against the wall in the tiny kitchen at one end of our apartment. I knew that Mom was somewhere in the back of the apartment, near the other end and would not be returning for a while. The backpack waited, a veritable treasure as inviting as the sirens of Odysseus.

I imagined how I might spend an unexpected $20; the sugar treats I could buy and enjoy unseen and unknown from my ever vigilant mother, the Matchbox cars of shiny colors and rubber wheels not yet bent in the pursuits of my imagination. The temptation was too much, the commission of the crime too easy.

Creeping to the kitchen, I realized that fate, luck, and opportunity had joined to welcome my good fortune. Mother had failed to place her purse in the backpack and close its Velcro-seamed sides! I knew instantly that the sound of ruptured Velcro no longer served as an alarm. I didn't have to peel back the Velcro, just carefully open two sets of snaps that protected the purse. I took my hands and, slowly pressing each side of the purse, unsnapped it in silence. My heart raced, feeling the same thrill as walking onstage to perform. I didn't think, I had come too far . . . I acted. As the purse opened, I saw a fat bundle of crisp, green $20 bills, more money than anyone could count. I grabbed one of the twenties and slid it into my pocket, then silently snapped the purse closed and put it back exactly where it had been.

I was in agony the rest of that day, certain that my mother knew what I had done. What would she say? How would my father react to the news that I was a thief? Would I go to jail? I wavered between confessing to my mother and reminding myself that I deserved the pleasures other kids seem to have without asking. The bill seemed to burn a hole in my pocket as I mentally repeated, "Don't even think about it, don't even think about it." It was all I could say to myself for the rest of the day. It was all I could think about that evening as I sat and ate my lentil soup. It was all I could think about as I practiced my violin and went to bed on the lower bunk of the bed that I shared with my brother.

The next morning, escaping from the scrutiny of my potential prose-cutors, I made a slight detour on my way to school. I bought five packages of Ding-Dongs at the corner newspaper stand, ate one and cached the others in my lunch bag, for once being able to show off my goodies to envious schoolmates. Better yet, I had received a huge amount of change, enough change, to get more than a few Matchbox cars after school, red, green, orange, cars of every color that were simply wonderful. Even so, I could not get all that I wanted. A twenty-dollar bill in New York City, even in 1978, could only get so many Little Debbie's and model cars. My money ran out.

There's something about crossing a line—once done, it is much easier to do again and again. No matter how hard it was the first time, the next time is always easier. Likewise, each additional time I stole twenties was easier than the last. I got away with it so many times, I figured my parents would never catch on.

The adventure continued for quite a while. I probably had more value in toys that were hidden from my parents than those purchased with their knowledge. However, like all childhood fantasies, this one, too, came to an end. Unfortunately, my memory of the outcome fails me; the memory of taking the first twenty, the first Matchbox cars and the Ding-Dongs is so vivid, but the end has become clouded by the veil of time. Whether my parents found the cars and the extra toys that I had hidden or whether they just noticed that the money was missing (I can only imagine they must have), they figured out something. My father's punishment was swift and brutal.

The method was simple. My parents did not do time-outs. I realize that those may not have existed back then (but I used them years later with my own sons). Simply put, there were certain "bad" things that I was punished for. If it was lying or stealing, I got a beating with a belt on the bare bottom. Anyone who has been subject to belt whipping knows that the first lashes are the most painful. By the third or fourth stroke, the buttocks become numb, saturated momentarily with pain. Barring the tearing of flesh, a whipping—if done quickly—is quickly over and bearable.

Whether or not it was the behavioral scientist in my dad with his theoretical calculations, he made sure that a beating was a terrible experience. He would not just beat me with the belt. He would time the strokes for maximum effect. My father would wait between strokes to let the cells and the flesh recuperate and rejuvenate so that when the beating resumed, the revived nerves would resend the message to my brain, "You were a bad, bad boy." Knowing his scientific mind, it wouldn't have surprised me to learn that he sat down and calculated the amount of time needed to maximize the pain of those beatings; for him, it would have been a chance to advance one's knowledge and awareness of the human body and the world in which we live.

When I was lucky, I could estimate the approximate number of strokes. For this one, the number was big, between fifteen and twenty strokes. They were slow and deliberate, but in the end, they did not outnumber the Ding-Dongs and Matchbox cars I had acquired.

Ironically, their years of training in behavioral science did them little good when it came to my desire for sweets. Those rules and restrictions led to my insatiable appetite for Ho-Hos. At times, it was other desserts like Little Debbie's, Ding-Dongs, and Ho-Hos. Twinkies—the puffy, orange-colored version with sprinkles—rivalled Ho-Hos for my attention whether squished down to a tiny little ball or just bitten into directly. They seemed to contain nothing but "air" and sugar, though I'm sure the recipe included other utterly frightening ingredients.

CHAPTER 2

VIOLIN AND MIDDLE PASSAGE

My early days in the double apartment also set the stage for the role of dreams in my life. In this case, not the actual dreams that one strives to achieve in life, like a successful career or family, but rather the dreams that provide a regular escape hatch from the fears, monotony, resentment, anxiety, or loneliness that life can all too often bring to an emerging human spirit. I began a routine that has stayed with me my entire life of architecting the trajectory of my dreams. When I laid down to go to sleep, I would ruminate on the troubles that had filled me with angst (usually related to my parents). I sought out an imagined refuge that would provide me with the freedom to unlink my soul from the pain. These began very simply with imagined amazing toys, idyllic deserted islands, fascinating foods, and intriguing people but quickly expanded in breadth to specific violin performances I would give, houses I would live in, places I would travel to, and other imaginary circumstances. The unique aspect and what invariably provided the pathway to unconsciousness and, ultimately, REM sleep was the micro perspective. I would go into extraordinary detail for each imagined scenario, down to the clothes I would be wearing, blemishes on walls, imperfections in people's faces, and nuances of sounds and colors. Ultimately, I was able to envelop myself in an alternate reality every night that provided an imaginary life, existing parallel to my "real" one. On occasion, when I created multi-episode storylines with my dreams, it became unclear to me which one was more real . . . and which one was more desired.

During that period of time, beyond stealing twenties, eating Ding-

Dongs, playing with Matchbox cars, or spending time with Leslie, I still had a desperate need for an outlet for the imagination that wove through my head. Music became that outlet, a channel through which to express inspirations that came from books that I read. In certain ways, I think music and the way in which I experienced it with my violin was a minor detriment to the development of my technique, although the latter soon began to grow rapidly, putting me ahead of the game. When I played, I inevitably found myself thinking of or imagining something specific. I rarely focused on the music alone. I did strive to learn the notes as quickly as possible in order to get past the "logistics" and reach the phase of exploring the feelings and emotions that I wanted to create in my mind. I suspect that this relationship with music in the early years enabled me to develop my love for it ultimately, and while I did not want to practice methodically, I always wanted to play as a means to escape. I closed my eyes and let the music take me on a journey to all of the places that I created in my mind. I *loved* the violin.

· · ·

Just before I turned ten, my parents made a decision that would change my life forever. Since this is a story about me, I feel justified to be egocentric and talk about the decision in that context, as opposed to what it may have meant for them or for my brother. We were living in New York, the Mecca of the United States, North America and the world. My father was offered a dream position for him and my mom to have their own lab at the Medical School for Penn State University, which, of all places, was located in Hershey, Pennsylvania. That's right, Chocolate Town, USA. The population of our surroundings went from millions in New York to tens of thousands in Hershey. Basically, the town of Hershey was comprised of the chocolate factory, its workers, and the Hershey Medical Center, which is the Medical School for Penn State, along with its employees. And that was the town of Hershey in 1980, when my parents decided to take a burgeoning young violinist trained by some of the best teachers in the world to a town with just a community orchestra.

I do not, nor did I ever, blame them for that decision. In retrospect, it obviously seemed to be the best move. Of course, the move to Hershey also affected my friendship with Leslie. When my parents finally told me that we were moving, it felt exciting. Moving to a house seemed so different than an apartment. I would have my own room! But I was losing Leslie—my best friend other than Nigel. At the time, that was my most serious challenge and my greatest fear. I was convinced I would never meet someone who would like me as much as she did.

When we first moved to Hershey, there were multiple items on our agenda. The first thing was to find a new teacher. They did not want me to fall behind. During a walk one night, they heard a violin being played. Yes, they still went on walks, but they were shorter. Thankfully, one simply could not go for long four or five-hour walks in Hershey because no matter which direction, all paths led to a cornfield. This was truly a grand bonus to my stay in Hershey.

My parents followed the sound of the violin down a street until they came to a house where the local violin teacher was playing. Although their immediate assessment was that this teacher might not be the best fit for me, he could at least give me the structure of lessons until we found somebody new. I started lessons in his home several blocks away in the same neighborhood in which we lived.

That lasted a few months until my parents found a teacher at a much higher level forty-five minutes away. Thus began the weekly hour-and-a-half journeys with my mom for my Tuesday lessons. With the violin dilemma solved the best it could be (for there certainly were no better teachers within a three-hundred-mile radius of Hershey), I was eventually able to serve as Concertmaster of the Hershey High School orchestra, as well as the Harrisburg Youth Symphony.

CHAPTER 3

CHOCOLATE CITY

"Your skin looks like this chocolate!" one white student said to a black student. "Are black people made of chocolate?" he asked. The child's tone of voice had a kind of playfulness and naiveté that is typical of young children, and so the question did not feel like a racial attack at the time, but I distinctly remember leaving class that day with the question, "What am I made of?"

   —LINCOLN A. HART, *THE CONSUMPTION OF BLACK BODIES AS CHOCOLATE*

For the first time in my life, I became aware of my blackness. Growing up in New York, we walked through diverse neighborhoods, not unlike my home, with White parents and a White brother. In school, I was surrounded by kids who were Black, Asian, and Hispanic. Hershey, in 1980, was predominately White. When I moved to Hershey, there was myself and one other Black family, the Waterfords.

During my first year in Hershey, I was still an elementary school student. Over the next six years, I learned about some early realities of "otherness," lessons that began in Mrs. Malone's fifth-grade class at Hershey Elementary School. On that occasion, she temporarily left the room. Immediately, bedlam began—some engaging in a frenzied spitball war with missiles of saliva-soaked scraps of Big Chief Tablet paper swooping through the air. In my defense, I was provoked into the fracas after ducking several squishy grenades tossed in my direction.

The battle was peaking when an angry Mrs. Malone strode into the room, her face contorted with indignation.

"You children have been ill-behaved and must be punished," she announced, pointing an extended index finger at those she believed to be the instigators of the affront against law and order. She marched seven of us, all boys, into the hall where we lined up against the corridor wall. Corporal punishment was still in practice at the time as parents abrogated their parental duties to official and semi-official representatives of the established social order.

We turned to face away, spreading our legs and bracing our outstretched arms against the wall. Starting at one end, Mrs. Malone went from one boy to the next, giving each three hard swats with a wooden paddle, especially made for that purpose. Her instrument of punishment was a two-foot length of one-inch board, beveled on one end to fit her hand and a series of small holes drilled in the other end to cut down the wind resistance to her swing.

When it came my turn, Mrs. Malone then leaned over and whispered in my ear, ever so softly but ever so menacingly, "I wish I could give you more, I really do. But I can't."

She swung, and the impact of each stroke on my jeans-clad bottom resounded in the hall. It hurt, but nothing like the precise lashes of my father's belt. I shuffled back into the room, almost chuckling to myself. She was an amateur. But the venom in her words stuck with me as a vivid memory that I will never forget. It was not the end of the discrimination I experienced, but a formidable beginning.

As the year passed, I made a few friends, mostly outcasts like me—a mixed-race, slightly plump violinist with a huge Afro and a funny name—trying to find some escape from loneliness among others considered odd and vulnerable. When Leslie and her family visited us that summer, it was wonderful. She still had the long, blonde hair, the same aura of goodness that brightened everything around her . . . if anything, time and distance had made her more beautiful.

After dinner, we walked alone through the neighborhood, strolling hand in hand until we reached the cornfield four or five blocks from our house. I thought about Hershey and the loneliness and isolation I felt with only Nigel seeming to understand my heartache. I had missed Leslie so much that I was certain that our relationship was beyond friendship. It had to be love, I was certain, a feeling unlike any.

"I love you," I suddenly blurted. "Will you go with me?"

She stared at me for a few seconds before shaking her head, "No."

I think she was wonderful and had fond memories of our childhood, but she had more sense than I did. Though we lived more than 150 miles apart and might never see each other again, our relationship had grown through trust, knowing that neither of us would lie to the other. I think she felt my pain, but she couldn't be false. She did not quite return my feelings.

I told her that I understood, but I didn't. I told her that things would be fine in Hershey, but they weren't. She knew. Her departure to New York the next day was filled with quiet sadness. This connection helped me begin defining the concept of love as a young person.

After we moved to Hershey, my brother and I began flying to California each summer to visit my grandmother on my mother's side. With Grandma Mona, summers were just incredible because they represented everything in my life that I missed or could not get at home.

Grandma Mona lived in a retirement community in Laguna Hills, a place called Leisure World. It was a perfect little village, a collection of four-story, white stucco buildings of apartments amid wide walkways, acres of green lawns, and trimmed flowerbeds that were always in bloom. Tall white walls protected the complex from the outside world; the only entrances were several large gates manned by uniformed security guards.

During our visits, usually one or two weeks, we had freedoms not allowed in Hershey. From 2:00 to 2:20 p.m. every day, we swam in one of five pools with other kids visiting residents. Older kids were not allowed during that time. I remember our adventures in the pool with great fondness.

Sometimes, we went to Laguna Beach where I tried to body surf on the big swells coming from the Baja channel. I liked swimming, but my favorite memories are of renting cowboy boots and horseback riding at the Equestrian Center. Every summer, I got the same horse—Sparky—and I loved riding him. He always galloped through the turn in the middle of the trail ride, but there was a gentle feel about him. He was never too fast and never left me at the back of the pack if we walked in a group.

At Grandma Mona's, we could watch TV. Not all the time, but we were able to watch a half-hour each day, sometimes up to an hour. We tried to never miss an episode of Starsky and Hutch or CHIPs. She also had different board games including Monopoly, my favorite. I pestered my brother Jon to play every day. I was consumed with the game, constantly proposing hypothetical property trades when we were together. Once in the swimming pool with other kids, Jon was horsing around with some girls and boys his age. I swam over and stood between him and the others, the water coming up to my shoulders as I bobbed up and down to keep my balance. I interrupted his conversation, intent on offering a property trade that I thought he could not resist.

"Hey, Jon, would you trade Boardwalk for Connecticut and Baltic Avenue?" I shouted.

The three of them just looked at me, no doubt wondering why I was bothering them. Jon looked at me, then at them, not saying anything. He suddenly reached out with both hands, grabbing my shoulders and pushed my head underwater. When I spluttered up, the three were swimming away, laughing.

Jon was, in many ways, a miniature, modernized version of my father—studious, serious, enthralled with science. Whenever I felt that I did not fit in socially, I thought of my brother—his physique, color, mannerisms and educational interests—all the things that proved he was my parents' blood, and I was not.

He was never really mean, at least no more than other older brothers stuck with a younger sibling by chance, not choice. Sadly, our different personalities would lead us down different paths, socially and professionally. But those summers with him at Grandma's home in California are some of my happiest memories from childhood.

Grandma usually baked cookies once or twice while we were there, something we never had at home in Hershey. She would wrap an apron around her waist and assemble her tools on the kitchen table—measuring cups and spoons, a big green mixing bowl, a rubber spatula, and two large cookie sheets. After she had the equipment needed to produce a superior cookie, she carefully collected the ingredients, always sacks of flour, sugar, dark brown sugar, vanilla extract, eggs, and sunflower oil. When she intended to make double chocolate chip cookies (my favorite), several packages of chocolate chips were within her reach.

As she sifted, then whisked the contents in the green bowl, I watched, sitting on one of the kitchen chairs, and listened to her stories of her childhood interspersed with hints on how to make the batter just right. She always doubled the recipe, empathizing with Jon's and my appetite for sweets (which were rare in our home). She then spooned and plopped little round balls of the sticky dough in evenly spaced rows on the cookie sheets and slid them into the waiting oven.

The rich aroma of baking chocolate would fill her little apartment, triggering my salivary glands in anticipation of the coming treat. Waiting for the cookies to cool before eating was an exquisite torture, a test of delayed gratification possible only because she protected her bounty, swatting eager trespassing hands with her wooden spoon until she deemed them ready to eat. She made chocolate, chocolate chip, and oatmeal cookies, each melting in your mouth with the sweetness of a grandmother's kiss.

My grandmother was a wonderful person. I did not fully appreciate all the interesting qualities of her character until later in life. She loved my brother and me to an incredible degree. Whenever I experienced a period of rebellion and angst, she was the only one who cared about and understood my feelings. She sent me a card on every birthday, a ten- or twenty-dollar bill tucked in the envelope. The money was nice to have, but more importantly, she showed me care at a time when no one else would. She was always there.

The long flights from Harrisburg to Los Angeles usually included a stopover. While I had previously experienced anxious moments in flight when the plane was buffeted by thermal winds rising from the uneven ground below, the rough air quickly passed along with my fears until a fateful morning taking off in St. Louis. When we turned from the taxiway to the main runway, the pilot accelerated the engines and began to race to takeoff. The roar of the engines filled the cabin as the plane stuttered down the runway, gaining speed. I leaned back and closed my eyes, anticipating that magical moment breaking the bounds of gravity and climbing swiftly to the blue sky.

Suddenly, the engines quieted, and everyone pitched hard against their seatbelts. The engines growled in fury, even louder than before, as the pilot reversed thrust to slow the speeding plane. We had almost stopped when the captain spoke over the intercom, "Sorry, folks, we seem to have a slight mechanical problem that needs to be checked. We're returning to the gate for a few moments, and we'll be ready to go."

The plane taxied up to the gate we had just left and parked. Several motorized carts pulled up and began looking at the jet engines under each wing. After a few minutes, the captain explained that the plane would be grounded so passengers should disembark while they arranged another plane to continue the flight. As Jon and I reached the front exit by the cockpit, I realized its door was open. The captain and copilot sat in their seats talking. I asked the flight attendant if I could say hello to the captain.

With her nod of assent, I stepped into the cockpit, awed by the number of different gauges, dials, and levers on the ceiling and dash below the small window. The pilot, hatless with head of white hair, turned in his seat, smiled, and asked, "Hello, young fellow, what can we do for you?"

"I just wanted to know what happened. If we had taken off, would we have crashed?" I asked.

Speaking in a more serious tone, the captain replied, "No, son. There is nothing to worry about. One of the dials was a little off and we wanted to check why." His smile returned. "There's nothing unusual and nothing to worry about. We're just being extra safe. We'll have a new plane here in a moment ready to take you to Los Angeles."

"But, if we had taken off, what would have happened? Did we have enough fuel to get back?" I persisted.

The captain replied, "Sure, we always double-check those things, and have a lot of extra safeguards. Even if something were to go wrong in-flight, we're always able to address it. But we like to be better safe than sorry."

I nodded. I understood. If we had taken off, we would have crashed and everyone in the plane would have been killed. During the next five hours playing Ms. Pac-Man with my brother in the airport waiting for the new plane, I had time to think about what could have happened and realized that I was powerless to change the outcome.

My worries over flying continued to grow. As I continued to fly, I became more aware of the various dangers that we could encounter. Whenever I read about a major airline accident, I was sure a similar fate awaited me. With each flight, I grew more and more anxious. Knowing that I was tempting fate, I battled my fear for the next decade, each flight a struggle between my phobia and my determination to control it.

Though the trips to California were the highlight of my year, they always ended with a return to Hershey. The friendships I eventually made in Hershey were mostly superficial, probably because being social outcasts was the only thing we had in common. By middle school, last names replaced first names in social conversation—Mike Stoner became "Stoner" while Philip Lefko was "Lefko." Those with hard-to-pronounce or multi-syllable family names learned to handle embarrassing, sometimes offensive titles. Nate Lookingbill was "lickin' balls" and I was "Dorkin," "Dorkmeister," "Dorkmaster" or just plain "Dork." These, in all sadness, were by my friends. Names from other kids could be far worse.

When we were together, we talked about everything from sports to something we had overheard from our parents. Sometimes, a Black/White issue came up. If it was negative, someone would argue with "Oh, yeah, well, dude, Dorkin's Black" or "I don't know about that stuff because Dorkin's Black and we're hanging." Then someone would say, "Man, Dorkin's not really Black." The first several times that I heard it, I did not know what to say and, frankly, I did not know if I made the connection. I did not process the concept of "not being Black." I thought if the comparison was to Black drug dealers, then I was not one.

Not really Black? A couple of years later, the meaning of the comments really dawned on me. I felt sick in the pit of my stomach, a shame that remains to this day. I not only allowed the stupid comments, but I did not complain when they said I wasn't really Black!

• • •

When I finally got to high school in Hershey, I did have a couple of friends, but my reputation for being the outcast was firmly established. Impossibly, it seemed to me, but the kids aggressively exploited my differences to show off to their friends. A late bloomer, I was shorter than the average freshman, still plump, and sported a large Afro. If my size, color, and different hairstyle wasn't enough to attract the bullies, playing the orchestra was another strike against me. I was bullied by the bullies whom other kids bullied!

One day as I walked through the halls to class, one of the football players grabbed my hair from behind. He reached almost to my scalp, scrunching a handful of my long hair in his fist, and jerking me backward. As I dropped my books and flailed to keep my balance, my attacker began to yell, "The Afro clutch! I'm doing the Afro clutch. I'm pulling Dorkin by the Afro clutch!" No one intervened, the crowd of boys and girls standing around us were laughing. I couldn't do anything. When the bully released me and walked away with his football buddies laughing, I felt like crying in anger and humiliation. No one helped me pick up my books; they just walked around me as if nothing had happened. But it had.

I learned to endure the Afro clutch when I couldn't get away. Each time it happened, I added more anger to my reservoir of hate for the town and its inhabitants—my parents for moving us to Hell, my brother too wrapped up in his own life to protect me, and my so-called friends too afraid to stand up for me.

Violence was not part of my personality, nor the lessons instilled in me by my parents. Even so, there are times when there are no other remedies. By the time I went to senior high school, I just could not take it anymore and I let loose. Experiencing the Afro clutch became unbearable. During my sophomore year, one boy tried one too many times to embarrass me. I went berserk, screaming as I attacked him, both fists battering him in my fury. Though he was slightly larger than me, he had no chance to fend me off. I pummeled him until I couldn't swing my arms, giving him a beat-down he wouldn't forget. Years later, I remain proud of what I did, fighting back when doing nothing meant accepting that I deserved the abuse because I was different. My determination to stand proud sent me to the office on more than one occasion.

Another time in German class, the kid sitting behind me, Sam, the biggest kid in class and the school's biggest football player, grabbed my hair when the teacher was not looking, whispering "Dorkin, Afro clutch!" I wrenched away and stood, thirty kids sitting around us, the teacher at her desk in the front of the room. I started screaming, "You better f*****g stop it, I'm going to kick your f*****g a**hole, and I f*****g hate you all, you mother f****r!" My tirade went on for five minutes using curse words and obscenities that I had never used.

The teacher had little choice but to send me to the office of the vice-principal, her husband, whom we called the Disciplinarian. This was not my first time to visit his "Gloom Room." Surprisingly, he never severely punished me, maybe because he felt sorry for me. I always ended up with occasional in-school suspensions and time in his office, but nothing worse than that.

Kids in my class were beginning to drive and a popular pastime was riding around with friends in the small town. Few of my friends had cars, so whenever someone was lucky enough to use their parents' vehicle, he would drive from house to house picking up the others. Whenever we pulled in front of someone's home, I was told, "Dorkin, Dorkin, just wait in the car, and we'll come back." Though the reason was never expressed, I knew it was not a good idea for me to come to the door with them, especially any girls' houses. There were no Black girls in my classes at Hershey.

I met Cathy when I moved to Hershey. She was more of an acquaintance than a friend. She was in a couple of my classes from time to time, but we never spent time outside of school. When I entered high school, I had a few more classes with her. Cathy, White with blonde hair was cute, though with the kind of attraction men typically overlook at first glance. She was not a part of the popular high school cliques—the jet-set crowd, the "in-crowd," the jock crowd. She was a little bit of an outcast like me. I think that was the part that drew me to her.

To me, she was beautiful, funny, and vibrant. I liked the time that we spent together in school. When we were around each other, I got a sense that she liked me, whether due to our similar social status or for other reasons.

Under the guise of schoolwork and needing to check on an assignment, I got her number and began to call her from time to time. We mostly talked about schoolwork but over several months, we eventually expanded the calls to other people and happenings at school. My freshman year, I asked her out on a date. She said yes, agreeing to have her parents drop her off to meet me at the theaters in the Hershey Lodge and Convention Center.

We met in the Center, spent some time walking around, and went to the movie. The title of the film escapes me; my focus for the entire evening was exactly when and how to put my arm around her. It was my first date.

I followed her as we entered the row of seats from the left aisle. She sat on my right side, a position that was good for me as my right arm, my bow arm, was the most comfortable to use. (My left arm   where the focus is on the fingers—would have felt awkward in the situation.) We watched the movie, neither of us speaking for the first half-hour or so.

My mind was focused on one thing and one thing only—putting my arm around her shoulders. As the minutes clicked by, I realized that I might wait too long and never have a chance to make my move. I fidgeted, starting to raise my arm from my lap but stopped—several times. I desperately wanted to curl my arm around her, but I did not want to be rejected. Unable to endure the tension, I yawned, raising both arms over my head, then dropped them on the backs of the seat left and right of mine, my right arm barely touching her shoulder.

She nudged forward, not to shrug off my hand, but to welcome it closer to her neck and bosom. I dropped my arm a little lower down on her shoulder and turned ever so slightly toward her. She turned and we kissed. It was amazing!

We continued to kiss repeatedly throughout the movie. Sometimes, she would initiate the kissing, and other times, I would. When the movie ended, we made our way to the rack of pay phones to call our parents to pick us up. While we waited, we talked for a little while knowing that our connection, at least for that moment, was real. For the first time, I forgot my grief of losing Leslie.

Her parents got there first and picked her up. I gave her a quick hug goodbye and they drove away. When my parents came, I jumped in the back seat. My mother asked how it had gone, I replied, "It was fun." My dad then asked, "How are you doing in school? Are you keeping up with your music?"

I didn't answer, upset that he constantly made our relationship about my playing or grades. In the silence, he said, "Son, I push you on practicing and schoolwork because you need to be the best at whatever you do. I'm less concerned with what you do than that you're the best at, whatever that is."

He glanced at me through the rear-view mirror and continued. "Unfortunately, Aaron, when you walk into a room, people are going to make certain judgments just because of the color of your skin. But if you're the best at what you do, you will overcome that. And that's why I want that for you. Because that is the way that you will defeat the prejudice. If you are the best on the violin, if you are the best at your schoolwork, no one will have the option to cast a stereotype on you."

In his own way, I think he tried to tell me that I might not be able to date her or any of the girls in the school, since they were White and I was Black. I thought, "Actually half-Black, but, as far as America was concerned, I was Black."

That conversation has stuck with me. I am not sure if that is part of what drives me now, but it is undeniably in part, who I have become.

. . .

One of my closest friends was Lori. Over my junior and senior high school years in Hershey, she became, in many ways, my closest friend. She played the flute in the orchestra with me. We not only saw each other in school every day, but once a week in the Harrisburg Youth Symphony. Parents would take turns driving the three or four of us in the Symphony each week.

With my advanced training and practice, I quickly worked my way up to being the Concertmaster of the Pennsylvania State Youth Orchestra. One duty of the Concertmaster was to lead the tuning of the orchestra. The process begins when the Concertmaster raises their hand and conversation is supposed to stop. In the silence that follows, the Concertmaster then points to the lead oboe player to blow a perfect "A" pitch. Then the rest of the orchestra tunes matching that "A," first the brass, then the winds, followed by the string instruments, then finally, the Concertmaster. I was the only African American in the orchestra. When I raised my hand for quiet, the kids ignored me, continuing to talk or play notes on their instruments. They refused to be quiet.

"Please quiet down, everyone," I would ask and hold up my hand to no avail. The process eventually became a joke because it was repeated so many times. Frustrated, but not knowing what else to do, I looked at Lori in the flute section. She knew what I felt. Those shared moments made me feel closer to her, unlike the other so-and-sos who comprised an ensemble that was incapable of playing the simplest Christmas music.

On the other hand, I loved playing my solos as Concertmaster. I was good, maybe I thought the best in the state, and I enjoyed showing off.

However, the icing on the cake was the stops at McDonald's on the way home. My parents, especially my mother, were strict about diet. We never ate commercially prepared food in the house. Chef Boyardee and Pizza Hut were as absent in our cupboards as a television set in the living room. Mom made everything from scratch, using produce from a local farmers market. Our household products—paper towels, soap, tissues—were the least expensive generic brands.

I dreamed about the incredible McDonald's fries and chocolate shakes on that weekly Monday night return home from the Symphony rehearsals. A bonus was the opportunity to sit with Lori and talk about a rehearsal, the music, or just about our lives. Those talks drew me closer to her.

Perhaps because of our interactions in school and music, I started wanting more from Lori. One day, in English class, I gave her a note, carefully written over two months. I outlined the importance of our friendship to me, the things that she had done to help me cope with Afro clutches, insensitive racial remarks, and overt prejudice. I wrote that she was a true friend, and I never wanted to jeopardize that. Finally, I told her that my feelings were beyond friendship, and I hoped she felt the same way.

She did not. Years later, I realized that she was bound by the expectations of her friends and social class. Unlike Cathy, who had little status in our class, Lori had more to lose and less freedom, being bound by the expectations of her friends and parents. She told me that she was sorry, but she didn't feel the same as me. She wanted to continue our friendship. So we did.

My days at Hershey continued with one date sputtering into nothing with Cathy. Perhaps the social pressure was too much, even for her. The fleeting friendships I grasped onto after were subject to a similar fate, but outside of Nigel, they were all I had.

CHAPTER 4

EUROPE

During the summers before my freshman and sophomore years of high school, my dad was a visiting professor at the University of Tübingen in southern Germany. Looking back, it was an amazing opportunity for me to learn about the world outside the parochial views of Hershey. While the first trip was only seven-to ten days (spent mostly sightseeing like other tourists), the second visit was for more than a month.

Tübingen's population was twice that of Hershey, and one-third of the population was college students. Unlike many German cities, Tübingen had largely escaped the destruction of World War II; its cobblestone streets, narrow alleys, and centuries-old stone and wood, multistoried buildings bisected by tributaries of the meandering Neckar River.

The relationship with my parents had been stormy my freshman year, probably due to the social pressures of high school and their insistence that I practice the violin for several hours every day. I had no time to be me, to catch my breath and escape the constant demands of others. Everybody seemed determined to make me into their image of a dutiful son, a violin prodigy, a compliant student, or a cool(er) friend. When the pressure became unbearable, I ran away, determined never to come back. Confronting the realities of being a fourteen-year-old with no money and few friends, I always returned chastened but not broken. Someday, I knew I would escape and never return.

On our second trip to Tübingen, my parents arranged for my brother (a recent high school graduate) and me to board with a Turkish family while there. They rented a flat on the opposite side of the town, so we only saw them occasionally for a meal. We were practically on our own!

My parents had arranged for piano and violin lessons with German teachers while there. The piano teacher was better than my violin teacher, but I appreciated the tutoring from both. During that summer, I realized that I could make real money with my violin. Busking—performing in the street for tips—is common in Europe. Everybody wins, with tips for the entertainer, a "real cultural experience" for tourists, and crowds of potential customers for the merchants.

Fueled by the imagined performances of the European artists of yesteryear, I ventured into the center square of Tübingen for a few hours almost every day to play my violin, effectively killing two birds with one stone. I accomplished the required practice and made spending money as passersby tossed pfennigs and groats (German coins) in my open violin case. Sometimes, I received coins from nearby countries—centimes from France and rappen from Switzerland. There were some days when I made as much as the equivalent of a hundred U.S. dollars for a few hours of playing. I liked the money, but the best part was standing on the street and watching people of all descriptions pass by.

My Turkish hosts had teenage children a little bit older than me. I had studied German for a couple of years in school. They had learned about the same amount of English as I had German. By the end of that summer, I was almost fluent, though they had progressed little with their English. I suppose, in part, due to my insistence on speaking German when we talked.

I was completely enamored with one of the daughters in the family, even though she ignored me most of the time. Her treatment didn't bother me since I had encountered similar disinterest from girls in Hershey. Presumably, her lack of interest was easier to bear because it was personal, not racial. I was too young and unsophisticated for a girl of more experience.

The friends of the family's teenagers were a bit tougher than those in Hershey. Every boy seemed to have a moped or scooter and a girl who perched on the rear, wrapping her arms around the boy as they raced between cars and up the narrow alleys, stopping occasionally to smoke or pass a bottle of wine between them. I couldn't imagine ever being as cool. When they were around, I pretended to smoke to be part of the gang. Trying to inhale always triggered a coughing fit—a sure sign that I was a novice—but I learned to turn my head when pretending to inhale, to hold the smoke in my mouth and let it out slowly. If anyone realized that I was faking, they were nice enough not to mention it.

When my father's term with the University ended, we took a trip across the Alps to Italy. The views from the highway were spectacular as we wound between snowy paladins guarding the entrance to the newly constructed road tunnel at Gotthard Pass. The 10.5-mile-long tunnel is one of the longest in the world, with a single lane in each direction. I suspect very few passengers make the journey without wondering, "What if the tunnel collapses?"

When we escaped to the sunlight on its opposite end, I breathed a sigh of relief, followed by a gasp of disbelief. Our view at the end of the tunnel was a vista of shimmering blue surrounded by craggy cliffs, each topped by the magnificent villas and private retreats of the rich and famous. The surface of Lake Como rippled with the movement of sailing ships and magnificent yachts. Even the air smelled of luxury and indolence.

We stopped at a café beside the lake for refreshments. I had the most incredible hot chocolate, so thick I had to eat it with a spoon. Our next stop was Bologna, which Italians called the "City of the Fat" for its rich foods. Arched arcades jutted from every building, it seemed, so that in the hot summer months, one could always sit in the shade for a meal of balsamic vinegar, Parmesan cheese, Parma ham, mortadella, and tortellini.

While Bologna is best known for its Parmigiano Reggiano (what Americans call "Parmesan"), fresh mozzarella was available on every corner. One of the things that my adoptive parents instilled in me was a fiendish appetite for the creamy, yellowish-white cheese with a slight tang. In Italy, the cheese is made from buffalo milk; in America, cow's milk is used more often. My parents loved it so much, they learned to make fresh mozzarella and my adoptive father taught me the craft I use to this day.

The food in Italy was very different than we had in Germany. Meat in a variety of forms is present in every meal, particularly sausages, usually served with sauerkraut, boiled or fried potatoes, and bread with a sauce of ketchup or mustard on the side. Italian food seems to be lighter with less emphasis on meat and heavy on pastas and vegetables, especially tomatoes. The most amazing thing to me as an American teenager was both countries' attitude about alcohol. Whether drinking beer in Germany or

wine in Italy, parents seem to have no qualms about their children participating in the respective spirits.

From there, we made our way up to Lido di Spina, one of the beaches
on the upper eastern coast of Italy. Unlike America, topless sunbathing is
not uncommon on many European beaches, and it is legal in Italy. (Total
nudity is restricted to certain private areas.) I'm not sure my parents realized the probability that we would see bare breasts on the sand, but they
took it in stride, ignoring it while we were there. For a fifteen-year-old
boy, the idea of a topless beach was almost too much to handle! I had the
time of my life, even though some of the topless women were my grandmother's age.

We then made our way north to Budapest, Hungary. The road at the
border between the two countries was blocked by armed soldiers checking the papers of those wanting to enter the country, tangible evidence
of the notorious figurative Iron Curtain that had existed since 1955. Giant
metal fences lined both sides of the two-lane highway into the country,
a view broken only by the square-shaped guard towers interjected every
other mile or so.

The ride was like being caught in an old black-and-white movie; the
color fading away by the sense of oppression that lay on the surface like
a fog. The feeling of malevolence discouraged conversation in the car.
When something was said, it was barely above a whisper. It was a relief to
finally arrive in Budapest.

Ironically, Budapest reminded me of our house, humorless and
very efficient. Since my mother never bought prepared foods, our
cabinets resembled stores of food bought for a fallout shelter. There
were no bright colors, elegant printing, or comical cartoon characters
decorating the tins and sacks of flour, sugar, salt and raw ingredients.
There were no Keebler elves promoting cookies or Snap, Crackle, and
Pop praising the nutritious value of rice krispies in our home. Everything was uniform, even while fresh; nothing stood out, in my teenage eyes.

The city was memorable because my parents found the pack of Marlboro Turkish cigarettes I had brought from Germany. I was surprised
when they called me to come to their hotel room. When I entered, I
immediately saw the red and white pack atop a dark wooden table beside

the single sitting chair in the dusky room. "No, no," I thought, trying to remember where I had hidden the evidence.

My parents were furious, the anger obvious in their clipped sentences and challenging stares, daring me to compound the transgression with a lie proclaiming my innocence. The three of us stood there, ignoring the object of our confrontation. My father, never considering that I might be an innocent party holding the cigarettes for a friend, began speaking.

"How long have you been smoking?" he asked.

"I really don't smoke. I mean I don't inhale. Just puff on one when I'm with my friends. Everybody does it." I could tell my explanation was rejected by the slight shake of his head and the upward curl of his lips. I tried another ploy.

"You and mom smoke. I see the two of you every morning and evening with a cigarette," I offered as a possible mitigation of my transgression.

As long as I could remember, my parents had privately smoked two cigarettes a day—one in the morning and a second in the evening—presumably escaping the growing public disdain for smokers. My father ignored my attempt to turn the tables. I realized that nothing I might say would excuse me in their eyes.

I prepared for the inevitable spanking that was sure to follow when I noticed he had not loosened his belt in preparation for his "discipline." Maybe I can skate on this, I hoped, though I didn't know the reason why.

"Aaron, if you want to smoke, then you smoke. Here's a cigarette. If you want to smoke, you finish this cigarette. If you don't, that's it. Not another cigarette, ever. And no matter what, you're going to sit here until you smoke it." He lit it and handed it to me, the end a bright ember with wisps of acrid smoke beginning to waft in the stale hotel room air.

I sat on the edge of the bed and took the proffered smoke. Holding it gingerly between my thumb and forefinger, I thought, "How bad could this be? Just sit and smoke this. I'm getting the easy way out." I puffed on the cigarette as I always had, turning my head as I drew in the smoke and began to exhale.

"No, no, if you want to smoke, you have to inhale. Pretending is not going to cut it," my dad said. I took a second drag, being sure to inhale as he had instructed. I started gagging and coughing, my eyes watering as the smoke and my throat burning.

Watching me, his face smug with satisfaction at my experience, my father said, "That's good. Keep going. Keep it up. I want to see you finish that cigarette." Mom said nothing.

"I'm fine, but I don't feel like smoking this." I tried to hand the cigarette back to him.

"You said you wanted to smoke, and you will," my father replied, refusing to take the burning fag from my hand. The two—my father and mother—watched me as I struggled to finish. Each time I inhaled, I doubled over coughing and hacking, with every toke, sure that I would throw up. My father watched my agony without speaking, though I am sure he felt righteous about his lesson. My mother might have intervened during the worst of it, but never did.

When I had smoked the cigarette down to my thumb and finger, my father silently put an ashtray in front of me. I snuffed out the butt and returned to the room I shared with my brother, still coughing and wheezing. The lesson didn't take. When we returned to Hershey, most kids my age smoked to be part of the crowd and to signal that they were old enough to make their own decisions. I discovered a cigarette that seemed almost like drawing air—Marlboro Lights—and practiced inhaling sitting on a hill behind my house at night. Years later, I still wonder at my foolishness.

Following Budapest, we returned to Germany, visiting a couple of my parents' friends in Munich. Munich is a beautiful city with a massive clock in the town square. At twelve noon, little wooden doors opened on the clock and an elaborate collection of elaborately painted wooden characters paraded above the square, delighting the children and fascinating the adults.

Our last stop that summer was Dachau, a small village outside of Munich. My parents were racially and ethnically Jewish, although they did not practice the religion. I suppose any thoughts about a Supreme Being or religion conflicted with their faith in science. Even so, they did expose my brother and me to some of the traditional rituals. We observed Hanukkah instead of Christmas, spinning the four-sided dreidel and eating matzo brei, a fried unleavened bread with eggs.

Whether due to their heritage or the belief that everyone should remember the atrocities committed in that little village, my parents believed that it was important for my brother and me to see what had occurred there. The village was the site of the first Nazi concentration camps, originally built in 1933.

Our visit happened more than a half-century after the camp had been closed. Even so, the sense of pure evil clung to the place; it was the most terrifying place that I have ever been on earth. Much of the camp is preserved in its original state. Tall fences topped with rusty barbed wire surrounded the compound. Seven wooden watchtowers where soldiers watched with machine guns for anyone attempting escape towered over the fence. Narrow dusty roads and footpaths snaked between the wooden dormitories and the few brick buildings that had served various purposes for the Nazi guards.

As we padded up the cold gravel drive to the entrance, I could hear the crunch of stones beneath my feet. It was a somber, almost holy place, sanctified by the thousands of martyred prisoners who were once there. It was a silent place. I do not believe I heard anyone speak above a whisper the entire time we were there.

Recalling that visit today, I realize it was a major turning point of my life. Most people of my generation do not remember our grandparents' war or the reasons for it. Our knowledge of the Nazis was from the images of old newsreels of goose-stepping soldiers, their arms stretched to salute a little man with a funny moustache. The true horrors of the Nazis—the stripping of their prisoners' possessions for resale, the inhuman overcrowding in the hastily constructed work dormitories, and the casual reference to the deadly gas chambers as prisoner showers—violate the sense that humans have evolved beyond beasts.

The photographs of Nazi medical experiments continue to haunt me today. Physicians in the name of science sought to understand the effects of high altitude and hypothermia, subjecting Jewish men, women, and children to excruciating, often deadly tests to find the critical levels of pressure and temperature on a human body. They watched, taking photos and notes, as their human guinea pigs struggled to breathe in low pressure or froze in mechanical freezing units. By the time we visited the ovens where thousands of bodies had been reduced to ash, the ash discarded in unmarked pits and forgotten, even the most callous visitor was stunned.

As I tried to grasp what I saw, I wondered what I might have done living in Germany at that time. Inevitably, I wondered, "What if this happens again?" Would I be considered Jewish and a potential victim? Would I declare that I was adopted, not really Jewish? What if the next time the victims were Black?

At that moment, I did not want to be Jewish. Ironically, when I returned to the United States and the small town of Hershey, one of my first thoughts was, "I think I'd rather be Jewish than Black."

CHAPTER 5

TARZAN, PRACTICING & SEARCHING

When we returned from Europe the second time, tensions with my adoptive parents became acute. The brief armistice during our overseas travel was over. In many ways, our antagonism was more pronounced due to the months of personal freedom I enjoyed during the trip. My rebellion began around age twelve, I think because of the unrelenting strictness my parents tried to impose. It seemed their rules controlled every minute of my life. Watching television wasn't possible since we didn't have a TV in the house. They didn't permit overnight visits to any friends since I would probably watch the TV like most families did in the evenings. I couldn't listen to any popular songs on the radio—the popular songs other kids in school could repeat verse by verse—except for classical music (a highly erroneous presumptive exclusion since classical music can use highly cyclical, sequential patterns). How many kids in Junior High School listen to Mozart's Serenade No. 13 for strings in G Major or Beethoven's Symphony No. 5 in C Minor? None, at least none that I ever met. They were listening to Michael Jackson's "Beat It," Run DMC's "It's Like That," and the Beatles. A teenager who doesn't know the names Madonna, Prince, or Bruce Springsteen was more than unique in the early 80s; they were the nerds, the oddballs, the sissies.

After school, I was expected to practice my violin at least four hours a day, every day. Malcolm Gladwell proposed that mastery of a skill requires 10,000 hours of practice. In my case, that meant four hours a day, every day, for more than six years. I suspect now that my parents believed me to be a once-in-a-lifetime prodigy destined to take my place among the best in the world. Was it for me or them, I wondered? Whatever their motive, their strict regimen of practice almost destroyed my love of the violin.

I despised practicing, even though I loved playing and making up my own arrangements. At that time, most of the musical things that I did were fundamental and very easy, making practicing an exercise in drudgery. My teacher did not inspire me or push me to more complicated works. My lessons were bland. Even so, I played rather far above the level of others around me.

Restricted from television and the radio, I turned to literature for entertainment and escape from the parental constraints of my everyday existence. Fortunately, reading was the one activity my parents approved of, and I quickly developed a voracious appetite for the imaginary worlds that books offered.

I continued to read everything from Tarzan to Thomas Mann. Surprisingly, my parents never bothered to restrict the subject of my literary works. I think censorship was antithetical to their scientific minds, or at least certain areas of life. Whatever the reason, I took advantage of their permission, searching the library on the weekends for books ranging from poetry to prose, including literary masterpieces and the trashy drivel of inept, soon-forgotten first-time writers. Whatever the subject or storyline, I reveled in the time away from the tedium of my real life.

My bedroom was my refuge, but not what you might expect for an average teenager. The room was a little larger than usual, probably 12 ft by 12 ft with a closet. Three of the four walls were bare since I had no interest in sports or popular teenage idols. A single twin-sized bed was attached to the fourth wall, hanging about four feet above the floor. Hanging the bed had been necessary to accommodate the old Grand Piano that dominated the room. The piano and the height of my bed created a perfect hiding place for a teenage boy, obstructing prying eyes and searching fingers who might try to learn my secrets.

When I climbed into bed and looked down at its dull ebony surface, the yellowed white and black keys of the keyboard looked like tobacco-stained and missing teeth in a grinning mouth. Ironically, the piano, which most people would consider a nuisance, became my ally as the years went by.

As most prisoners do, I began to find ways around the conditions I found unpleasant. For example, I resented my parents' ban of television. My brief moments of TV through school or at friends' houses were wonderful! I wanted to watch more TV; I needed to watch television regularly to talk with my classmates.

By happenstance, the father of one of my close friends, Pete, worked for Magnavox. The company had a 5" portable color TV that Pete's dad could get at cost. Having some money from working part-time at a local theater, I bought the TV and hid it under the covers of my bed, sure it would not be discovered if I was careful.

Despite my hiding schemes, my parents found and confiscated the TV. When I wouldn't explain how I had gotten it, my father threatened to punish me with a beating with the belt. He didn't because I hadn't broken his two big rules: No lying or stealing. My dad settled on the punishment being the permanent loss of the object.

We were at a stalemate for several months as I tried to find a smaller TV that would be easier to hide or a hiding place that might not be discovered. The Sony Watchman gave me the advantage I needed. It was small enough to hide anywhere and I could take it with me in my backpack when I thought a search might happen. When I look back today, my father must have spent an extensive amount of his time exploring my room in search of the various things he rightfully assumed I was hiding from him.

My efforts to avoid the 4-hour violin practices became an epic contest between my father and me. My first attempt was simple: I did not practice if my parents were not home. Unfortunately, they soon deciphered that ploy.

"I know you're not practicing when we're gone. Because I can't trust you, I want you to record your practices from now on, so I can listen to them when I'm back," my father said.

This was before small, portable tape recorders were available, so he bought a large, reel-to-reel tape recorder and set it up in my room. I began taping my practice and my father always listened to the tape. Unbeknownst to him, I figured out how to copy and splice the practice tapes, taking pieces from older tapes and mixing their sequence to appear as if they were recorded during a real practice session.

When my father realized the charade, he purchased a massive electric tape eraser and began erasing the entire reel of my practice after confirming its validity. Since he erased the entire reel beginning to end, I couldn't counterfeit my practices. I realized that no technology was available where I could continue the sham. I had no choice except to practice the required number of hours. As an avid Sherlock Holmes fan, I recalled Holmes's famous explanation to his friend Watson: "Once you eliminate the impossible, whatever remains, no matter how improbable, must be the truth." My father had won the battle of wits, an accomplishment I am sure he relished for some years.

Practicing meant playing scales and arpeggios in different tempos, passages that I knew inside and out and could perform in my sleep. My musical development stalled as the work became more and more boring. I tried reading as I practiced, placing the book on a music stand. Having to turn the pages left constant breaks in my playing, a pattern that my father would be sure to note and eliminate. If I stopped turning the pages to keep playing, I lost interest in the story; if I turned the pages, a break in my practice was inevitable. I couldn't accept the possibility that my father had outplayed me again, and I spent hours devising ways to read and practice simultaneously.

One day, out of the blue, an idea popped into my mind. What if I could turn the pages with my toes? I moved a stool from the kitchen and removed my shoes and socks. It worked. I began practicing barefoot, looking down at the pages as I bowed the strings of the violin resting comfortably in the crook of my neck. Whenever I reached the end of the page, I rested my left foot on the book to stop any movement and swiped my other foot across the righthand page, then repositioned to left foot to keep the book open. Reading and practicing simultaneously enabled me to focus on the written page even as my subconscious mind fixed any mistakes in my music.

One problem did arise—the sound of the turning page. I wasn't sure that my father would notice when he listened, but I didn't care to find out. I got my books from the public library, lacking the funds to buy them. I began searching for volumes with softer-textured pages that I could turn without making a sound. I also learned to open the books before starting the recorder because their plastic book covers crinkled and crackled each time the book was opened or shut (My one complaint about the Hershey Public Library was their insistence on those noisy covers!). To my knowledge, no one in the family ever learned of my duplicity.

. . .

When I was eleven or twelve years old, I began to have nightmares along with severe pain in my groin at night. My parents, being behavioral scientists, assumed the cause was psychological, most likely from the new tensions I was experiencing with the move to Hershey. They were certain that most illnesses and pains were psychological rather than physical and delayed going to physicians for advice. After months of nightmares and terrible pains in my lower abdomen, they took me to the hospital for diagnosis.

The doctors concluded that I had two hernias in my lower abdomen, the cause of my pain. They also discovered I had an undescended testicle. As an adult, I think "undescended testicle" has a bit of a humorous ring to it. Back then, I dreaded that anyone might find out. I was certain that I would be the famous young Black-and-White kid with an Afro who played the violin and had one ball.

The doctors elected to do both operations—removing the hernias and relocating the testicle—at the same time in day surgery. I was nervous, but the doctor assured me I wouldn't feel a thing. The nurse gave me a local anesthetic in my wrist and put an IV in the back of my left hand connected to a bag of clear liquid on a portable stand. They wheeled me into an operating room and another doctor, the anesthesiologist, injected another anesthetic into the IV tube between the bag and my wrist. I remember him saying, "Count backwards from ten. I guarantee you won't make one." As I counted, of course, I did not, in fact, make seven.

When I woke up, still groggy, my scrotum ached from the two incisions from the operation. The top of my wrist where they put the IV hurt more and lasted longer. Nearly a year later, I could still tap the injection spot and feel the IV in my arm. The best thing about the operation was the recovery room and its juice and graham crackers for those who survived their surgeries. Under the circumstances, my parents could hardly object to my taking advantage of those wonderful, commercial, sweet-tasting crackers that were never allowed in the Dworkin household. I decided that I was more than willing to undergo another operation or two if it meant a few more packs of those graham crackers.

During my middle school years, I became close friends with Dave, a White kid who lived right around the corner from me. I think we recognized a kindred soul in each other because he, too, had problems with his parents. Everything seemed normal there when I visited him, but you never know what goes on behind closed doors. Dave and I fed off each other, each coaxing the other to take risks that we would never do alone—sneaking out, hitchhiking, going to the local arcade to play video games. He was the person and friend who was there when I needed to talk to or yell at someone. He understood more than anyone my feelings, something my parents never did. Dave was a good sounding board for me in those years, an ally that every kid needs at times.

Dave went to the Catholic school in Hershey and shared his difficulties fitting in with the other students. As we grew older, the problems each of us faced in our respective schools escalated. Sometimes, we snuck out in the middle of the night to visit an abandoned depot by the town's main railroad tracks. Freight trains were constantly coming and going in Hershey, boxcars on the way in loaded with jute sacks of raw cocoa beans competing with boxcars filled with chocolate candy going out.

The depot, a red brick building constructed in early 1921, attracted a regular stream of hoboes who hid in empty boxcars and moved from town to town. Dave and I would meet them and learn about their adventures and crazy travel. Desperate to escape the miseries of Hershey, we imagined riding the rails to Las Vegas or to some other faraway point on the rail system. We never attempted our break-away, but I often dreamed about it when I fell asleep at night, especially when the battle with my father escalated.

Our fights began with an argument that continued until I angrily retreated to my room, wishing I could retaliate in some way to even the score. As I grew older and more desperate, I would leave the house, stomping out and slamming the door to ensure that everyone knew the depth of my fury.

"I'm going to run away." My declaration was sure, I thought, to show him how unhappy I was with his rules and constant pressure to practice.

"Okay, fine. Go ahead," my father replied. He stared at me, daring me to put up or shut up.

"I will! I really mean it. I will run away. You'll never see me again," I screamed. On some level, I realized my threat to run away was nonsensical. Where could a twelve-year-old with no money, no clothes, no car go? Frustrated at my helplessness, I began pummeling our steel mailbox with both fists as hard as I could, ignoring the pain in my hands.

During my tirade, my mother had joined father at the front door, both parents silently watching my self-punishment. My arms aching, my hands beginning to swell, I stopped to catch my breath. I realized that my knuckles were cut with blood leaking down my wrists. I turned to the two of them, held up both hands with the bleeding knuckles facing them, and yelled, "I cut myself, see? Now I'm bleeding. I'm just going to bleed to death, and you don't even care."

My father shook his head in disgust, whether at me or his aversion to overt emotion, I don't know. As he turned and walked into the house, my mother, wordlessly, led me into the kitchen to bandage my hands. I had not run away, that time.

The first time I left home, I stayed with some friends whose parents knew about the situation with my parents. I realized that they did not want to be caught up in my parental conflicts, so I never stayed more than a few nights. I occasionally slept in a local movie theater where I worked part-time, stretched across a row of seats after everyone left. I never volunteered where I had been when I returned, and my parents never asked. When I returned to the house, the routine of practice and expectation that I would follow the rules continued as if I never left.

My longest period away was more than a week. I had saved some money from work and moved into the Brinser Motel, a cheap motel on the outskirts of Hershey that rented rooms by the hour. The parking lot was faded asphalt with tiny cracks that meandered from curb to curb, a fitting setting for the non-descript two-story building with staircases at each end and a sparse hedge of holly in need of a trim. My room was very basic, thin carpets and thinner towels, a lumpy mattress with dingy sheets, and an ancient color TV bolted into the wall. But I loved it. I ate Ho-Hos, Little Debbies and the other foods forbidden at home, washed down with bottles of RC and Mountain Dew.

My freedom ended when school officials tracked me down. As I lay in bed one morning eating a hearty breakfast of pop-tarts and warm soda, I heard a tap on the door.

"Aaron, we know you're in there." I recognized the voice of Dr. Summers, head of the Gloom Room, vice-principal of our school. Having missed school for a week and learning from my parents that they did not know my whereabouts or seem to care, they determined to find me. Only a few of my friends knew my hiding place and they were sworn to secrecy. One of them must have given me up, I thought. I didn't respond, hoping that they would give up and go away.

"We know you're in there. We just need you to come back to school." Since there was no other exit from my room and Dr. Summers wasn't likely to retreat, I opened the door. I was surprised to see the coach of the football team with him. The coach knew me from the mandatory gym classes. He knew I was a frequent target of bullies and the last to be chosen for any team activity.

"Alright, Aaron, why don't you come back with us?" the coach asked.

I hadn't preplanned running away when I left and wore the same clothes for a week. I hadn't showered either, a condition apparent from my appearance and odor.

"Why don't you come back to school and clean up?" the coach asked. "I'm pretty sure I have clothes that fit you, and you will feel better."

I agreed since I had no other choice. After showering, I returned to classes as if I had never left. At the time, I didn't realize the kindness shown to me by both teachers. They didn't have to search for me or treat me as kindly as they did. No one asked them to get involved, not even my parents, but they had spent hours to find me. I wish I had been mature enough then to thank them; perhaps they will read my book and realize my belated gratitude.

At the end of the school day, I just went home. There was no welcoming celebration when I walked in the door, no questions about who I might have been with, what I might have done, or why I left. Their reaction to my return was the single admonition: "Well, we hope you learned your lesson. You shouldn't do that again."

After that, things went from bad to worse at home, climaxing in another argument with my father. I don't remember the subject of our disagreement or how it started. As we stood face to face in the kitchen, each of us snarling at the other, my father shoved me in the chest. I stumbled backward into a heavy butcherblock carving station. The station was on wheels for convenience. When I hit it, I fell to the ground, my legs sprawled out full length. The carving station careened into the wall cabinet, banging with a loud "bam" and fell over.

Afraid that he might attack me, I struggled up and grabbed one of the stainless-steel kitchen knives from a wooden knife organizer on the kitchen shelf. In a complete fury made up of anger and fear, I thrust the blade in the space between us and screamed, "Stay the Hell away from me! I hate you!"

My father, in that cold, calm tone that I could not stand, turned to my mother who had run into the kitchen after the crash and said, "Susan, call the police. Tell them that there's an armed Black man in our house."

I know my father knew exactly what he said and the impact it would have on me and the police responding to the call. There was only one Black family and me living among the Hershey White folk. I imagined the reaction of the police when they received a report of a strange, armed Black man in the home of a White family. I panicked, dropping the knife and sprinting out the door to a friend's house two blocks away. I ran through the door of his house, shouting, "I'm in trouble. We gotta go upstairs now!"

Bounding up the stairs, I explained, barely able to quit shouting. "My dad and I had a fight, and I got a knife to make him stay away. They called the cops."

As we hid in the attic, we heard the sirens of four or five police cars, maybe more, racing past his house. My friend, wide-eyed and finally grasping the potential of a police encounter, turned to me and said in a shrill voice, "Man, this shit is just too intense. I didn't sign on for getting shot. Look, there's no way you're getting out of this. You should give up if you don't want to get hurt."

He stared at me, his eyes blinking and sweat popping out on his forehead from fear or the heat in the attic. He licked his lips but said no more. I knew whatever I did, he was going downstairs to meet the cops and I couldn't blame him. I knew he was right. There was no way I could escape and hiding would certainly make it worse.

I followed my friend downstairs and walked out the front door of his house alone, expecting to be shot or tackled within seconds. No police were visible, so I continued to walk to my house. I heard a police car rumbling behind me and a quick whoop of the siren, a warning to anyone within hearing of police presence. When I turned around and put my hands up, the White, middle-aged police officer opened the door holding a shotgun pointed into the air. Standing behind the opened door of the car, the officer motioned for me to come to the car. As I approached, he told me to lean face-forward over the hood of the car, spreading my legs and hands so fast movement was not possible. He patted me down, but did not handcuff me, possibly because he knew I was more boy than man. He sat me in the passenger seat of the squad car and drove me to the police station.

During the ride, he asked, "What happened here? What went on?"

I told of the fights and the troubles I had with my parents, especially having to always obey them, practice for hours every day and never getting to visit my friends' houses. I told him that I hated them. I thought, but did not say it, that I felt like a slave having to obey the White man!

When we arrived at the police station. I sat alone in a little room, wondering what would happen. After an hour or so, the cop who had brought me came into the room.

"Aaron, I've been talking to your parents. You have two choices. You can listen to what your parents say and agree to their conditions or go to juvy (cop-speak for juvenile detention)." He sat back and waited for my answer.

While I was rebellious, I was not stupid. I sat and listened to their complaints about my behavior and their demand to obey them if I returned home. As I sat under the lights in the police station, I knew I would obey every command, but they could never break me. I felt free in that moment. I despised them more than anything or anyone on the planet. Nursing that hatred, I could obey, and I would. And I did.

The silent ride home in the back of our Chevy Citation to 435 Leearden Road was the apex of my rebellion years. The lights of the police station set the stage for my next life-changing moment, but it would be a change for the better.

CHAPTER 6

INTERLOCHEN

The requirement to obey my parents and their rules, inevitably, led to continued simmering of fundamental resentment. Tensions remained high, no doubt encouraged by my hateful stares and unwillingness to make any effort to bridge the gap between us. I accepted the likelihood that I would remain a prisoner in their house until I reached eighteen, the legal age in Pennsylvania to be recognized as an adult.

Since the environment was as uncomfortable for them as it was for me, they began searching for a boarding school where I might spend my last years before maturity. Fortunately for me, they discovered a private boarding school in northern Michigan recognized for its preparatory arts curriculum. Four hundred high school kids from around the world attended classes, living in dorms on the 1200-acre campus to study theater, dance, music, creative writing, visual arts as well as conventional academic subjects. The school also offered a popular summer program for young musicians that drew hundreds of attendees each year.

The 1200-acre campus of the Interlochen Center for the Arts was located between two small lakes—Green Lake and Duck Lake—on the lower peninsula between Lake Huron and Lake Michigan not far from Traverse City. In the decades since its founding, the school has produced notable artists and entertainment industry leaders, including Meredith Baxter (Emmy Award winner for *Family Ties*), Linda Hunt (Oscar winner), Josh Groban (singer), Peter Yarrow (Peter, Paul & Mary singing trio), Mike Wallace (the *60 Minutes* newsman) and Christie Hefner (the daughter of *Playboy* founder Hugh Hefner who succeeded him as CEO).

My first reaction when learning they wanted to send me away to school was anger. I finally had made friends with several schoolmates (even though they did not consider me really "Black") after having endured so many challenges in Hershey during my first years there. I had gone on a date for the first time. While I detested Hershey, I knew my way around and began to understand what to expect.

The thought that I would experience the same trials in a new place turned my stomach. I didn't want to find myself in some unknown, God-forsaken place to attend school with truants, misfits, and worse. When my parents first broached the topic with me, I made it clear that I wasn't interested. They wouldn't give up, maybe in part because they saw promise in the prospect, whether for my future, or theirs. They pressed and pushed until I agreed to go for a visit.

I rendered my decision before I realized that the trip required flying. I never understood the cause of my anxiety, but it was real. My father accompanied me on the trip, which included an entrance audition. I wasn't worried about the audition, having a very high, if not exaggerated, opinion of my skills. After all, I was the concertmaster of the student orchestra and earned money playing on the streets of Germany! But the idea of flying worried me as the date of the trip approached.

My father thought my fear was foolish but decided to determine its cause so he could end my anxiety. When we were aloft, he periodically checked my blood pressure and heart rate. Past being elevated, the indicators were through the roof and remained high for the full hour-and-a-half trip. While neither of us understood the basis for my fear, he recognized that it was significant, given my body's extreme reaction while airborne.

Interlochen was a surprise. Although it was spring in northern Michigan, the air nipped at my face and hands as we walked across the frozen tundra. Budding beech, maple, and oak trees competed overhead with tall white pines, remnants of the old forests before Paul Bunyan and his Blue Ox ravaged the Michigan forests (to which I would eventually acclimate). More than 100 small cabins populated the scenery, temporary homes for young students training in orchestral and solo performance in the summer programs.

Four hundred high school students in residence for the term lived in four dormitory buildings (two for male students and two for female students, upper and lower class-level, with practice rooms in the basements). A central cafeteria with guest rooms on the second floor, a nurse's station, and several halls were connected by white, curving walkways.

The large indoor auditorium accessed two large outdoor amphitheaters, one rumored to have been built on ancient Native American burial grounds. The larger one, Kresge Hall, was the place of my audition. It is a beautiful, covered pavilion with a seating capacity for over a thousand people. The stage, a huge wooden platform in the front featured huge glass doors that opened to a narrow balcony overlooking the campus lakes.

As my audition neared, I had little concerns or anxiety over how I was going to perform. Instead, I was much more fascinated with the place, its geography and the way the surroundings made me feel. Thinking of my life in Hershey, I walked onto the stage and through the back doors to the balcony to gaze at the lake. Though the wind hardly fluttered, emerald waves slowly lapped the shore in a rhythmic, almost inaudible beat. I felt like I was lying in a baby's cradle, far away from heartache, ugliness, or anger. The sound was so soothing.

I looked out on the water, thinking about what I had seen—the dorms, the teachers, and, especially, the food in the cafeteria. (There were Cheerios, Fruit Loops, and other delicacies I never ate at home.) I decided that meals would be good and the teachers far superior to any in Hershey. For the first time, I would be surrounded by kids my age. Naturally, I had not seen anyone who was Black.

I sat by the water, calmed by the relentless rolling of the waves. And I thought, *"No matter what the unknowns are here, I could always come right here to this place, and everything would be okay."* The lake that day convinced me that no matter what, I could overcome any new challenges. I recognized on a visceral level that attending Interlochen would be the path to take.

Upon my return, I shared my decision with my friends, Lori, Dave, Pete, and Tim. They were surprised, but not terribly disturbed by my pending move. Except for my buddy Dave . . .

I had been through a lot with my parents and Dave had been there for me. Since my episode with the police, problems between Dave and his parents had escalated. Having experienced the loneliness and loss he was feeling, I should have been there to help him. Leaving Dave was my greatest regret.

At the end of summer, I traveled to Interlochen to begin my junior year in high school. I convinced my parents that taking a Greyhound bus was not only less expensive than a plane ticket, but stress-free for me. So, with some final hugs, especially with dear Dave and Lori, I boarded the bus for Interlochen.

Everyone should experience an extended bus ride through the back-yards of America to understand its past. It was a grand adventure, twenty-two hours through small towns and big cities with intermittent stopovers in seedy, dirty, dark bus stations signaling the border between bustling business districts and the shabby neighborhoods of the poor, addicted, and homeless. But I loved it. I loved every Twinkie-eating, cigarette-smoking, Mad Dog-drinking minute of those bus rides with the truths of Bob Dylan and Peter, Paul and Mary pouring into my conscience. It was during those bus rides to and from Interlochen that Simon and Garfunkel's *Homeward Bound* became my favorite song.

When I arrived at the school, I seesawed between excitement and anxiety. Would I fit in? Would I make friends? Had I made a mistake agreeing to come here? I checked into my dorm and walked apprehensively to my assigned room where an unknown roommate waited. As the door swung open, a young Black man sitting on the left bed turned to stare at me. Thomas Slaughter.

I could not believe it. Could this be right? His name was Thomas Slaughter. He was a vocalist, a musician who used his vocal cords as I did my violin. We began talking about music and composers we liked. Amazingly, within the first forty-five seconds of meeting, I had found someone who had more in common with me than anyone I had encountered my entire life! It was a portent of a place that was to change my life forever.

Over the course of the first couple of weeks, I met many people, probably the majority of the four hundred students who shared this new home with me. I met fellow students in the rooms on the floor, then everyone living in our dorm. I met the people who played in the orchestra, and others sharing my classes.

Everyone attended classes in a complex of three round, domed buildings connected by a long, covered walkway that also linked with the Library and Administration office. Classrooms filled the outer section of each building, the center reserved for study and quiet conversation. Most classes were arranged to encourage communication between students and teacher, a semi-circle of chairs and tables with the instructor in the center.

My classes, each with only twelve to fifteen students, were incredible with teachers who truly cared about their students and the subjects they taught. They challenged me! For the first time since leaving New York City, learning became an emotional, transformational affair. It was a dream.

Each dorm had several areas for students to gather and relax. Massages were popular expressions of friendships, though mostly between the genders. Day in and day out, people would give each other back, arm or foot massages. There was comfort and compatibility with so many people. The unique thing at Interlochen was that, literally, everyone on campus knew everyone else. My mind was opened to so many new ideas.

After a week of classes, I knew there was no chance there would ever be an Afro clutch within a hundred miles of this glorious place. I began new friendships with three classmates—Joe, Phil, and Helen. Joe was your average hippie, a Jeff Spicoli character from the movie *Fast Times at Ridgemont High*. Phil was just the opposite, bouncing with nervous energy and happiest when he was outdoors. A little undersized, he was surprisingly athletic and moved with the grace and quickness of a ferret. He loved trees and would scrabble up through their limbs without invitation. Looking up at him through a canopy of dense greenery reminded me of the squirrels in Central Park chuffing at the pedestrians on the paths below. He was always climbing trees. Whenever the group walked around the campus, we would look around to find that he was gone, only to discover him sitting in a tree. He was great!

And there was Helen. Helen was tall, maybe a little heavyset, but to me, one of the most beautiful women I had ever met. She had an unbelievable spirit, dealing with setbacks and disappointments in an incredibly loving manner. I had never known anyone like her. She was the embodiment of love and acceptance, making me feel safe and strong and capable, feelings I rarely had in Hershey.

Right before I left for Interlochen, my mother's sister, Aunt Laura, gifted a meditation pillow to me from one of the exotic places she had visited in her travels around the world. She also taught me the rudiments of meditation, a wonderful way to deal with my flying anxieties. At Interlochen, the objects of my meditations expanded, disintegrated, and reassembled in new, exciting directions.

My friendships with Joe, Helen, Phil were intense, and they played a role in my metamorphose. I was closer to them than I had been with anyone during my entire life, and we talked about everything from music and the arts to spirituality. We listened to New Age music, a genre intended for meditation, inspiration, and introspection. Ray Lynch's *Deep Breakfast* album was a particular favorite. We sat for hours and analyzed profound phrases like, "Welcome, my friend, into my apartment, and we shall suffer through a deep breakfast of pure sunlight." We would talk about what it meant, not on the surface but deep in one's soul. What secrets were hidden behind the hypnotic repetition of natural and electronic tones and sounds?

Our examinations transcended spirituality, awakening new feelings about the meaning of life and our place in the universe. Our meditations infused our interactions and our studies. For me, those conversations introduced new revelations and emotions to express in my music.

For the first time in my life, I could focus on me and discover who I was. The people who surrounded me were comfortable in themselves, unconcerned about what others might think, uninterested in the social games played by the insecure. They were just themselves. They liked me for who I was, all my good, bad, and ugly. With their example, I began to like myself, too. I learned to accept that some people would not like me, and I was okay with that.

So much had changed for me in just a few short months at Interlochen. I remembered a terrible fight with my parents over something. I ran from the house, certain that they cared nothing about me. I had no true friends, the kind you could tell your most intimate fears and they would understand. I ran until I collapsed, exhausted and sobbing in a cornfield, surrounded by broken stalks and misshapen ears from the harvest. I promised myself, lying in the dirt that dark fall night, that I would never, ever treat anyone who loved me the way I saw people treat others in Hershey. With Joe, Phil and especially with Helen, I knew that I would never break that vow.

Midway in my first semester, I became close friends with Phil O. Everyone called him that because his last name started with an "O" and was too long to pronounce. Phil O was an academic major from a relatively affluent background. Unlike my other close friends, he was not the hippie type. But fun-loving he was and popular among the female students, so popular that his nickname quickly became "Casanova."

The five of us—Joe, Phil, Helen, Phil O, and me—were an odd group, but for some reason, we just fit together. That such different people could be good friends was beyond my experience. In Hershey, cliques were common, but the members shared a common denominator. There was the jock group, the playboy group, the brainy group, the nerds, and then, a mix-match group of outcasts. At Interlochen, everyone interacted and, if there were any groups, they were based on an art form. I was in music, Phil and Joe were in creative writing, Helen was in visual arts, and Phil O was in academics, though he dabbled in dance and theater.

That first year at Interlochen—my junior year in high school—and the incredible friendships I developed completely altered the arc of my life. My relations with women benefited from being a good friend of Mr. Casanova, Phil O, the boy everyone wanted to date. Even though my conversations with the opposite sex typically began with "What do you think Phil thinks of me," I didn't mind. To be able to sit and share a massage with a woman was wonderful, which minimized any concerns about the actual topic of our conversation. After all, we were talking about a great friend of mine whom I also loved, so it just did not matter.

Of course, some things never change, including my dislike of practice. I spent most of my time enjoying these friendships and, of course, watching endless television in the general area of the dormitory.

My first trip back to Hershey was for Christmas Break—"Spring Break" at most schools—a long bus ride that was as entertaining as my first trip. I decided I really preferred bus rides over other sorts of transportation. The sense of independence is similar to Jack Kerouac's adventures on the road but not as dangerous as hitch-hiking.

I reconnected with my Hershey friends and settled into a mutual armistice with my parents for the period. The truce, I think, was possible due to my new self-confidence developed and nurtured by the Interlochen community. That first Spring Break was memorable for another reason; I lost my virginity to a casual acquaintance during a party at my house when my parents were away. Since it was my first time, it was a big deal to me, confirmation that I had finished the last phase of puberty.

I returned to Interlochen, eager to reconnect with my dear friends who were changing my life. During that first year, my friendships introduced and encouraged personal reflection and self-expression. I was learning who I was and what I could become, with their help. I also learned that discretion is often preferable to confrontation. For example, Interlochen's administration had rules that students felt were unnecessary, including the prohibition of permanent alterations to dormitory rooms. We thought that the regulation was contrary to the collective artistic temperament and infringed on our personal freedoms to express our nature in our own space.

Phil and I determined that beautiful mosaics on the ceilings of our rooms would reflect and inspire our true natures. I decided a glowing, fire-breathing dragon best reflected my self-image while Phil felt a panorama of the Zodiac expressed his intent to live life to the fullest.

Luckily, we had friends studying Fine Arts with the creative talent to create our visions and shared our rebellious nature to break the rules. Even so, there were limits to our insurgency. A blatant disregard of the regulations would force the administration to react, even expelling us from the school.

Our solution was glow-in-the-dark paint. Over a few weeks, our friends drew the entire Zodiac on Phil's ceiling. A magnificent two-headed dragon circled the center light in my room. If Mickey, our RA and the only Black Resident Advisor on campus, visited our rooms after dark, we just turned on the lights to become the conforming students we pretended to be. Joe and I liked Mickey, but he was an authority figure, and we were always in a contest of cunning intellect, breaking the rules that we were able to break without getting caught. I do think that he respected our abilities, and if we didn't cross the line, everything was fine. We liked our relationship. One evening, we talked him into a "Confession night." I wasn't sure I would be back for my senior year and Joe was graduating, and it seemed like a cool thing to do. We wanted to share with him the rules we had broken where he hadn't caught us, knowing he would not impose any retroactive punishment. In the spirit of the moment, he revealed some of the crazy things he had done, including his fondness for some students. I guess his attraction was to be expected since, at most, he was in his early twenties. Even so, the realization that a female student could attract an authority figure was something we had never considered. In hindsight, I think our friendly relationship with the RA was handy later in the year.

During the winter semester of my first year, our orchestra was invited to perform at Lincoln Center in New York and Kennedy Center in Washington, D.C. The plans included a flight from Interlochen to Washington, a bus ride to New York City, where we would fly back to Interlochen after the last concert. I had not flown since I had auditioned for Interlochen and never expected to fly again. My anxieties returned, becoming intense as our departure date neared.

With the introspection gained through meditation, I realized that the dread of flight was not from a physical fear of flying or the absence of personal control that affects other aerophobians—people who are afraid of flying—but a fear of death itself. I was sure that turbulence would sever a wing from the plane's cabin, and the aircraft would plunge to earth in a fiery explosion.

As the tour date approached, I had numerous calls with my dad exploring my temptation to refuse the flight. Having experienced my trauma on our initial visit to the school, my dad was sympathetic but insisted that I confront the situation head-on.

"You have no choice, Aaron. You must face your fear and learn to control it. I'll tell you what. Your mother and I will wait for you. We'll be in D.C. when you land."

Appreciating their concern and hoping that flying again would end my problem, I got on the flight, sitting between Helen and Sonia, my good friends in the orchestra. After takeoff, I never said a single word to either seatmate. Closing my eyes, I sat rigidly in the middle seat, my fingers welded to the ends of the armrests. I was oblivious to the efforts of my companions to talk or offers of refreshments from the solicitous flight attendants. I was completely unresponsive to anything around me from the moment the plane left the ground until we returned to the ground in

Washington, D.C. When we finally touched down in Washington, D.C., I was exhausted. Helen and Sonia helped me from my seat and down the aisle.

"You were right, Aaron. We really don't think you should fly," they advised as we walked down the concourse to the terminal. I mumbled thanks, knowing I would never again voluntarily fly on a commercial airline.

As I hobbled into the airport terminal, I found my parents waiting by the baggage claim. I gave them a big hug in gratitude that they had made the trip. When my father asked me how the flight had gone, I grimaced and shook my head, finally slurring my answer, "Well, you know."

He did and, thankfully, didn't try to get more from me. I did not return with the orchestra from New York by plane. Although the school was reluctant to allow it due to various liability issues, I returned to the campus in my trusted and safe Greyhound. It would be decades before I again set foot on a commercial airliner.

During that spring semester, I discovered my love of practical jokes and pranks. To this day, I have no complete answer for why I pulled so many pranks back then. I've wondered if the years of feeling like an outsider was the source.

I realized that friendly teasing and joking only happen between people who are comfortable with each other. A stranger calling someone a dork would have triggered harsh words, if not violence. Among friends, the sobriquet is typically considered a sign of affection or friendly exaggeration. Before Interlochen, I was probably regarded as uptight and straitlaced by those who only knew me casually. I suspect the camaraderie and bonhomie of Interlochen freed a part of me that I did not think I had.

At the end of each school year, students eagerly participated in the "sign-in," a tradition at Interlochen that went back to its early years. The activity began with the students in each dorm confirming that they were in residence at the designated curfew hour, typically 10:00 p.m. on weeknights and 11:00 p.m. on weekend nights. At a pre-designated time, all students would leave their rooms, assemble, and kidnap the RAs in each dorm. One group after another, the laughing students would then haul their counselors to the boat dock behind the dorm and launch them into the lake. It was a wonderful tradition that was good-natured and fun for the RAs and students.

Unfortunately, someone in the administration thought the activity was too rough, unnecessary, and inappropriate for future artists. They banned the event and threatened to expel any student caught outside their dorms after curfew.

As might be expected, the students were upset about what seemed to be an unacceptable extension of authority over our personal rights. Many had older brothers and sisters who had sign-in during their residence without complaint from participants, "victims" (the RAs), or previous administrations. The banning was considered a personal insult to many, including me, since it was to be my first time. With the spirit of revolution wafting into the nooks and crannies of each dorm, a cabal of rebels decided to take action.

The solution, we believed, was to dunk the counselors under the guise of an unscheduled campus event, more specifically, a fire drill. During the confusion, the crowd of students would be encouraged to continue the banned activity—dunking the RAs—under cover of anonymity. I admit that most of the planning and organization was my responsibility.

Our plan called for co-conspirators to pull fire alarms in each dorm precisely one half-hour after sign-in. After evacuation, the same designated students would begin chanting, "Do the Kresge challenge! Do the Kresge challenge!" "Head for the Lake!" Kresge was the name of the lake abutting the campus. Excited by the moment and governed by mob mentality, the fuse would be lit, and the unofficial sign-in would occur.

The last step in the plan was to identify who would pull the alarms in each dorm and begin yelling outside. As planners, Joe and I agreed to set off the alarm in our upperclassmen dorm, HU-4. We decided that two people in each dorm would share the task to ensure no one lost their courage. Part of our espionage had revealed that the fire alarm, when triggered, spewed a cloud of red paint on the hand of the person pulling the alarm. I remember thinking at the time that the designers of the alarm system must also make those little packets of exploding indelible paint packets bank tellers hide in packs of currency.

Precisely at 10:30 p.m., Joe and I moved to the hallway upstairs where the fire alarm was located. Using old cotton socks, we completely covered the fire alarm with extra padding next to the handle to absorb any paint that might squirt one of us. We also positioned two buddies on the stairwells at each end of the building as lookouts. When they signaled the coast was clear, Joe and I stared at each other, silently mouthing the numbers: *one, two, three*. We pulled down on the fire alarm and raced to the nearest stairs to the outside.

Fate intervened at that moment. Just as we sprinted down the stairwell, two and three steps at a time, our RA, Mickey, opened the exit door to come in. We almost crashed into him in our haste, the alarm shrieking its bell, its strobe light pulsing brilliant light through the second floor's staircase door. Startled, he asked, "What's going on? Why are you in a hurry?"

Pausing, I yelled at him, "Don't you hear the fire alarm? There's a fire. We need to get out of the building. This is serious, Mickey."

"Alright, keep on going," he replied and sped up the stairs to ensure everyone was safe.

There was no one else outside. No alarms rang in any other dorms. We had been the sole conspirators that had performed our duties. Since no one had pulled the alarms in the other dorms, only residents of our dorm had evacuated, and some were in a surly mood for the interruption in their evening. At that point, abstaining from yelling "Do the Kresge Challenge" seemed to be the wisest action.

The ringing ended about thirty minutes later, and we were ushered back into the dorm. Joe and I trudged in, keeping our eyes down and trying to be inconspicuous. Maybe, I hoped, no one would realize it was us.

As we passed the head RA talking with Mickey, he said, looking at us, "Would you come into the office for a moment? We need to talk with you."

We followed the two into the office and sat in two wooden chairs in front of a desk. The head RA walked around the desk to the chair on the other side. Mickey stood behind him, glaring at us.

"Mickey tells me he saw you guys running down the stairs when the alarm went off. Since your room is on the first floor, it seems strange that you guys would be running from where the fire alarm was."

"No, we had no idea. We didn't see anything," we responded, talking over each other. "Someone else must have pulled it. It wasn't us. When we heard the fire alarm going off so late, we thought that there could be a real fire, and just wanted to get out of the building as soon as possible, sir."

Skeptical of our explanation, the two RAs separated us and continued their interrogation. Having learned from my many confrontations with my father, I knew the safest approach was to never admit anything and adopt an "I don't care" attitude. I recognized the stakes were exceptionally high for Joe, a graduating senior. I was determined not to throw him under the bus if I could help it. Even though the possibility of expulsion terrified me, I felt like our motive in planning and executing the fake fire drill was justified by the school's arbitrary banning of what should have been (at least to me) a sacred tradition. Despite my inquisitor's threats, I held to my story.

They continued their questioning, taking turns with each of us, one being good cop to the other's bad cop. When they told me that Joe had confessed, I thought it was just another interrogation ploy. They explained that, without a confession, they would expel him before graduation. Neither of us was prepared for the higher stakes in the game we had started. For Joe, failure to graduate would have been devastating and a waste of four expensive years of education. Worst of all, Joe would have faced his parents' disappointment when they learned the cause. We were right at the end of the school year.

When they told me they would let me finish the year if I confessed, without any guarantee for attendance the following year, I realized I had little choice. Although I believed the administration had overreacted to the incident, I couldn't let Joe bear the brunt alone. *In the end, they probably know, so why not just fess up?* I thought. And so I did.

True to their promise, they allowed Joe to graduate and me to finish out the year. However, they would not allow me to return the following year. Over that summer, a period of terrible apprehension that I might have to stay in Hershey, I wrote the administration a long, pleading request to reconsider their decision. I wrote how Interlochen had changed my life and how important attending the school was to my future. I closed my letter with a statement of fervent hope they would allow me to return.

My writing skills paid off, and my request was mercifully granted with a caveat that any violation, even smoking a cigarette, would mean automatic expulsion. With the sword of Damocles hanging over my head, I returned to Interlochen for my senior year, a year that was even better and more rewarding than I could have hoped.

Phil, Joe, and Helen had graduated the previous year, one of the reasons my friendship with Phil O blossomed. We shared various interests and activities, which helped cement our friendship. Oddly, some of the strongest personal bonds that I have ever experienced occurred during those months in the middle of the woods of northern Michigan. Phil and I have remained the best of friends since those days.

I became close friends with two new students during my senior year, Dwjuan, an African American student from Detroit, and Heidi, a Jewish girl from New York City.

Dwjuan, a very tall, thin, slightly gawky African American with a funny walk, had difficulty adjusting to his new environment. There were less than a handful of Black students at Interlochen then, and Dwjuan was uncomfortable in the predominately White culture.

Fortunately, he was good-humored with a distinct style that over-came bad first impressions. His predilection for an exceptionally white coat with a fur collar coupled with a wee small, white hat slightly askew on his head made him instantly recognized anywhere on campus. All in all, he had a wonderful, indomitable spirit, and we soon became good friends, too. Since Phil and I were Interlochen veterans, we were able to show Dwjuan the ropes.

Heidi was a bubbly girl with a knack for asking personal questions without seeming nosy. She could challenge someone and make them feel her only concern was their welfare. Seeing her in action always brought a smile to my face. We became friends through her attraction to Phil, still the Casanova of Interlochen. Since we had become upperclassmen, Phil's popularity had increased exponentially. Heidi certainly was attracted to him and remained so the entire year. At first, he tried to ignore her, but he fell for her by the end of the year.

The four of us frequently had intense conversations over what-if situations and how we might react. I enjoyed proposing different scenarios to see how people would respond. I realize today that none of us appreciated the difference in stress and our reactions between a theoretical and a real dilemma. Still, it was fun to imagine how we might respond in the fantasy.

One time, while sitting in one of the blocked-off rooms near the backstage of Kresge Auditorium smoking cigarettes and having a drink, someone proposed that we had been trapped in that same room by the Russians who had taken over America. They had placed a pistol with one bullet in the chamber with instructions that one person had to die before they returned. If they found the four of us alive, they would execute everyone.

As we pondered the proffered scene, I asked, "What would you guys do? That's the situation, that's the scenario. What would you do?"

Phil, always the gallant, didn't hesitate. "I would pick up the gun and shoot myself." His answer implied that he would save the rest of us by shooting himself.

"Yeah, yeah, that's easy to say, but when it comes down to actually pulling the trigger and blowing your brains against the wall, would you really do it?" I realized that I probably couldn't shoot myself.

"I'm not scared of dying," he replied. "Death just doesn't scare me. I wonder about what comes next. Besides, if I didn't do it, they would kill me anyway. Why not go out a hero? Maybe it would save the rest of you or maybe it wouldn't. But I would die, thinking I had saved you, why not?"

No one replied. I broke the suddenly somber mood, answering, "Thank you, Phil. I and the others appreciate that you would die for us. That's nice to know if we ever have to make a choice."

As everyone laughed, I turned to Heidi. "OK then, what about you? Would you kill yourself for us, too?"

I felt her flush in the darkness, hesitating before she replied. Giggling a little uncertainly, she said, "I don't know, Aaron. I hope I would do the same thing, but I really don't know. Maybe I would just leave the gun there and hope one of you acted."

"Yeah," I said. "But if we leave it there, then we all die. Doing nothing guarantees our deaths."

She surrendered, clearly not interested in further questions. "I just don't know, Aaron. And I hope none of us will ever find out what we would do in that situation."

As she finished speaking, Dwjuan jumped up and began pointing his thumb and forefinger like he would hold a pistol, "Pow! Pow! Pow!" He turned and shot several imaginary Russians, growling, "Man, I would grab that gun, and I'd be blazing. If they came back in here, I'd be like, blam, blam, blam. Pop those mofos."

"Dwjuan, that's why we only have one bullet. That's not an option." I interjected.

"That doesn't matter," Dwjuan sneered. "I would grab the gun. I'd be popping 'em. Run out of bullets, I'd grab their gun, I'd be popping them, and we'd be out of there."

I gave in. "OK, Dwjuan, OK. You are kind of defeating the purpose of the question." But he really wasn't because I had proposed the scenario to see how their minds worked.

The table turned when they asked me what I would have done. Because most what-if discussions ended before my turn, I rarely considered what I might do in any of my what-if games. I responded with the first thoughts that came to mind: "I think the first thing I would do is grab the gun, before anyone went crazy. I wouldn't want anyone to shoot me so I would make sure I had the gun. Then, I'd suggest that we talk and try to figure out a good solution to the problem,"

Ignoring that I really had not answered the question about the death of one or all, I think my imaginary response reflected my true character. I want to be the person in control. I know I am not good at following orders unless I understand and agree with their purpose. As I have recalled the question in the years since, I hope I would have acted more like Phil than Heidi, but I don't know. I am pretty sure that I would not react like Dwjuan. Conversations like these, along with a variety of other experiences and circumstances, forged a close relationship that year.

Despite my intent to walk the straight and narrow after the previous year's disaster, the boredom inflicted by days and days in the middle of hundreds of acres in the frozen tundra demanded a counterpoint. The only benefit of being artists and musicians in that frigid space was the juxtaposition and fusing of diverse talents. However, even creativity has its limits, perhaps the reason Van Gogh lopped off his ear for love.

At Interlochen, the result was a series of pranks directed at the administration and fellow students. A popular gag was tilting a trashcan half-filled with water to rest against a door. When the door opened, the trashcan fell into the room, flooding the floor with a half-inch of water. The gag was funnier if the victim was a poor housekeeper who left clothes, books, and papers strewn on the floor. Unwary sleepers were the favorite targets as few people were alert when answering a knock at the door in the middle of the night. A successful effort always ended with a blood-curdling scream and a stream of profanities echoing down the hallways from the victim's room.

While I was a target from time to time—maybe, from the victims who blamed me for their disaster—I never fell for the prank. I learned to test the weight against my door by slowly and cautiously moving it a tiny bit at a time. A door with a boobytrap opens easily with the dead weight of the trashcan against it; a safe door requires a little more effort. Knowing what awaited, I had three choices: I could 1. try to catch the can before it fell over; 2. close the door until someone came by and rolled the can away; or 3, slowly inch the door to the point that the can might fall forward, then suddenly slam the door to upset the can into the hallway, keeping my room safe and sound. I preferred the third option because I could play the victim, evidence that I was not one of the culprits in the skullduggery.

In the interest of civility, I have not described the various pranks or their victims we successfully performed during that year. Our most satisfying trickery involved Mickey, my RA of the previous year who became the head RA of the dorm during my senior year. Our two-floor dorm had a Resident Advisor on each floor. A third RA referred to as the head RA supervised other RAs and had the nicest room downstairs. Mickey was the head RA and head honcho or, as he liked to say, since he was African American, the HNIC (which, for those unfamiliar with the term, was the "Head Negro in Charge"). He was also the only African American RA on campus at that time.

We occasionally snuck out after curfew or broke other minor regulations. Even though we considered Mickey a friend, he was the natural opponent in our ongoing conflict with authority. He suspected that we regularly participated in illegal outings but couldn't prove it. In the spirit of competition, Phil and I devised a scheme that would drive him crazy with little risk of our being caught.

We had discovered the plan of the ventilation system for the dorm. Unsurprisingly, rooms on one floor connected with rooms on the second floor through the ventilation system. In other words, odors in one bathroom flowed to a second bathroom unimpeded. "Hitting the vents" was the practice of standing in one bathroom and blowing cigarette or marijuana smoke through the vents into a second bathroom. Success depended on knowing which rooms were paired and whether the vent doors were open.

Our covert investigations indicated that Phil's room on the second floor was connected to Mickey's room on the first floor. We knew that anything coming from the vent could seriously irritate Mickey. We filled a bottle of tap water and began pouring it down the vent in Phil's bathroom, expecting that Mickey would believe there was a leak and call the school's maintenance department. We did not intend to damage anything but to be a royal pain in Mickey's ass.

After we poured a little bit of water, I rushed down and listened at Mickey's door for a reaction. I heard him say, "What's this?" When I heard him on the phone to Maintenance, I ran upstairs to stop Phil's pouring. We then went down to the lobby outside of Mickey's room as if we had been there a while and killing time. When the maintenance man arrived and went into Mickey's room, we cracked up. It wasn't one of our bigger pranks but one of the most satisfying due to its victim. I'm not sure whether the head RA even realized he had been pranked.

Toward the end of our senior year, Phil and I decided to execute the most elaborate gag of the year. (It wasn't the scale of the fake fire drill of my junior year. I had learned there are limits to practical jokes, and I did not want to risk expulsion again!)

Inspiration struck after watching the movie *Billionaire Boys Club* one night in the dorm lobby. The movie's plot featured a group of rich kids in a club with fast cars, fast women, and fast ideas. "Wouldn't it be great to transform our dorm into the Billionaire Boys Club?" we thought. It was our last year at Interlochen. If we wanted to be remembered, we needed to do something on a massive scale. We began planning that same night.

When we shared our plan with Dwjuan, he wouldn't participate. In his first year at Interlochen, he wasn't anxious to rock the boat. We insisted, telling him, "Dwjuan, you gotta be down with this."

"No, man. That's too big, man. You're gonna get in trouble. That is just too big. I ain't doin' it," he replied and walked away. We were disappointed and a little miffed that he refused to consider the idea, but we continued ahead.

To transform the dormitory into the Billionaire Boys Club meant replacing the giant cut-out lHU-4 letters of bubble papers hanging on the front wall of our Housing Unit 4 dorm. They were the first thing people saw when they walked in the front door. Executing our plan required a new sign with "Welcome to the BBC."

To create the visual effect we wanted, we intended to move or reverse everything in the room. Late that night, between one and two o'clock in the morning, we snuck out while everyone was asleep. We were ready to make changes. There was a giant pinboard behind the main receptionist station. We took it and turned it around. Stacking chairs on top of each other, we climbed up to the "Welcome to HU-4" sign and replaced the letters. We unscrewed and reversed the fire exit signs in the dorm and the massive bulletin board behind the receptionist station.

We then moved to the furniture, initially placed in a conventional lobby setting. We moved an ironing table from the utility closet and set chairs around it to resemble a dining room just outside Mickey's door. Placemats on the table were pictures of the RAs that we borrowed from a locked display cabinet.

We worked for over two hours before we were satisfied with the transformation. It was splendid. It was glorious. It was sure to go down in the folklore of the school. Although no one could "prove" the identity of the provocateurs, we had little doubt we would get the credit among the students.

As we turned to go back to our rooms, I remembered Dwjuan's refusal to help us. It seemed only fair that his disloyalty be repaid. He had accidentally left his coat, the signature white coat with the fur collar, in my room earlier. I suggested to Phil, "You know, since he wouldn't help us, maybe Dwjuan should get the credit for our work."

I went by my room, picked up his coat, and left it lying on the floor to look like someone had taken it off while they were moving the tables and forgot it. Excited and waiting for the morning's news, we then returned to our respective dorm rooms.

Since it was the weekend, I figured everyone would get up late, and a description of the new look would spread quickly across the campus. Ready for the accolades that were sure to come, I sauntered into the hall around 10:00 a.m. The first thing I noticed was the exit sign at the end of the corridor. It appeared as it always had. I paused to wonder, How did we miss that sign? I must have missed it thinking Phil would do it. He probably thought I had done it, and we hadn't noticed it when we returned to our rooms.

As I walked through the lobby doors, I was stunned. Nothing was out of place. The pieces of furniture rested in their normal positions; the signs looked as they always did. The ironing table was gone, and the RA pictures sat in the locked display cabinet. There was no evidence of our hard work the night before.

I hurried to the front doors, hoping that somehow our work on the front wall had been missed. Our carefully crafted "Welcome to BBC" had become a simple "Welcome." What happened? I wondered. How had our plans been thwarted in this way?

I rushed upstairs to tell Phil what I found. He was incredulous, throwing his clothes and asking, "What are you talking about? That can't possibly be." It was in the same condition I had found it earlier—nothing had changed. The two of us sat in the lobby, fuming but helpless to do anything. Our expected glorification never happened; everyone was walking around like normal. Inexplicably, our planning and work were wasted.

We trudged back to my room, too depressed to talk. Shortly afterward, we found a furious Dwjuan banging on the door. He was wearing his white coat, the one we left as a red herring for Mickey. When he stormed in, I thought he might attack one of us. His eyes bulged as he jittered from one foot to the other, trying to gain control.

"What the Hell are y'all doin, Man, trying to get me in trouble? I thought we were friends," he took a deep breath. "I just got my ass chewed out by Mickey and the maintenance man for shit you guys did. I told you I wasn't interested, so you decide to pay me back by framing me?"

"Wait a minute! Wait a minute! Tell us what happened?" I said, still upset that the plan had gone awry and looking for someone to blame.

"Man, this morning, it must have been like seven or eight o' clock, Mickey called me to come to his room. When I was slower than he liked, he came up and got me. He told me that he and the maintenance man, Larry, had been up since 5:00 a.m. fixin the mess in the dorm. They found my coat and knew I had something to do with it. They kept questioning me about it, but I said it wasn't me, that I didn't know anything about it."

Forgetting that it was my fault that Dwjuan was even involved, I pressed him to be sure he hadn't ratted on us. "Are you sure you told them that you knew nothing?"

"Yeah," he replied. "But this is screwed up, man. I didn't say anything, although I thought about it. You guys weren't worried about what might happen to me at all. I took the heat, but you guys have a problem."

We began to chuckle with relief, then laughed. Dwjuan didn't see the humor in the situation. I told him he was right; we hadn't considered any blowback in our determination to write out names in the unofficial history of Interlochen. We apologized to Dwjuan, and life went on. We were sad that the prank had failed but curtailed our gags for the rest of the year.

. . .

During my senior year at Interlochen, my lack of practice caught up with me. With my natural talent, I easily occupied third chair in the orchestra. In my arrogance, I believed that I could be first chair any time I wanted it, and the others in the orchestra knew I could. Confident that they knew I was the best, I didn't feel like making an effort to prove it.

One day in my last term, the Concertmaster, other top players, and I were discussing how attitude—the power of the mind—affected one's musical skills. I believed anything was possible if one puts their mind to it. They disagreed, countering that no one could learn one of the complex pieces for the violin just because they wanted to. They had a valid point, but I continued to argue.

"Well, no, but given basically realistic circumstances, yes, one could."

"You couldn't learn the Bach Chaconne, a thirteen-page long solo movement for violin, in a week," she challenged.

"Of course, I could." I wasn't prepared to give an inch in the argument.

"No, not possible," she said smugly, clearly throwing down the gauntlet.

Not one to turn aside a challenge, I said, "I'll bet you I can learn that piece well enough to perform it in one week."

Knowing I never practiced and more than a little tired of my bragging, they agreed to take the bet. I knew that all I needed to work was the proper motivation. I practiced two-and-a-half hours each day during the week and played the Chaconne. Not particularly well, but I did deliver, on Saturday. That silenced them for the rest of the year.

I continued rule-breaking my second year at Interlochen despite my precarious hold on matriculation at the school. I have no explanation for my willingness to skate close to the line or over it at times. Fortunately, my exaggerated sense of self-confidence led me to the second love of my young life.

Melissa was the most beautiful woman I had ever seen in my entire life. She had a statuesque model's body, captivating green eyes, and flowing dark hair that cascaded over her shoulders and perfectly framed her delicate face.

Do you believe in love at first sight? I met Melissa when she dated Ned, my roommate, that year. The moment that I saw her, I felt our perfect synchrony. In the brief moment our eyes met, I thought she knows me, and I know her better than anyone else ever could.

We became friends initially, but relationships mature quickly at Interlochen. Within a couple of weeks, we spent almost all our free time together, taking extended walks along the beach, talking, and exploring the meaning of our life. We spoke of our beliefs about spirituality and the purpose behind our existence. My talks with Melissa gave me a hunger for the metaphysical.

The spiritual union that we felt developed quickly into a wonderful, amorous connection. On the beach, by the water, amid a gusty wind kicking—the kind that heralds a soaking rain—we kissed for the first time. I remember the moment felt like an eternity, but the cliché diminishes the impact of that moment.

I loved Melissa dearly and passionately, but she was from Texas, and her parents had regressive views on race. They would not tolerate our dating, and I wasn't sure how much Melissa told them about me. Melissa went on tour with the choir, so we didn't see each other as much.

I realized I wanted to spend the rest of my life with her. Only a gift of a ring would do. As a senior in high school, I had no money. Nevertheless, it was critically important to show her how I felt. I went to one of the dollar stores and got an electroplated gold ring.

When she returned, I found a moment to tell her that I loved her when we were sitting alone on the beach. I explained that I wasn't asking her to marry me then, but I hoped she would someday. She put the ring on her finger, never asking me if it was real. It was symbolic of our togetherness, not a pledge of future matrimony.

For a time, life was perfect. We made love in private places, including a hidden alcove above the stage of Kresge Auditorium. I still remember the experiences today, not for the sex, but the intimacy of two souls intermingling, touching, feeling, lost in the exquisite pleasure of being one.

Melissa's grandmother passed away, and she left school for a week to go to the funeral and be with her family. Something happened during that trip, but she never told me of it. After she returned, we began to drift apart, occasionally recapturing what we had for a moment, but it never lasted.

We parted ways at the end of the school year. After that term, she left Interlochen, became engaged, and married before year end. I will never see her again, I thought. I have many recollections of the incredible things about Melissa, the joy—the spirit—the wisdom that she brought into my life. Decades later, we reconnected and rebuilt a friendship, which remains to this day.

• • •

At the end of the school year, my parents came to pick me up. For me, it was the end of a significant chapter in my life. As we pulled out of the campus in our little Chevy Citation, I mourned for the family I would miss. In my mind, I said goodbye to Phil O, to Dwjuan, who had forgiven me for the dorm incident, to my other friends in classes, and to the orchestra. I thought of Melissa and hoped she would have a good life. Again and again, I realized what I was losing and feared what awaited me in Hershey, two places not only miles apart but existing in different worlds. Would I ever find another Interlochen, a place where I could be me and others accepted me unconditionally? How could I return to the site of much unhappiness and loneliness? I didn't know if I could.

CHAPTER 7

A LOVE AT PENN STATE

Looking back, the summer after graduation from Interlochen seems like an intermission in my life, a time of no movement, almost like catching my breath before starting a long journey into the unknown. Leaving Hershey to begin my senior year at Interlochen had severed any emotional link I had with the town. Going forward, it meant nothing more to me than the place my parents lived. In that sense, I was homeless, untethered from any physical location that I considered home.

Melissa dominated my thoughts and my sense of loneliness. I spent hours in my room listening to songs of lost love, wallowing in my melancholy. I think I cried a little each day for my loss, doubting that I would ever again capture the magic we shared. My parents, oblivious to my emotional trauma, insisted that I stay busy doing odd jobs, fixing and building things. I built a wine cellar. I built a stoop in the front of the house.

During my final semester at Interlochen, I applied to several colleges to continue my education. Going to college was never a question in my house, a reality for most kids whose parents are college graduates. My older brother attended Swarthmore College, and my adoptive parents expected that I would end up at a similar prestigious institution. As he pursued his academic interests, I would continue in music studies.

After receiving my audition tapes or hearing me play during a personal visit, some of the top conservatories in the country invited me to attend their programs. By then, I realized that I hated to practice, no longer loved the violin, and was unable to express myself through my music. I realized that I needed another vocation, so enrolling in a place whose purpose was to train future musicians made little sense. I wanted a school that could provide more career options than work as a musician.

Penn State was an obvious choice, with in-state tuition plus an additional discount due to my parents' employment at the Hershey Medical School. The school also offered a summer orientation program, mostly designed for inner-city school kids to help them prepare for the culture shock in a predominately White, small community known as "Happy Valley." I attended the program, though I was already familiar with a similar environment from my life in Hershey.

I lived in a dorm with kids coming mostly from the inner cities of Philadelphia and Pittsburgh. For the first time in my life, I was surrounded with more Black people than ever in my life. My classmates used slang and expressions that I had never heard. I pretended to understand, but I felt awkward and out of place. Unsurprisingly, they thought I talked White and, occasionally, teased me for something I said. Some suggested that I wasn't really Black, much like my Hershey friends who claimed the same things. Though I never felt the comment was meant to hurt me, I couldn't help but think, "Who am I? Where do I belong?"

When the fall semester at Penn State began, we settled into our dorms (or "halls" as they were called at the school). The university paired halls of men and women for joint activities. I befriended an African American female student named Michelle from my sister hall. Almost as attractive as Melissa, she was athletic and popular with both genders. The guys in my hall really wanted to date her. I kept getting questions about her, like, "Man, how did you get to be friends with her? Could you hook me up?" I told them that we were just friends.

Because of everything that I had gone through with Melissa, I was not interested in dating anyone at the time. But Michelle and I were close friends, playing sports and going to parties together with other people from our halls. Still thinking of Melissa, I did not want to be close to anyone—male and female friends—at that time. Even so, I was attracted to her, the first time I felt close to a woman of color in my life.

Michelle had a White roommate from Pittsburgh. I had seen the two of them at volleyball games, but never talked to her. Our relationship began when I called Michelle and Sherrie answered the phone.

"Hi, Sherrie. Is Michelle there?" I asked.

"That's right. You just call to talk to Michelle. No one ever calls to talk to me," she teased.

"I'm sure that's not right. I bet you get plenty of calls from guys trying to take you out," I replied.

"If you only knew," she answered, laughing.

"Well, I'll talk to you. What should I know about you? Where are you from?" We ended up talking for about thirty minutes until Michelle came in. Before Sherrie handed her the phone, I continued to flirt, saying, "Maybe we should hang out sometime." I heard her giggle as she passed the phone.

After that conversation, when I went to their room, I would stay to talk to Sherrie when Michelle wasn't there. We became close friends, sometimes giving others the impression that we were dating, though we weren't.

I was also friends with two Black students, Sandy and Monica. Unplanned, Sandy and I eventually hooked up, but only once. We liked each other, but nothing more than that. My relationship with Monica was more complicated because she did not like Sherrie. Monica had many of the stereotyped habits of an aggressive Black "sister," pointedly shaking her head and shaking her finger when she wanted to make her point. If Sherrie visited me while Monica was there, she would immediately leave without any apology and return only when Sherrie was gone.

Eventually, her hostility included me. Concerned, I asked Monica, "Why don't we take a walk and talk about this?"

As we walked, I said, "Monica, you've got to tell me what's going on because you know that I like to be up-front and resolve issues directly."

She didn't respond immediately, then said, "I know that, and I'm going to be direct with you. I have a problem with you hanging out with Sherrie."

"Why? We've talked about these things, and you know that I don't care whether someone's White or Black. I just care who they are. You don't choose the color of the person when falling in love. You should also know as a friend that I don't date anyone because of their color. I developed a friendship with Sherrie, but now it seems like I've fallen in love."

"Aaron, I believe you when you say color doesn't matter to you. But it matters to me. You're an educated, attractive Black man who should be with a Black woman as far as I am concerned. If you choose to be with Sherrie, I don't care what your reasons are or may be. I will always believe that it's because a Black woman isn't good enough for you."

"But you know that's not how I feel," I protested, unsure how to respond.

"Yes, Aaron, but you have a choice. This is one of those times in life you have to decide who you are. Not with me, but with other Black women. You can't be with Sherrie and have friendships like the one with me or other Black women."

I begged her to not ruin our friendship, but she gave me no choice. I never saw Monica again after that evening.

Over the previous months, my relationship with Sherrie had skyrocketed. Although it took me almost a year to tell her I loved her, I had known for some time what she meant to me. Our relationship began as a friendship, a connection that magnifies the feelings that love brings. Friends rarely punish each other, even in arguments, perhaps because they know that friendships are voluntary, and they don't want to risk their relationship. People in love often hurt their lovers deeply and intentionally when they are angry or disappointed as if "love" is an excuse for punishment.

Initially, Sherrie and I went together for the mutual joy of being with a kindred soul. Occasionally, she would drink too much, ending the evening with a tearful apology during the long walk back to her dorm. I think the beginning of our serious connection began on September 22nd of our freshman year. It was a typical fall day in Pennsylvania. The trees had begun to don their red and yellow fall clothes, the air just nippy enough to warrant a sweatshirt or a light jacket. Walking by the university's vacant baseball fields, we found an empty dugout to sit in and talk. For hours, we shared stories of our lives, me telling her about Interlochen and my friends, Phil and Heidi.

As the night grew darker, shadows from the full moon began to creep up the dugout walls behind us, as if an unknown intruder was silently listening to our conversation. Strangely, it was not a malevolent presence but more like a friendly sentry keeping us safe, a Man Behind the Wall on guard. We kissed that night, only holding each other to confirm the innocence and purity of the moment. Even now, we agree that evening was the beginning of a connection that lasted for years. I kissed her the next day in her dorm room following a pillow fight.

While I continued to play the violin, I had registered as a business major. While I had a full social life, I had no confidence in the direction of my life. I was lost. The Greek community—the name for the collective members of fraternities and sororities on campus—was a big draw for incoming freshmen, establishing an identity and an established social network in an otherwise anonymous existence. I considered joining one of the Black fraternities on campus—Alpha Kappa Alpha or Kappa Alpha Psi—but their tradition of branding the symbols of their Greek names on arms—a protest of when slaves were branded involuntarily—and their militancy turned me off. From my perspective, there was just no need for overt identification to signal one's racial status.

A White friend invited me to visit the Alpha Tau Omega (ATO) fraternity on campus. The fraternity had been founded at Virginia Military Institute in 1865 by Confederate war veterans. I became the first African American pledge of the ATO chapter at Penn State.

My Greek affiliation did not last long, discovering after a pledge meeting that I would never fit the model of brotherhood they sought. At an early meeting, a fraternity officer explained the goal of the pledge term: "It's very important that we mold you, and I repeat, mold you, in the image of an ATO brother."

If there was one thing I knew, no one or organization would ever again force me to become something I was not. I had spent my childhood trying to be the child my parents expected at a heavy cost to me and them. I told them that I was sorry, but becoming a pledge had been a mistake and I left.

Over a phone call, I confessed my unhappiness to Phil O who had enrolled at University of Florida in Gainesville. When I told him that I had considered joining a fraternity, he laughed. The idea of becoming a clone of a typical American college student was abhorrent, especially following the nature-loving, "everybody love each other" type of philosophy and anti-commercialism I had adopted at Interlochen.

"I'm not doing my music and I'm a half-assed business major," I complained.

"Hey, I know. It's the same for me," Phil replied. "It doesn't make any sense. We're totally lost. We need to find ourselves. Aaron, why don't I drive up, pick you up, and we will go out to Michigan and just see if we can find ourselves?"

Although my quitting school was likely to hurt Sherrie (and probably enrage my parents), I knew that finding myself was something I had to do. I had no qualms about leaving Penn State.

My parents and friends warned me that few people who quit college return, losing the opportunities that are afforded college graduates. I considered the consequences but realized I would never be able to concentrate on my education until I knew myself. I wasn't giving up on college, I told myself, but taking a sabbatical until my uncertainties were resolved.

No matter what I promised or explained to Sherrie, she was inconsolable, certain that I would never return. Our passions would cool, she said, and our love would wither away from abandonment and regret. Desperate to receive her understanding, I considered how I might be able to convince her that I would return for her. I finally realized that leaving my violin with her was my only choice. Sherrie knew my violin was an integral portion of my self-image. My devotion to that exquisite blend of human artistry, physical beauty, and emotions was complete and infinite. Through our tears, we said goodbye, her pain softened only by the security of my violin.

• • •

Phil and I drove to Lansing, Michigan and boarded at his mother's house. After trying several minimum wage jobs, we found a canvassing job for an environmental group. From October through December, we knocked on doors to get signatures and donations to save the natural environment. Those three months proved to be a major influence in my adult life. I learned more about people and myself than I would ever gain from a classroom.

Each time I rang a doorbell or rapped on a door was a new adventure. At least one-half of the time, no one answered, or they cracked the door open to growl, "Not interested." Occasionally, a resident would invite me inside to ask about the cause and how their contribution would be used. Success, measured by a signature or a donation, was statistically low based on the ratio of positive responses to the number of attempted contacts.

I quickly realized that door-to-door solicitation was, first and foremost, a numbers game, i.e., the more doorbells I rang, the greater signatures or donations I could obtain.

I also learned that spiel and performance—when given the opportunity to speak personally with a potential donor—significantly affects their monetary response. I believe that most people want to do the right thing; they want to help the common good, but they are jaded and skeptical due to exaggerated, meaningless promises from slick-talking promoters and over-the-top TV advertisements. I believed in the goals of my employer and my belief, I think, was evident in my work. Phil felt similarly, so we felt good about the job and trying to make a difference.

Despite the distance between us, my relationship with Sherrie deepened and expanded. We talked almost every day on the phone, and there wasn't a day that I didn't think about her. I knew then that I was truly in love with her.

• • •

At the end of the year, I returned to Penn State for the spring semester. I knew I had to be with Sherrie, and I wanted to get back to my music. I registered as a music major and rose quickly through the ranks to become Concertmaster of the Penn State Philharmonic. I enjoyed being a music major and Concertmaster. For the first time in years, I practiced regularly, not from duty, but because I wanted to play. The connection with my violin that I had as a little kid playing for my mother in our New York City apartment reawakened, resurrected after years of neglect.

With my return to Penn State, my relationship with Sherrie led to conflicts between her and her family. Her parents were racist and, from my perspective, the worst kind of racist. Some White people, a relatively small percentage of the population, are especially vocal about their prejudice and belong to fringe supremacist groups. Their hate is overt and easily recognizable, a characteristic that blunts their effectiveness.

A much larger group of people hide their racist feelings knowing that ordinary people would be disgusted by their beliefs. While they do not participate in Ku Klux Klan meetings or attend White supremacist rallies, their silent approval encourages the truly evil people to advance their racist position. Why racism exists, I don't know, perhaps to have a scapegoat for their own failures. The Nazis targeted Jews and racists target people of color.

Sherrie's parents were solidly situated in the second group. Her dad was a middle-management businessman, while her stay-at-home mom occasionally cut hair and babysat. To them, Black people were lesser, probably stupid, and most likely drug dealers and criminals. The thought that their daughter might date a Black man was inconceivable. Even the suspicion of such in the minds of friends and neighbors was intolerable.

Sherrie knew her parents would not approve of our relationship and kept them in the dark about its seriousness. She told them of our friendship but kept its details secret.

In the months following my return, I had taken her on hour-long trips to Hershey to meet my parents and friends. We agreed that going to Hershey with me for Spring Break would be wonderful. To avoid a confrontation, she lied to her parents about staying with a White friend during that time.

When her parents discovered the lie, they called her at my house and insisted that she return to her parents' home in Pittsburgh immediately. Feeling that she had little choice, she tearfully obeyed. The following day, she called to tell me our relationship was over and she could not see me again. As I later learned, her parents demanded she end it, threatening to cut off her school support if it continued.

Even though I suspected her parents were the cause, I was heartbroken and enraged. Her parents knew nothing about me, what kind of person I am, or how I felt about their daughter. They were breaking us apart for the sole reason I was Black. I lost control, throwing furniture across my parents' living room as my dad tried to calm me. I suspect he was happy to be the peacemaker in that incident, rather than the instigator.

Still angry and depressed, I returned to school at the end of the week unsure what I should do. Sherrie must have felt the same since she called me that evening. We met and she explained that her parents had given her no choice. Unless she broke up with me, she was on her own. Since we loved each other, we agreed to see each other on the sly. Sneaking around as if we were a pair of love-sick adolescents embarrassed me. I told her that I had no respect for her parents and their prejudice. I wished that she had been honest and told them that she loved me, but I understood her situation.

• • •

The plan worked until my friend Dwjuan from Interlochen visited later that spring. Sherrie had her parents' car and offered to drive us around campus to show off the school. Her older sister Lyn (Sherrie is the middle of three sisters) also attended Penn State and happened to see us. She immediately called their parents to report that Sherrie was alone with "several Black men," one of whom had to be "that Aaron guy." By the time Sherrie returned to her dorm, her father had called several times, leaving a message demanding she call him at once.

I was proud of her when I learned of the conversation. She admitted that we had been seeing each other and she loved me. Since the term was almost over, he told her that the matter was to be discussed when she returned home. I foolishly thought the situation would improve. She had repeatedly told them how happy we were and my importance to her. I couldn't imagine that a father or mother would try to keep us apart in those circumstances. I would never again underestimate the viciousness of racial hatred, even to the point of disowning one's children for loving a person of another color or race.

After Sherrie rejected a transfer to another university far from Happy Valley, they disowned her. The following day, Lyn—the sister who shared her childhood and blood—knocked on the door of Sherrie's and Michelle's dorm room. I happened to be visiting at the time. Lyn didn't say a word, striding across the room to Sherrie's bed. She ripped the sheets and blanket off the bed and stuffed them in a large duffel bag along with the pillows, then went into the bathroom and grabbed the towels.

The three of us were dumbfounded. We just sat there in amazement as Lyn opened and slammed dresser drawers and closet doors, seeking anything Sherrie's parents might have given her. She didn't say a word, just glaring at us as she continued her looting.

When she left, Sherrie began to cry. Michelle, embarrassed to have witnessed the humiliation, reached out to touch her and promised, "Don't worry. I'll give you some of my sheets."

Unlike me, Sherrie had lived most of her life in a happy home, her parents taking very good care of her. The rejection of her parents and sister over our relationship stunned her, exposing a hypocrisy in her family's character that she did not know existed. The combination of their repudiation and withdrawal of any financial support devastated her. I was overwhelmed by my own guilt for having caused (unintentionally) so much pain to her. I wondered how I, penniless, could possibly make the situation better.

The three of us—Sherrie in the middle with the arms of Michelle and me around her—sat on the stripped mattress. Lyn barged through the door and unplugged the television bought by the parents. She grabbed it and snarled to Sherrie, "Help me carry this downstairs."

Sherrie began to rise and help her when I pulled her back down and said, "Do it yourself." It took every ounce of my willpower not to add a few select curse words or choke the vile, despicable witch as she exited the room.

Even now, I will never forgive or understand Lyn's behavior that day to her sister. My adopted brother and I were never close, being too different, but I knew he would never treat me the way Lyn treated Sherrie that afternoon. I didn't agree with nor respect her parents' prejudices but recognized that I had grown up in a country just beginning to acknowledge the wrongs of racism. Lyn had no excuse for her wickedness, being of my generation.

In my eyes, she was Cain to Sherrie's Abel, so twisted with her perceived superiority that she would come into her sister's room and steal the sheets off her bed just because her sister dated a Black man. She showed not a sliver of compassion or empathy for her victim. To me, her actions were a betrayal most heinous, making her one of the most contemptible forms on earth. I will never understand those like her, young and educated, aware of tolerance, yet choosing a racist and intolerant path. I consider them the greatest obstacles to peace in our world. Every time I listen to Martin Luther King, Jr.'s "I Have a Dream" or hear stories from the Civil Rights Era, I think of people like Lyn.

For the next several years, Sherrie endured a brutal, cruel treatment from a family that made my parental challenges seem like a cakewalk. I had little money, but I was in school, thanks to my tuition discount, music scholarships, and student loans. I shared with Sherrie what little I had or could borrow, so we barely eked by. But we made it and resolved to work that summer to save money to get her through school.

I shared my dorm room with a White suburban kid named Nat. He acted as if he came directly from the streets of Compton. Like many middle-class White kids, he adopted the pseudo toughness of the rap culture, its slang, dress, and impudence without understanding the culture of its inner-city roots. We were nothing alike and I considered him as one of the most obnoxious people I had ever met. By the end of the semester, I truly detested him.

Our problems began with Sherrie occasionally spending the night. I had explained our situation to him and asked if he would object to her staying over time to time. He said her being there was not a problem, suggesting that he too might have an overnight visitor.

Sometime later, Sherrie was spending the night and began to feel ill. Nat was out for the evening, and we went to bed early. About one o'clock in the morning, Nat and a couple of his friends burst into the room, slamming the door, turning on the lights, and yelling, obviously very drunk.

"Yo, man, we're sleeping. You need to chill out, dude, she's sick. Either crash, or go hang out in someone else's room," I called from the bed.

"F*** that S***!" he yelled. "This is my f***ing room, too. I'll make as much noise as I want."

"C'mon, Nat. Let's just go to my room and let them sleep," said one of his friends. I knew the guys and appreciated their help.

"Nah, F*** that," Nat said. He stumbled across the room and turned on the TV. We didn't have cable then, so nothing was being broadcast that late. The white glare from the screen added to the room's brightness, its static punctuating the tension between the two of us.

I lay there, hoping that he would realize that he was acting like an a**hole and leave. After about ten seconds, I said, "Nat, you need to shut that off immediately and get out of here. Otherwise, we have a problem."

"No, man, F*** you and F*** her. I don't want her staying here anymore," he sneered, staring at me, sure that I would back down.

Without thinking, I leapt out of bed in my underwear and hurdled toward him, determined to knock that look off his face. He backed up, almost falling through the door as he realized my intention. He had not expected my reaction and desperately wanted to escape. As he moved away, I grabbed his shirt, intending to hold him as I hit him with my other hand. Before I could do any damage to anything but his shirt, the other guys grabbed me, wrapping their arms around me and tried to cool me down.

I still wanted to shove my fist into his pasty-white face. Certain that he was safe, the obnoxious little grin returned. I continued to struggle against my captors, screaming that I would kill him.

The noise of our confrontation woke up people on both sides of the hall and brought the Resident Advisor running to our room. Sherrie had woken and was crying, as much from the raw violence that had erupted as worry about me. The two of us were separated and I eventually calmed down. Nat realized that he had provoked the fight which could lead to punishment if the RA reported it. Neither of us wanted to deal with the Dean of students, so we apologized. I went back to my room with Sherrie and Nat went to a friend's room. We never made up and I was glad when the semester was over.

CHAPTER 8

FINAL YEAR AT PENN STATE

At the end of the spring semester, we realized that we needed to earn some money for the next year's tuition and expenses. Sherrie's parents had not changed their position on our relationship and refused to give any financial aid if she was with me. I remembered an old joke I'd heard about marriage—"Two can live as cheaply as one, but only half as long"—and agreed with the sentiment. We were tired, barely eking by and afraid what the future would hold.

Through a friend, we learned about a book company looking for salespeople to sell encyclopedias door-to-door. In those days before the Internet, many parents would buy a set of reference books for their children, paying for them on an installment basis. The Southwestern Book Company hired clean-cut-looking college students, trained them for a week in Nashville, Tennessee, and then shipped them around the country to different cities. The company offered room and board plus a commission of the books sold, each salesperson earning $5,000 to $7,000 on average for the summer, we were told. Part of the pitch was that we would be a team sent to work in California, Florida, or Hawaii. Thinking we could return to Penn State at the end of the summer with $10,000 in savings, we applied. With those savings, we could cover our sophomore year costs, Sherrie could stay in school, and everything would be perfect.

After completing the training program, we learned that business promises are not always kept. Instead of being on the sunny beaches of Florida or California, we were assigned to the eastern side of Washington State. Neither of us was prepared for the combination of sweltering summer heat and high humidity that soaked clothes and frizzed hair.

Even though we had made our relationship and our desire to work together clear from the onset, the company assigned Sherrie to work in Spokane and me in the Tri-City area of Pasco, Kennewick, and Richland, about 140 miles south. Each of us lived in a company apartment with other team salespeople of the same sex.

At 8:00 a.m., six days a week (Sunday was an off day), a company representative would collect a group of salesmen, each with a 30-pound pack of sample books, and ferry them to different residential areas of the city. The salesperson was expected to go door-to-door in the neighborhood trying to sell a set of encyclopedias for the next thirteen hours (with a small break for lunch) until the company returned at 9:00 p.m. to take them back to the group apartment.

I am sure there are worse jobs, but I never discovered one. A salesperson was lucky to give one sales presentation a day, most homeowners either refusing to open the door and quickly dismissing us with a curt, "Not interested." I was luckier than most, making a commission on a couple of sales. In retrospect, when I consider the hours worked and the pay, I think I would have made more at McDonalds's flipping burgers.

Sherrie and I talked each evening, and her experience was the same as mine. We had made a horrible mistake, being too naïve to question the results being tossed about the company or the ease of selling the books. The physical part of the job—carrying around the equivalent of four gallons of milk all day—tested my stamina; I can't imagine how the girls in her group felt each night.

To ensure people actually worked, the company forbade any salesperson to return to the apartment during the workday. Toward the end of the third week, hot, tired, and disgusted at the futility of selling books we didn't have to strangers we didn't know, I decided to quit. I went back to the apartment and called Sherrie to leave a message. To my surprise, a message wasn't necessary. She and her roommates had reached the same conclusion and intended to quit.

Phil was still working at the environmental company in Lansing, Michigan, where we had worked the previous fall. I was pretty sure I could get both of us jobs there. We would still be going door-to-door, but just five hours in the evening Mondays through Fridays. Just as important, it would be working for a cause that aligned with our values. If we didn't make much money, we would be doing good at least. Sherrie didn't hesitate; she asked, "When can we go?"

• • •

A couple of days later, Sherrie and I piled into a friend's car and made the nonstop journey to Michigan. Confirming that we had a job, the two of us stayed at a cheap motel until I found a sublet, a furnished apartment above a laundromat in East Lansing. Without air conditioning, it was a bit warm but a paradise to us since we were together and had jobs. Since I had experience, I was hired as a field manager and added Sherrie to my crew. Sherrie did a passable job, but really disliked walking up to strangers and starting conversations.

The occasional letters from her parents berating her in the most despicable terms for our relationship saddened and frightened her. They claimed that I was interested in her only because she was White. When the novelty grew old, I would leave her like Black men always left their women. In reaction to the possibility they might be right, she lost her self-confidence and grew more dependent on me. I understood the pressures on her and tried to avoid adding to her misery. That summer, we had a few harsh arguments between us because of all those external pressures.

We returned to Penn State, cobbling together what pennies we had for tuition. Sherrie went to class and worked part-time in Ben & Jerry's Magazine Shop, then as a waitperson at a franchised Roy Rogers restaurant. With the little money she earned and what I could give her, she rented a bedroom in a two-bedroom apartment off-campus. Her landlord-roommate was anti-social and especially jealous of her property, unwilling to let Sherrie use any of her things.

We couldn't afford to buy any furniture including a bed for Sherrie. The roommate kept a little ornate bed in the room, but forbade Sherrie to touch or use it. Sherrie slept on the floor next to the bed, using a pair of folded blankets as a mattress. To be sure Sherrie didn't lie down or sit on the bed when the roommate was out, she spread a roll of butcher paper between the mattress and the bottom sheet. When she returned, she lifted the sheet to find any crinkles in the paper, a sign that Sherrie had broken the rules.

Sherrie didn't have a phone. Her roommate did, but she refused Sherrie to use it. If she wanted to talk to me late at night, she had to leave the apartment and use a pay phone down the street. As a young man, I did not appreciate the hopelessness and anger Sherrie must have felt and was willing to experience because of me. I loved her certainly, but I was too wrapped up in my own problems to think about those around me.

Sherrie's parents stepped up their pressure on her after we returned to Penn State. Having been at odds with my parents over the years, I couldn't understand how she held on to her fantasy that they would suddenly change, welcome me into the family, and life would be what little girls imagine when they grow up. Each time a card or letter arrived, she rushed to open it expecting to find good news. Instead, they asked, "How can you do this to the family? What are you doing? Come back to the people who really love you. You know we're the ones who really love you." On her birthday, they sent a cake signed, "From the ones who really love you," the message implying that I didn't love her. Even holiday greeting cards included hand-written questions of "How can you be with that drug dealer?" ". . . that pool hustler?" or another stereotype they picked up on the street.

Telephone conversations always ended with Sherrie's attempts to show them that they were wrong about me. "He has White parents. He plays the violin. He's Concertmaster of the Penn State Philharmonic."

"Well, so what about playing the violin. Anyone can do that," they replied. "And he's lying to you about his parents."

Sherrie's mother was most often on the other end of the calls. The only conversation with her father that she told me about was his claim that they had given Sherrie and her sisters all that they could, even helping them to go to college. In return, they only asked that each girl behaved "decently." Going with a Black man was certainly not decent behavior, so her predicament was not their fault, but hers.

Apparently, they believed that my assertation about White parents was a scam. Somehow, I had the means and money to rent a pair of White, middle-aged actors and a house in Hershey just to convince Sherrie to believe me. That is the truth of racism: When the reality doesn't align with the stereotype that feeds the prejudice, the only option is pure idiocy.

Sherrie's distress with her parents and the conditions forced upon her rebounded on me. I didn't know what to do. I realized that the distance between her and her family was due to me, but I didn't understand why she seemed unwilling to confront her family and move on with her life. She eventually dropped out of school, the burden of paying her own way and trying to study was just too much.

As the relationship with her parents deteriorated, I felt like she began to cling to me more tightly. I didn't want the responsibility of fixing her life. I had a hard time trying to keep my own life on track. I resented her dependence and felt guilty as I pushed her away. We began to argue more about meaningless things, usually ending in my anger and her tears.

I loved her, but her inability to fight back frustrated me. The girl that captured my heart was upbeat, funny, and independent. We bonded because it was fun, glorious, exciting, and comforting. I longed for her to be the person I thought she had been—her own individual unaffected by the prejudice and persecution of her parents.

When I look back at that time, I realize that neither of us were mentally nor emotionally prepared for the pressures of the situation. We were just kids, only two years from graduating high school. I like to think that today, given a similar situation, I would be more sympathetic, more comforting, and less self-centered than that boy finishing up his sophomore year in college.

Even with our problems, we stayed together, the good times and memories masking the unpleasantness with forgiveness and the possibilities of the future. The coming of summer opened up new possibilities, opportunities to get on a better financial footing for the fall semester so Sherrie could get her career back on track.

Our possibilities included staying at Penn State and taking whatever jobs we found or returning to Lansing and working for the canvassing company again. The problem at Penn State was the lack of employment options due to the small community. On the other hand, Sherrie hated the canvassing, and I did not want to have to deal with her complaints. We agreed that the Lansing option would only be exercised if other opportunities failed to surface.

I also knew of a good summer music program called Penn's Woods. The program administrators wanted me to play in the orchestra. I thought participating would be my best career option, giving me the opportunity to show my skill at the final recital. The problem was that I needed to work over the summer to cover our expenses the next semester.

Reluctantly, I asked my parents for financial help, explaining the benefits of the program and my need to work due to Sherrie's situation with her parents. They were sympathetic, but non-committal. To my surprise, they proposed to pay me a lump sum equal to what I would earn working a minimum wage job under two conditions: (1) I promise to practice (They remembered my previous dislike for repetition, not knowing my attitude had taken 180° turn,) and (2) the payment would come at the end of the summer.

It seemed to be a perfect solution. I could work on my musical skills and get a wad of money at the end of the summer. Added to what Sherrie would earn, we would be able to eke by. While we couldn't live in luxury, we wouldn't have to worry about a roof over our heads or food.

I participated in the program that summer, practicing two hours a day as promised. Sherrie worked part-time as the desk clerk for a local motel. She didn't earn much, but every little bit helped. My recital at the end of the summer went well and we were excited to begin the fall semester.

When it was time to receive the money that my parents had promised, they changed their commitment. Instead of the lump sum of money we expected, they sent me a note: "We've decided not to give it to you all at once because you're not good at budgeting. We will divide the money we were going to give you by twelve and send it to you each month."

Their decision infuriated me, especially since they never talked to me or asked how the change might affect us. I felt that they had planned it all along since it was another way of controlling me. Despite my fury, I had no choice but to accept the new arrangement. Arguing with them could end with them giving me no financial help. I had trusted them and participated in the summer program instead of working. As much as I wanted to throw it back in their face, I realized rejecting the new arrangement would only hurt Sherrie and me. I swallowed my pride and accepted the new condition.

• • •

The combination of the check from my parents and Sherrie's savings allowed for us to live together for the first time in months—no roommates, no worries about pleasing anyone else. Though we lived right on the edge, we made the most of what we had.

Our apartment was better than the worst, but considerably less than the best. We paid $700 a month for it, but made it look and feel like it cost much more. We were resourceful, hunting for cool tapestries and vivid posters that brightened the space with an aura of character and original- ity. I felt like, at last, we had a home, a place of refuge from the trauma and tension of the world beyond its walls.

Unfortunately, there is never a lasting escape from reality. Despite our improved living conditions, we couldn't cover Sherrie's school expenses. My education costs were low due to the discount on tuition for my par- ents' employment in the Penn State system. I also earned several music scholarships, which significantly offset the burden. Sherrie had to pay full tuition for an in-state resident. Her parents refused to help her but continued to claim her as a dependent, a condition that prevented her from applying for student loans.

Sherrie decided to drop out of school and take a full-time job, intend- ing to return after a semester or two. She found a full-time job as a nanny for a couple of physical therapists with two young kids. She also took a Penn State online course, an innovation just beginning to gain traction at the time.

Not content with abandoning their daughter financially, her parents revoked her car, leaving us dependent on public transportation and the charity of friends. I think by then she had accepted that we were on our own, our fate being up to us. While she wasn't the happiest, she had con- fidence that we could make it.

• • •

That semester, the first hint of what my career would be appeared. Two aspects of my being are my love for music and my empathy for those who are persecuted for their difference. The two led me to a vision of a non- profit Pennsylvania Council for the Arts that would sponsor a competi- tion to inspire young kids, especially urban kids, to play music.

My relationship with music has been rocky at times, especially during my teens. Even so, I have never denied its hold on me. Music allowed me to express emotions I could never articulate how it resonates deep in my soul, the hidden spaces known only to me and what one may refer to as god. Music is the story of mankind with its melodies and beats—the tragedies, the triumphs, the loneliness, and the wonders. It is a part of me that connects me to the rest of the world.

Growing up different—biracial and adopted—indelibly colored my attitude for those who suffer the terror of prejudice, stereotypes, and isolation. I know what the little boy with the huge Afro feels in a class of White bullies or the skinny girl with glasses who is tormented by the popular kids. I've experienced the guilt of being unique, and I will always, always fight for the underdog, the child others disdain, ridicule, and avoid.

At the time of my first effort to unite music and opportunity, I knew nothing about organization, the importance of financial sponsorship, or how to begin. Unsurprisingly, my idea never got off the ground. Today, there are a variety of programs encouraging young classical inner-city musicians, including some that I later played a part in starting.

For most of the semester, Sherrie and I enjoyed a period of normality. While her parents continued to be estranged, the money from her job and my parents' check kept our heads above water. Over the Thanksgiving holidays, my parents surprised us with a new condition to our agreement.

Even though I had fulfilled the conditions for the full gift during the summer, they had arbitrarily decided to split the amount into twelve payments. Their note added a new component to the agreement, a requirement that I made grades acceptable to them if the previously agreed payments were to continue. At the time, they had sent three of the monthly payments (September, October, and November), but the rest depended on the new condition.

I despised them for the change and myself for having trusted them to live up to their word. They knew the difficulties we had with Sherrie's parents and trying to stay on an even keel financially, but it didn't seem to matter. To me, their actions were unfair. However, as before, we had little choice but to accept the new condition.

Even though our future was uncertain, I wanted to surprise Sherrie with a special Christmas. My family never celebrated Christmas, my only experience with the holiday was with Phil and his parents in Lansing when we attended Interlochen. Sherrie's family always made a big deal of the event as she was growing up—house decorations, Christmas tree, hanging stockings—and she missed those times.

Knowing that cutting down a tree would be the least expensive, I drove to one of those cut-down-your-Christmas-tree plots scattered around Happy Valley. After searching for hours, I found the perfect tree. I borrowed a handsaw to cut it and hauled across the three-acre site and loaded it in the trunk of the car. I admit driving back with the green branches extended out for the world to see really person- ifies the Christmas spirit and the anticipation of the joy to come. I hurried home and spent the evening hanging lights and decorations. My effort was worth it when Sherrie returned home from work and opened the door to see the tree in its glory. The smile on her face lasted the evening.

My grades arrived in the week before Christmas, and I forwarded them to my parents. My 2.6 GPA was not unexpected, but I had hoped they might have been a little better. Even though I had not studied as I should have, I expected my parents to consider the stress I had experi- enced during the semester. As always, I expected too much.

That Christmas Eve, I received an envelope with the December check with a Post-It note saying, "This is the last check.", and their initials. M&D. That was it. There was no other message, no card, no suggestion that I call them for an explanation.

I was furious. I never wrote or talked to my parents about why they had done what they did. They knew what Sherrie's parents had done to her, the way we felt about each other, and our financial situation. Know- ing that they chose to punish us for my GPA. I vowed never to forgive them for that cruelty. After that night, six years would pass before I spoke to or saw my parents again.

ATM

Did I forget
my last deposit?
That check was cashed last month.

Why must I withdraw twenty dollars?
I only wanted ten.

Please, someone's lookin', give me somethin'
other than a receipt.
Vile contraption,
evil fiscal temptress!
Why can't you make mistakes? "Insufficient funds
for transaction."

During that fall semester, I was determined to confront my fear of flying. The last time I flew had been the Interlochen orchestra's trip to Washington, D.C. and New York City, which ended in a bus ride for the return trip. I realized an unwillingness to fly would negatively affect my career, whatever it might be. I hoped the problem was limited to the large commercial planes where any personal control over the outcome was impossible.

Penn State offered many opportunities for various extracurricular activities, including a course for a glider plane's pilot license. Happy Valley was one of the glider capitals of the country at the time. The Canadian autumn winds confronted the temperate atmosphere of the dying summer and crashed into the slopes of the Blue Mountains. The atmospheric turmoil produced a series of irregular updrafts that drew glider aficionados across the region.

Glider planes are motorless, very light with abnormally long wings designed to exploit the turbulence like a great soaring bird. Glider planes gain altitude by riding pockets of rising air—what pilots call "elevators"—or increasing airspeed by gliding through them. Experienced pilots perform maneuvers of "ridge soaring," plunging down an elevator of upward flowing air to gain speed until leveling off for a long glide. The simplicity of design and use of natural forces, distinctly different from the huge commercial jets that bludgeoned the air with powerful jet engines, appealed to me.

Excited and a little apprehensive, I enrolled in a class to learn to fly. Walking to the airfield, I saw the plane, essentially a long, silver tube with giant narrow wings extending on both sides. The glider rested on two small wheels used solely for takeoff and landing. It was beautiful, perfectly designed to soar and frolic with the clouds above. A nylon strap stretched from its nose to the tail of a single-engine Cessna waiting to pull us into the sky.

A typical glider has seats for two people, one behind the other. Students are in the front seat. As I waited for my instructor to get settled, I nervously clapped my hands, thinking, "This is crazy . . . this is crazy . . . this is crazy . . ."

Once we were in the glider, the tow plane began rumbling down the runway, pulling us behind until both aircraft broke free from the ground almost simultaneously. As we rose in the air, the glider piloted by the instructor swang in smaller and smaller arcs, much like stock cars in the pace lap before a race. There was the slightest vibration and only the sound of the wind passing over the cockpit.

I felt my heart racing, not from anxiety but exhilaration. When the instructor said, "Okay, let's let her go," I pulled the red knob release handle in front of me, cutting our link with the tow plane. We were on our own!

Every sense of the vibrations and the sound of engines just vanished; the front of the plane dipped slightly and then came back up, and it was like we were floating. It was one of the most beautiful sensations that I've ever felt.

"So you want to do some ridge soaring? We're lucky. Sometimes, the winds are too weak to get enough lift. It looks good today." By the time I answered "Sure," he had already turned us to the ridge.

We slowly drifted down to the ridge. The boundaries of the ridge's wind currents were invisible, the only sign of their presence being a slight bump and rock, like going over a speed bump in a car. The instructor lowered the nose to gain speed as we approached the ridge. We raced across the landscape, the tops of trees and barns sliding by faster and faster until he pulled up the nose, and we began to soar again, slowly making our way back to the airfield.

As we swooped into the final turn for landing and gently touched the ground, I think I knew what it was like to be a bird. Unfortunately, with our finances and the subsequent turmoil of that year, I never finished the program to become a glider pilot. But I did confirm that my fear of flying had to do with commercial planes.

• • •

The winter semester following my parents' reneging on their promised payments was challenging. Money worries never ceased. We maxed out our credit cards, struggling to make the minimum payments, with interest not much better than from a local loan shark. Sometimes, I exploded in fits of rage. My inability to find enough income to make ends meet frustrated me. I desperately wanted to give Sherrie the security she needed, but I couldn't.

People in our situation sometimes think irrationally, the objects of our affection becoming the objects of despair. On the one hand, I loved her, and the hardship we faced drew us together. On the other, I resented the responsibility that she unconsciously imposed on me. I had not asked her to choose me over her family; I didn't want that responsibility nor ever expected it.

Nevertheless, I felt our being together was the cause of our problems. During our time together, my obligation to Sherrie had become a third member of our relationship. In my worse times, I wondered if being together—no matter how much we might love each other—was worth the pain I felt.

"If she would just go home and accept her parents' demands, we would both be better off," I thought. "I wouldn't have any problems taking care of myself."

Each time the temptation to end it crept into my thoughts, I was ashamed. I ignored them as much as I could until we were caught in the middle of the next crisis. To those naïve enough to believe that love conquers all, I would say that there are times when it is not enough. You make it by sheer willpower, the determination not to give up no matter what.

Towards the end of that semester, we realized that we would not, could not make it by ourselves. We needed five to six thousand dollars to pay our overdue bills and finish the semester. With our credit history, borrowing from a bank or a credit union was not a possibility. Finding an angel was our only recourse if we wanted to stay together.

The only people who we believed might help us were Sherrie's employer. They were a young couple who had hired her as a nanny for their young children. In desperation, we arranged a meeting. Asking anyone for money is embarrassing, especially from people who barely know you. We realized that their help was unlikely, but we had no other alternative.

Early one evening, we sat with them and explained our situation, including the difficulties we had with our respective parents. They clearly empathized with us, becoming distraught about the parental-imposed estrangements. To our great relief and eternal thanks, that wonderful, caring couple co-signed a loan for us for over five thousand dollars.

With that loan, we could pay our bills with enough remaining to get through the summer, we hoped. By the time we got the loan, my grades had fallen, so continuing in school didn't make sense. We both had lost any good feelings about Penn State. After a long conversation, Sherrie and I agreed that a relocation might bring a new start, a step away from the unhappiness and the anger associated with Happy Valley. It was an easy decision since there were no decent-paying jobs around the school.

CHAPTER 9

JUMPSTARTING THE HOMELESS

We decided to move back to the one town where we knew we could make some money—Lansing, Michigan. We packed what little possessions we had in an old white van, the last in a series of jalopies we bought after Sherrie's parents revoked her car. Our previous employer, the canvassing company, hired us, and we found a cheap sublet in East Lansing—$300 to rent a room in a house for the whole summer.

The canvassing job didn't work out, primarily due to the lackadaisical effort we put forward. We were often late and frequently missed whole days when we didn't feel like working. With the remaining money from the loan and rent of only $300 for the summer, we foolishly did not consider the future or the consequence of our irresponsibility.

Towards the end of that summer, after notifying the company we were taking the day off, our supervisor said, "Don't worry about it. We've learned not to count on you. You need to find other employment."

Our termination was a cold dash of reality. As fall approached, our favorable lease was also ending. I realized I had to find another job and soon. Luckily, a former country commissioner in Kalamazoo founded a new consumer alliance organization to promote insurance reform. With my experience, I was a perfect match.

Since the organization was new, it had no infrastructure. Aside from the commissioner (whose help was sporadic at best), there were two employees, both of us hired at the same time. The two of us were expected to build the organization by canvassing citizen-consumers for support. The task was not much different from my work years before with the environmental company. After a few months, I persuaded the commissioner to let me open a new office in his hometown of Kalamazoo.

Sherrie and I moved to Kalamazoo, Michigan, in the fall of 1991, right before my 22nd birthday. We agreed to share an apartment with two friends, the nicest we had lived in since being together, with a rec room, hot tub, and swimming pool. After moving to Kalamazoo, we sold our white cargo van and bought our first new car, a Mercury Topaz.

Sherrie and I were expected to build a self-supporting organization in Kalamazoo. A portion of the donations we received would pay office expenses and wages, essentially commissions. With overall responsibility, my primary duty was to recruit volunteers and canvassers. At the same time, Sherrie focused on people to do phone solicitations.

In my enthusiasm for the new position and convinced that the organization's purpose was needed, I grossly underestimated the difficulty of finding qualified people willing to work on a commission basis. Getting donations was a struggle every day. Sherrie and I were paid an override on the donations received and a commission on our direct contributions. Our combined income averaged $100–$150 per week.

The remaining money from the loan the year before was quickly spent. By the start of winter, we were in deep financial trouble again. Our roommates also struggled and couldn't pay their share of the rent. Sherrie and I couldn't carry the rent alone, and we were evicted at the end of the year. We found a much cheaper apartment and continued with the consumer organization.

During the hard times when I felt especially vulnerable and alone, I thought of the summer visits with my grandma Mona in California. She was the only one in my family who cared about me and tried to stay in touch. I was estranged from my adoptive parents and brother, who purposely distanced himself from me. Every couple of months, Grandma Mona would send me a card or call. She would always send money on my birthday, which helped us and meant something emotionally. Her gifts seemed to arrive when they were needed most—after an eviction or during times when generic mac and cheese or ramen were luxuries—and gave me hope that I would someday achieve the dreams of a young boy riding Sparky the pony. My grandmother was indeed an angel, and I will never stop missing and loving her.

Though often overlooked, living on the edge of poverty has its benefits. People who never want or worry about life's essentials rarely see mankind at its best. Pride and pretense often accompany wealth and possessions, substituting selfishness for charity, prejudice for community. Poverty strips away non-essentials and, more often than not, replaces resentment with grace.

As a door-to-door canvasser for community and environmental causes, I found those who lived in the poorer, blue-collar neighborhoods were more likely to listen and support a cause. While the monetary amount of their donations was low, it represented a significant part of their income. Many times, during those canvasses, I recalled the Bible story of the poor widow giving two pennies in the temple offering, all she had, and the contrast with the rich who often give nothing.

One of our new neighbors was a young Korean man, named Terry. We would see him in the neighborhood and stop to talk. He explained that his dad in Korea had established a trust fund for him to use in America, requiring him to periodically go to the bank to make a withdrawal. We finally realized that he was homeless. The trust fund story was invented to "save face"—an important aspect of Korean culture. We invited him to stay with us in our tiny one-bedroom apartment. At the time, we barely eked by. Nevertheless, we felt called to share what little we had with someone who had less.

Sherrie eventually stopped working for the organization to take a receptionist job in a new retail cell phone store. The pay was higher and more consistent and lifted some of our financial stress. Even so, our income was not enough to sustain us and forced another decision about the direction of our lives. We decided to move to Ann Arbor, the home of the University of Michigan. The town of 100,000 plus was about the size of Hershey. Still, its proximity to Detroit 30 miles east offered numerous business opportunities.

We arrived in Ann Arbor in the late spring of 1992. Walking down the main street, I heard a violin playing. I had not touched my violin since we left Penn State. I felt being with Sherrie should be my main priority without the competition of the violin. I missed the spirituality of playing, but I knew that I did not have the discipline to keep playing without the structure of regular lessons and playing in the orchestra.

Even so, the sprightly notes of a stringed instrument wafting through the air as we walked on that soft spring day in Ann Arbor brought joy to my heart and purpose to my steps. The high tinkling notes of bells perfectly integrated with the melodic tones of the violin seemed of another time and place.

We finally reached the player, a young gypsy woman, her colorful dress accented by the large hoops on her ears and the bells hanging from her boots. She twirled and bent as she coaxed an old fiddle to recall nights of gaiety and romance.

The two of us listened with an appreciation of her skill, then took the little change we had and dropped it in the battered case at her feet. As we walked away, I whispered to Sherrie, "This is the place we need to be."

The following week, I moved to Ann Arbor, finding a telemarketer job and leasing a cheap one-bedroom apartment, paying $600 for the summer. Sherrie followed me two weeks later.

Unsurprisingly, I hated telemarketing—hours of soul-sucking tedium making one call after another that usually ended in a hang-up or an obscenity. When someone was kind enough to have a conversation, I was required to repeat a rehearsed response, essentially ignoring questions and interruptions. The duration of each call was tracked, and a roving supervisor continually stalked through the call center to ensure that each telemarketer met their assigned quota of calls. By any definition, call centers are sweatshops.

Since a trained monkey could do my job, I had plenty of time to think about the future and what I wanted to do with my life. Ann Arbor was beset by homeless people at the time, an irritant to the City Fathers since their presence contradicted the city's image as an ideal place to live and work.

Most people are unaware of the possibility of falling through society's cracks, whether from unemployment, under-employment, addiction, or mental health issues. Sherrie and I had lived on the edge for years, kept afloat only by minimum-pay jobs and credit. We were lucky; others, like our friend Terry from Kalamazoo, were not so much.

We realized that creating shelters where desperate people could find a bed or meal was a step in the right direction but was, at best, a temporary solution. People need tools and resources to rebuild their lives, including mental, physical, and vocational assistance. They need to have an opportunity to get decent jobs and help to reconnect with the community.

I can't explain why Sherrie and I felt a responsibility to get involved when we were fighting to keep our own heads above water. What makes some people see a need and try to help while others turn away? Is it nature or nurture? Are some people born with tendencies of empathy and altruism? Is it the result of the environment—a loving family, religious devotion? Perhaps there are no easy explanations.

As for me, I always remember the story of Hillel the Elder, a Jewish rabbi and scholar who lived between 110 BCE to 10 CE. The wise man wrote, "If I am not for myself, who will be for me? And being only for myself, what am I? And if not now, when?" Variations of his questions have been repeated for the last 1100 years, always calling individuals to accept personal responsibility for others less fortunate and to act now, not in the future.

I believe that a successful solution to the homeless population requires living in a place of their own, not crammed together in a public shelter with little privacy and, in some cases, actual danger. We believed that a transitional housing program and accompanying training and employment help subsidized by public funds was a better solution than human warehouses. Energized by the promise of making a difference in the lives of the unfortunate, we established "Jumpstart," a nonprofit organization to turn our concept into reality.

Nonprofit organizations need funding for administrative costs and the fulfillment of their missions. While we were willing to expend our time and energy on the effort, our ability to finance the program was limited. Our plan was to raise funds from individuals initially through canvassing, then pursue more consistent financial support from foundations and corporations.

Shortly after the launch, we confronted our first problem. The car we purchased in Kalamazoo was repossessed due to nonpayment. Determined to make Jumpstart a reality, we invested in newspaper ads to find canvassers, riding to the local library on the bus to meet prospective employees. Luckily, one of our new hires had a station wagon and was willing to use it for canvassing. With the generosity of Ann Arbor patrons, we rented an office in downtown Ann Arbor and a minivan for Jumpstart business.

We slowly but surely built up the organization. Our personal financial situation didn't improve since we kept the donations in the organization. Our most important objective was getting enough money to get our first family—a single mother and her children—into an apartment that we subsidized. Money was tight, so we stayed in the apartment we had initially sublet.

Despite our efforts, problems for Jumpstart continued. While we were experienced with telephone and door-to-door solicitation, the cutthroat competition among charitable organizations came as a surprise.

Charitable organizations are forced to compete for the same contributions for survival. Dollars that flow to one are not available to others, so programs and overhead must be cut. As we reached the stage of seeking foundation and corporate contributions, we attracted the attention of a larger nonprofit that ran an Ann Arbor shelter.

Since our purpose was to replace shelters with transitional housing, they considered Jumpstart a competitor even though each organization aimed to help the homeless. In their minds, there was only room for one charity focused on homeless housing, and it wasn't Jumpstart.

Our competitor persuaded an Ann Arbor newspaper to author an article about Jumpstart. One morning in the fall, we woke to a front-page article titled "Jumpstart Organization: Help or Hindrance?" Though they had never talked to Sherrie, me, or any of our workers or volunteers, the gist of the piece was ridicule (referring to me as "21-year-old Penn State dropout Aaron Dworkin") and claiming that the donations were used for our personal benefit. We were livid, especially since we continued to live hand-to-mouth to support the organization. I tried to find an attorney who would sue the publishers for the lies and misinformation that had been printed, but none would take our case. The typical response was, "Suing the paper? Good luck. You're not going to find an attorney in town that's going to be willing to do this for you pro bono."

The article demoralized the staff and destroyed any hope of corporate donations. Within weeks, we had no canvassing staff and no donations. Our last hope to survive was a celebrity mailing. Surely, I thought, famous people with all of their resources would be willing to step in for a program everyone recognized was urgently needed.

Using *The Celebrity Directory*, a database claiming to have the home and business addresses of more than 7,000 famous people, I drafted a letter describing Jumpstart and its importance. I included personal stories of those we sought to help. With little resources, we used the public computer system at the library to print and mail 120 personal pleas to the ones we thought were most likely to respond.

Not everyone responded. Most returns were standard rejection letters ("The project sounds like good work, but we can't help."). We did receive some unusual responses, including the Prince of Monaco's offers of a couple of items for a celebrity auction. While appreciated, we didn't have the resources to sponsor or hold an auction or a public fundraiser. Despite our hopes and efforts, Jumpstart was doomed. We lost the office and the minivan. Facing reality when you have invested so much of yourself is hard. The day we finally shut Jumpstart shattered my self-confidence.

For almost three years, Sherrie and I had faced one disappointment after another. We were estranged from our families, barely making enough to live at the poverty level, school dropouts. "Were we done?" I wondered. "How much stress can a couple take? How much could I take? Could I get back on my feet one more time?" I didn't know.

CHAPTER 10

DUNGEONS, DRAGONS & MIRACLES WITH ROBIN WILLIAMS

The demise of Jumpstart coincided with a notice of eviction from our apartment and constant calls from collection agencies for overdue credit card payments. Of course, we were both trying to find jobs, so answering the phone was necessary. The verbal sparring with the collection reps became a recurring consequence.

During one of Sherrie's turns to answer the phone, she received a call from a woman asking to speak with me. Hoping to head off another collector, she asked, "May I tell him who is calling?"

"My name is Marsha Williams. I'm calling about a letter to my husband." Sherrie covered the phone and whispered, "Marsha Williams, something about a letter to her husband?"

The name did not trigger a reaction for either of us initially.

I grabbed the phone, stammering, "This is Aaron Dworkin."

Over the course of my dialogue, I came to realize that Marsha Williams was married to Robin Williams, the comedian starring in the popular television show *Mork and Mindy*. Our conversation lasted almost an hour. I thought, after explaining the original purpose of the letter—seeking funding for Jumpstart—no longer applied, our discussion would be short and sweet. She sympathized when I told her that we had to close the charity. With no resources, we couldn't make it work. To my surprise, she asked me about our plans and background. Before long, I was pouring out my worries, frustrations, and hopes, including why we had moved to

Ann Arbor and our hopes to return to college. We couldn't enroll due to the overhanging student loans at Penn State since they wouldn't transmit our transcripts until they were paid.

At her urging, I explained the whole story—the relationship with my parents and Sherrie being disowned by hers. I told her about our experiences together—the cheap apartments, questionable jobs, and insufficient credit lines to eat. As she listened, Mrs. Williams would interject stories of the difficulties they faced when Robin broke into the entertainment industry and the conflicts with their own children.

Though I expected nothing to come from the conversation, I found healing in the process of talking to one of the nicest people I've met.

She ended the conversation, saying, "I'll tell you what, Aaron. Let me give you our address. Send Robin and me copies of your student loans, and we'll see what we can do. Maybe we can help you out a little bit."

I told Sherrie about the possibility that the Williams might help us. We collected the latest information on our student loans, added audiotapes of my last recital at Penn State as well as copies of my poems. We included a letter detailing our plans and why going back to school was important. We sent the material to her, trying not to get too excited. We realized that Mrs. Williams knew little about us, initially contacting me to learn about Jumpstart.

When we didn't hear anything for several weeks, we assumed she or Robin had found a better avenue for their philanthropic outlets. After our eviction, we moved to a cheaper apartment and continued our job search. Sherrie found a receptionist job in a local law firm that paid almost $1500 per month, more than the two of us had earned in a single month previously. We were beginning to imagine and perhaps see that light at the end of a long tunnel.

Two weeks later, Super Sales, a national marketing company, hired me to work in the mailroom. The company promoted weekend markets for vendors of all types in small to medium-sized towns around the country. The week before the show, the company flooded the region with local television and radio commercials advertising "Microwaves for $49 . . . VCRs just $99 . . . Discounts you will not believe. Don't miss it . . . Only available this Friday, Saturday and Sunday . . . Come to the Super Sale."

Within a few weeks, we had gone from being indigent to a combined income of $3,500 a month. Worries about rent payments and meals of ramen noodles and boxed mac and cheese subsided, though the battle with bill collectors persisted. Most of what we earned was needed to pay off endless debt, but we could go to the occasional movie and strategically purchase food at the market without the anxiety of examining the price label first.

One evening, I came home from work to find an official-looking envelope from the Joel Faden Financial Company. "Another bill collector," I thought, adding it to the bottom of the stack. We made headway on the bills and tried to pay those most willing to work with us first.

Upon opening, the envelope was to reveal a short note with copies of several printed checks. The note read: "Enclosed please find copies of checks made out on your behalf from Robin and Marsha Williams' account."

I did a double-take, unsure if I had understood the message correctly. I yelled for Sherrie and handed her the note. We passed the papers between us, carefully reading each line. There were four or five pages of copies of canceled checks signed by Robin and Marsha Williams. The two had graciously paid off the Penn State direct loans and other student loans in default, altogether an amount over $8,000.

We were stunned, looking down at the paper then at each other. Suddenly, we were on our feet, hugging fiercely and screaming with pure joy. Raised voices were not uncommon in our home, generally in anger or frustration over poverty, our parents' coldness, or the horrible minimum-wage jobs we were forced to take. Our screams that evening were a combination of surprise, relief, gratitude, and happiness. Not only had the loans been made, but we were beneficiaries of immeasurable kindness from strangers, two people who knew us from a single one-hour telephone conversation. The moment felt overwhelming!

We celebrated the event with dinner and drinks that evening at a nice restaurant. Realizing that returning to school was genuinely possible, we considered what we should do. Despite our student loans being paid, we had outstanding debts. Borrowing money to attend school while paying the debt could quickly leave us in the same position as before—living at the poverty level. We were not prepared to face those conditions again, especially after the past months of decent income. We decided to continue working until our debt was paid. When we did go back to school, we would indeed be free and clear—no credit card debt.

I rose rather quickly through the ranks at Super Sales. The company grew from 30 employees to over 80 within my first year. Through Jump-start, I learned about starting a nonprofit 501(c)(3) organization and applying for a charitable solicitation license. At Super Sales, I added word processing, spreadsheets, and database skills to my repertoire, eagerly soaking up the knowledge I had missed from my focus on arts and music and lapsed time.

I thrived when I joined Super Sales, rising to the regional coordinator for the southeast region within a few months. I seemed to have a knack for administration, developing multiple Excel applications to better assess the company's profit margins and allocation of advertising between traveling and local vendors. The president, Bart Loeb, noticed my work, a connection that proved beneficial later, in more ways than one.

Hoping to get better insight into show mechanics—the tasks and problems associated with setting up a massive, though temporary show-room floor—I attended my first show at the giant I-X Center at the Cleveland Airport. As I walked down the aisles, occasionally stopping at the booths that drew the most attention, I heard someone calling my name. I turned to find Danielle, the girlfriend of an old roommate.

As we hugged, Danielle let me know she was working a booth for the show.

Gesturing at an ornate display of electronic equipment, she asked "What are you doing here?"

"I work for Super Sales, the company that sponsors the show," I replied.

"No way! You must know Bart!"

"You mean, Mr. Loeb, the President of Super Sales?"

"Yeah, I know him," Danielle said. "He's totally cool. A few of us are hanging out in his room tonight. You gotta come."

That night, I discovered that I was the only employee at the gathering of vendor reps in Bart's room. Bart was surprised to see me and called me over.

"I really try to avoid socializing with my employees," he said, his tone suggesting I had crashed the gathering. I explained that I was there at an old friend's insistence so we could catch up.

"Well, since you are a friend of Danielle, you can stay, but don't talk about business. These people are not just customers, they're friends of mine," he cautioned.

The party went on for hours, as people came and went. I thoroughly enjoyed the evening, meeting people and drifting in and out of conversations. When someone learned that I worked for Super Sales, they invariably praised Bart for the help he had given them and their respect for him as a person.

Until that night, Bart Loeb was as much a stranger to me as the others at the party. I grew to have a great deal of respect for him. I've encountered a multitude of different personalities in my life. Certainly, there was those who claimed to be a part of the hippie culture, the free spirited, indulgent, shamelessly relying on kindness and generosity of others to survive. On the flip side of the coin, there were the super-productive business geniuses, generally impassive and uninterested in other people, unless they offer an advantage to be exploited.

Bart is one of those rare beings who seemed to have both qualities—responsibility and a genuine care and curiosity about life, while accomplishing things that improve the world around them. Bart's example continues to inspire me. In the ensuing years, we were to become great friends.

• • •

At that time, my friend Phil decided to move to Ann Arbor. He came down, staying with us in our one-bedroom apartment. When the college kids left town in the summers, rental prices for homes dropped significantly. The three of us, with some friends, moved into a huge seven-bedroom house in downtown Ann Arbor, costing us only $700 for the summer.

The game Dungeons & Dragons obsession was at its peak. We were all avid players. Phil's role was Merlin (for his love of sorcerers and magicians), Sherrie was Lady Godiva (for her love of chocolate), and I was King Arthur. Naturally. We christened the house "Camelot," the mystical kingdom of King Arthur.

We had some great times that summer, adopting the hippie lifestyle in many ways. Through our friendship with Bart, I learned about the Rainbow Family, a counter-culture group that emerged after the Woodstock Festival. The Rainbow Family was a loose-knit collection of misfits and outsiders of all ages who eschewed corporate profitability and focused on ecology and New Age spirituality. They were best known for their large, spontaneous gatherings celebrating peace, love, and unity on public lands. In other words, they were a giant family of individuals reflecting the flower culture of Haight-Ashbury, the home of the Grateful Dead band. Rainbow houses—someone's home that is open to Rainbows as they traveled across the country—were available in different communities. Bart's house was the Rainbow House in Ann Arbor.

While I had worked my way up the Super Sales organization, no doubt with some help from Bart, I wanted to be my own boss. The government had recently broken up the AT&T telephone service, encouraging new suppliers. I realized the confluence of antitrust legislation, the appeal of ecology, and Super Sales' sales channel of vendor shows created an unusual opportunity for a business.

Enter "EarthPro" (the name of my new company). This initiative would encourage people to switch telephone suppliers for a cheaper service, an introductory green plant, and a designated donation to an ecological group in the community. EarthPro would receive a commission from the new telecom for each switched customer. With its success, I could leave Super Sales with the security of a regular income.

Phil believed in me and in the concept of EarthPro, initially providing free booth space and the funds to hire extra help to man the booth. I solicited agreements with many of the new telecoms in my spare time. From time to time, Phil helped by working in the booth, demonstrating the right way to sell for my new employees. He had been a car salesman in his past and had not forgotten the tools of that trade.

Phil was the best salesman I had encountered up until that point in my life. He possessed a unique ability to connect with people, gain their trust, and advocate for whatever he was selling in a way that pleased the person about their purchase. He would sell only those products he believed were suitable for a customer, one of the reasons I respected his craft.

Despite my ambition, intentions, and effort, I couldn't make EarthPro profitable, Bart's mentorship and assistance notwithstanding. I believe EarthPro was ahead of its time—a sound marketing approach—without a reliable, well-funded telecom partner.

The impact of AT&T's breakup triggered massive competition between its behemoth offspring, each being a giant company in comparison with their regional phone company competitors. Every switch to a new telecom was bitterly contested, eliminating or delaying commission payments to EarthPro, its only revenue source. When I finally closed the doors, I owed Bart money which I repaid through deductions from my Super Sales salary.

EarthPro had reinvigorated the spark in me to move beyond Super Sales, which I knew I couldn't be in for the long term. Sherrie was doing well as an assistant to a professor at the University of Michigan's Institute for Social Research. The job reinforced her interest in sociology and intergroup conflict resolution, which she intended to study when we returned to school.

Few Super Sales employees were committed to the company, working solely for the money while they waited for an evening or weekend to party with friends. As soon as the workday ended, they rushed to Chi-Chi's, a popular chain restaurant and bar down the street. (All Chi-Chi's restaurants in the U.S. closed in the early 2000s following the deaths of several customers from hepatitis.) Fortunately for the Super Sales employees, their goal was to drink to forget the misery of their lives, not eat. Repulsed, I promised myself that I would not spend my life doing something that I didn't love.

Bart told me he was thinking about selling the company and retiring to Jamaica, one of his favorite places to visit. He really wanted a more stable home life, his residence in constant turmoil in its function as a Rainbow House. The summer sublet of Camelot was ending, so we needed to find a new place as well. The three of us decided to get a house together, Bart's old home solely dedicated to the Rainbow Family.

• • •

Earlier that year, I had returned to writing with a focus on poetry. With EarthPro shutdown and my enthusiasm for Super Sales waning, I had the time to consider what the next step in my career might be. Whatever I might do, I was determined that it would resonate with my interests as an artist and a community activist.

Ann Arbor is a great community with an avid interest in education and the arts. It probably had more bookstores per capita than any other city in the United States. But it didn't have a literary magazine, an outlet to highlight the works of emerging authors and poets reflecting on their lives in the 20th century. "There is clearly a need," I thought. "And I'm just the person to fulfill it."

After some thought, I developed the perfect plan to launch the new magazine featuring new and emerging authors. Once they knew of us, I was confident that the writers would submit their work in the hope of some publicity and a boost in book sales. Credibility would naturally follow the establishment of a qualified literary review board selected from the notable authors in the community and the faculties of the local colleges, especially the University of Michigan and Eastern Michigan University. The magazine would be free to readers, with revenues coming from advertising.

An added benefit was the chance for Sherrie and me to work together, something we had not done since our last experience canvassing. When I told her of my idea, she appeared enthusiastic. To this day, I am not sure if it was because she believed in the magazine or in me.

While still working at Super Sales, I developed a business plan for our new publication, *The Bard*, named after the great William Shakespeare. I knew the typical magazine takes five years to break even, but I planned to use Hugh Hefner's strategy to start up *Playboy* in 1953 with $8,000 (about $45,000 forty years later) of beginning capital.

Success depended on a minimal dollar investment, free labor, and suppliers willing to wait for payments until the magazine was published. I underestimated the complications of advertising revenue versus magazine sales, compounding the magazine's cash flow difficulties. I also didn't have a nude picture of Marilyn Monroe as a centerfold, probably the single reason *Playboy*'s first edition was a big success.

We took what money we had saved plus a loan from the bank and began operations. Both of us continued to work full-time jobs, spending evenings and weekends on the magazine.

Sherrie served as the chief editor, and we used friends for the necessary design and layout work. We were swamped, taxing the capability of our literary review panel to select the best papers for each month.

By then, I realized how much work was needed to produce a publication each month. If *The Bard* were to survive, I needed to devote full-time to the effort. I left Super Sales that fall and dedicated myself wholly to the magazine. We published a magazine for four months—October through January—eking by as advertising revenues slowly increased. Advertising dollars were hard to come by, with several small publications in Ann Arbor vying for the same resource.

The February issue was extraordinary. The theme was Black History Month and included some of our most exciting work. Dwjuan, my friend from Interlochen, had been immersed in the Chicago hip hop culture for years. His piece was the feature article of the issue.

Most of our vendors knew our situation and tried to work with us. An exception was our printer, who put us on a COD basis after being late on previous payments. When they delivered the February copies, I didn't have the funds to pay them. I explained that our advertisers paid their fees after the magazines were distributed, allowing us to cover the bill the following week. The printer refused to give us the publication and subsequently sued me for non-payment, adding other costs and fees that seemed exorbitant to me. Unable to afford an attorney, I represented myself in the trial. Despite representation by one of Lansing's most prestigious law firms, the judge cut the amount owed in half, a bittersweet victory and small consolation for the demise of *The Bard*.

CHAPTER 11

RECONCILIATION TOUR

Early February 1996, Michigan's cold, overcast winter days perfectly reflected the disappointment of closing The Bard. I had failed again, despite Sherrie's commitment and my effort. The financial wolves at our door were not so vicious since we rented a couple of rooms in our friend Bart's house. He had exponentially greater means and covered most of the household expenses.

That winter was a time of introspection. Sherrie and I had dropped out of Penn State, our financial situation being untenable. We had tried a new start and wound up in practically the same conditions that prompted our move to Kalamazoo and Ann Arbor. Amid my unhappiness, melancholy, and frustration, I realized what I missed most—the part of my life that grounded me, the gift of music. I had cheated, dismissed, and abandoned my talent, chasing false idols and selfish goals.

"Sherrie, I think I need to go back to school," I told her one morning as we lay in bed, listening to the wind whistle against our bedroom window. "I need to play my violin again. I miss it so much."

"You're not the only one thinking about the future," Sherrie replied, rising on her elbows to look directly at me. "I don't want to work at the Institute for Social Research anymore. If I work there, I want to be a researcher, someone who can solve problems between White and Black people. I want to understand why my parents and their friends are the way they are. If I knew that, maybe I could help change their minds."

I stared at her in surprise. I never suspected that she had her own goals separate from mine. I was happy to see her in the new light. When she turned away, I whispered, "Let's do it. Let's go back to school, only not to Penn State and all the bad memories. I want to go to the University of Michigan here in Ann Arbor."

She grabbed my head with her hands and kissed me. "I'm ready. I love you."

By the end of the week, we had completed our applications. Since the Williams had paid our student loans, we could enroll. I picked up my violin for the first time in over four years, practicing feverishly for an audition scheduled for just a week later. My audition went well, and I was accepted into the University of Michigan. Sherrie also made it, so we were set to return in the fall of 1995.

At the time, I was studying Silat, an Indonesian martial art form. Combining the hand strikes of karate, joint manipulation of aikido, and throws of jiu-jitsu, Silat is a cerebral, passive form of self-defense learned by practicing a series of fixed hand positions and rhythmic slow, controlled moves resembling a dance. Gamelan (Indonesian) music generally accompanied our practice. Once each week, the session ended in Zikr, meditation while listening to a series of recited prayers of Sufi Sheikhs, specially trained guides in Sufism, a branch of the Islam faith based on peace and forgiveness.

When we celebrated our eighth anniversary together that year, almost seven years had passed since Sherrie's parents had disowned her. I hadn't spoken to my parents for over six years. That summer, things were to take a different turn.

During one of my meditation sessions, listening to soothing words and music, I thought about the deep-seated hatred of my parents that I nourished and hoarded for years. As I swayed back and forth, my eyes closed as I caressed my prayer beads and listened to the chants and wisdom pearls, I wondered, "Why?" In a moment of clarity, I realized my anger didn't serve me, suit me, or the world around me.

I resented my parents for what I felt was a betrayal, if not the cause of the challenging times that Sherrie and I endured. In my mind, even their token assistance would have made our circumstances more bearable. Yet, they had deliberately abandoned us. I made the decision to forgive them, rationalizing that they didn't truly understand me or realize the impact of their decisions. "The past is the past," I thought. "And nothing we do now will change it. Perhaps I can change the future."

The next day, I wrote them a conciliatory letter stating that I wanted to reconnect and move forward. They responded that they, too, regretted the distance between us. There were no apologies to suggest that their actions were wrong, naturally. Yet, it was a start. Sherrie and I decided to visit them during the summer.

I also wrote to Sherrie's parents, hoping to put the past behind me with a new start. If they were not ready, I promised to respect their privacy and never bother them again. They never responded to me. However, a few weeks later, Sherrie told me that her mother had finally agreed to meet me. We subsequently planned our "Reconciliation Tour of 1996," a single trip back to Pennsylvania to see our respective parents and, hopefully, bury the hatchet.

When we stopped outside of my parents' house, I tensed, unsure how I would act if the old wounds were opened. Sherrie shared my apprehension, saying nothing but tightly holding my hand as we walked to the front door and knocked. Suddenly, the door opened, and my parents appeared.

To my surprise, I was happy to see them and couldn't help smiling. I had missed them, despite the anger. Sherrie and my mother lightly hugged as my father and I approached one another in an awkward yet connected manner. I think each of us was a little anxious, but everybody was determined to avoid controversy if possible. We had a pleasant visit that included a history of our past six years when we were not speaking. As we talked, I realized that there was no way that they could understand the pain and challenges we had overcome, especially the embarrassment and shame of eviction. Nevertheless, the visit carried meaning, and they made it clear that they regretted the estrangement.

As we were leaving to meet Sherrie's mother and younger sister at a restaurant off the turnpike in Pittsburgh, Sherrie's mom called. When she got off the phone, her face smiling with happiness, she said, "Aaron, you won't believe this. My mom talked to my dad, and they said that we can come for dinner."

Just the way that Sherrie described it concerned me. From my perspective, their permission to "come to dinner" implied that they were offering us a bone. I kept silent. No matter how I might feel, I knew the pain they had caused Sherrie over the years and would have done anything to help bring her some peace.

"Okay. That's great. Are you sure your dad wants that?" I asked.

"That's what my mom said. She said that she talked to him, and he said, 'Okay, they can come to dinner,'" she replied, unable to keep the eagerness from her voice.

Sidney Poitier's *Guess Who's Coming to Dinner* flashed across my eyes. Our visit was going to be rough. It was the price I was willing to pay for Sherrie's sake.

As we were loading the car, my dad came out and said, "I heard the news."

Knowing me and how I reacted during my rebellion with our arguments, he knew how "expressive" I could be with words.

"Now, Aaron, I really wouldn't feel a necessity on your part to be honest with them about how you feel. You really don't have to be righteous here, you know. You can just sit back and be cool."

"Be cool, huh?" I repeated.

"Yes, in this case. You don't need to let them know how you feel. Just go, be nice, and let it go," my father advised. I thought about it, and, even though it was against my instinct, I knew that he was probably right.

I thought about the meeting during our four-hour drive to Pittsburgh. I had silently decided that I wouldn't make a scene unless they attacked Sherrie. I said to myself: "You need to keep your self-respect and show your love for Sherrie by making peace. It was that simple."

We pulled up to their home in a well-to-do suburb northwest of Pittsburgh. The lawn was neatly mowed and trimmed, and a candle glowed literally in each window. It was a scene out of a storybook, the perfect representative of middle-class Americana imagined on television family sitcoms. In contrast, my parents' home was older and plain, almost spartan. It did, however, look like a place where real people lived. As we walked from the car to the porch, my mind screamed, "You don't belong here. You're not like us. Why are you here?"

It was too late to retreat. The front door suddenly opened, and Sherrie's Mom and Dad were there. Sherrie's youngest sister waited behind them. The three were well-fed and nicely dressed. The mother and daughter wore pastel-colored sundresses, and the father wore dark slacks with a light blue, open, button-down collared shirt.

Sherrie hugged her mother as we entered. I held out my hand to shake her father's hand. "Nice to meet you," I said, thinking, "You're a real hypocrite." I then shook her mom's hand as well and gave her younger sister a hug. To my surprise, no one spoke of the past nor questioned how our life had been during the past seven years. It felt unnatural.

Sherrie's father had grilled a whole chicken for dinner and began carving pieces for each diner. When it came to me, he asked, "Aaron, would you like white or dark?" As soon as the word "dark" passed his lips, he realized that his question might be the match that lit the simmering undercurrents of the room.

I've never liked dark chicken meat, so without thinking, I answered, "I only eat white meat."

Everyone froze. Had I just thrown down a gauntlet to the father? How would he respond? My answer might have caused a chuckle or a witty repartee in other situations. That evening, it was as if someone had tossed a grenade in the room, and everyone waited for the explosion. The air was so thick the butter knife on the saucer would have cut it like a straight razor.

Sherrie's father didn't react, keeping his eyes focused on the bird and slicing one piece after another. He just kept cutting until Sherrie changed the subject, attempting to lighten the mood.

When we left, I hugged Sherrie's mother—a big step for me—and told her I was glad to meet her. She whispered in my ear, "It's about time."

"Exactly. Why did it take so long?" I thought. Instead, I verbalized, "Yes, I agree. It's nice to meet you."

We returned to Ann Arbor, ending the Reconciliation Tour. With the return of our parents in our lives, we hoped the worst was behind us. For a time, we moved forward with a sense of naïve confidence.

CHAPTER 12

THE ANGEL

It was getting into the spring of my first year back at Michigan, and I took some time to really think about my relationship with Sherrie. We had always told ourselves that since we had become more immersed in the hippie lifestyle, there was no reason to be married. Why did we need a slip of paper from the government telling us that we loved each other? We also always felt that marriage wasn't necessary because, at this point, our two paths seemed to go side-by-side in the same direction. Why then go through the hassle and trouble of formalities when we don't know what the future holds?

We had been together for going on eight years. I thought about all of the different possible futures for myself, but I couldn't grasp any scenario that didn't include Sherrie. That left me with the certainty that I should ask her to marry me. I stowed away a little money without her knowing it. I went to a well-known jewelry store in Ann Arbor and could not help reflecting back to what had happened with Melissa so many years prior. This time, the ring would be a genuine symbol—emotionally, spiritually, and financially.

As I looked at the rings, I realized that none of them made any sense. They weren't *us*. I realized that the only way to do it right would be to make one. I went about designing a ring that would be like Sherrie and me, white and black. In all of that, I saw yin and yang, so I designed a ring that incorporated those symbols. For me, an impatient person, it was hard to wait the six-to-eight weeks to have it made and also save up the money; it was a torturous time for me. When I finally saw the end result of their work, though, it was all worth it. The ring gave me an indescribable feeling because it made me think about the joy that it would bring her. In a strange way, although it's a different story, it made me think of *The Lord of the Rings*, which had gained all of that fame with the movies. I used to read the entire trilogy every year, and it pleased me to know that Sherrie and I would have "one ring to show our love, one ring to bind us, one ring to seal our love and forever entwine us." At that point, I was trying to figure out the best way to ask Sherrie. I decided it could not be some dull moment; it had to be some point in time that was exciting, new, and different. We had plans for an upcoming vacation to the Bahamas, so I thought that might be a good time to propose. We had visited in the previous year and really loved it. We found the opportunity to go very cheaply, so we decided to get together with a couple of friends—Sherrie's friend from the Institute for Social Research along with a friend of ours—because they had started dating. We also thought it would be great because Phil, who lived in Florida then, could travel on his boat and meet us there.

On the way to the Bahamas, I thought, *Okay, on this trip, there is going to be the perfect moment, and I will do this.* Before we went, I purposefully didn't even tell Phil, my best friend, what I was about to do. I didn't tell anybody, and, for me, that was also very important because, in the end, this yin and yang had only two parts to it: Sherrie and I. While I wanted to share that excitement with others, I had to share it with her first.

• • •

When we finally got to the Bahamas, I thought, *Okay, what we need to do is have a wonderful dinner, and at that dinner, I'll do the traditional thing because Sherrie would kind of like the traditional thing, and in the middle of dinner, I'll get down on one knee and I'll ask her.* I told them that there was just one thing that I wanted to do while we were on the island, and that was to have one nice meal. After Phil got there, we went to what must be one of the nicest restaurants on the island. We had this fantastically expensive but wonderful dinner where, at the end, they brought these delicate crepes and lit them on fire by the table. It was great, but, somehow, I felt like it wasn't right. Maybe the restaurant felt like a sterile environment. Something just didn't seem right. So, when dinner was over, I said, "Well, you guys, why don't we go take a walk by the water?" *Maybe the water*, I thought. The five of us ended up walking on the beach together.

The sun was about to set. As I looked out on the water, I was reminded of the feeling I had when I first looked out on the water at Interlochen, the moment I knew that would be the next step in my life. I walked in front of Sherrie, then stopped her, and knelt down. I'm not the steadiest person, so I wound up on both knees. I pulled out the box that I had been saving in my pocket all night long and, looking up at Sherrie, I said, "Although we never really thought it was necessary, and we didn't know if our paths would always lead in one direction, I do believe now that they will, and I want to celebrate that. Will you marry me?" I opened the box and held it up to her.

At the same time, Phil was emitting a nervous exclamatory chant . . . "Holy Smoke! Holy Smoke!" He was quite surprised by what he saw transpiring before his eyes. Lyndie, our other friend, was too busy taking pictures. And Sherrie, dear Sherrie, the girl with blonde hair and blue eyes, just stood there. I had totally stunned her.

Then, the silence became a little too long for me, and I became a bit concerned. I said, "Well . . ." I wanted to make sure that she wasn't feeling pressured, and I guess it hadn't occurred to me that maybe she might not want to say yes, so I added, "Now look, I know this is a big shock, so why don't you take some time before you decide?" I rambled, "You can put the ring on, but you can take some time. Why don't you, and let me know?" But she did say yes, and it was wonderful. At that moment, I knew I loved her more than anything or anyone on this planet.

• • •

Given our shared fascination with castles and the Renaissance period, our betrothal took place a couple of years later at the only formal castle in North America, Casa Loma, located in Toronto, Ontario, Canada. With full Renaissance attire worn by the bride and groom (as well as the majority of their guests), our love, which had sprung from youthful beginnings at Penn State, was declared, and Sherrie and I were wed.

She and I were continuing on our unified path together. Earlier, I described our friend Bart as a Rainbow. In some sense, Sherrie and I came to realize that we were also Rainbows. The next annual Rainbow Gathering was coming up around July 4th, and we decided to go. Leading up to the gathering, literally tens of thousands of hippies, members of the Rainbow family gather from all over the country in one place in the middle of the woods in a national forest. It's an amazing gathering of groups of people from all over the country who set up kitchens in the middle of the woods to live for a while, some of them for up to two weeks. Sherrie and I had always thought this would be a pretty exciting thing to attend.

We drove all the way to some place well outside of St. Louis, Missouri. I remember driving in the woods for a while on these back roads until we finally got to that place, and there were police checkpoints on the way in. We ended up parking in a lot with thousands of other cars. We grabbed our packs and wondered what we could bring to help contribute to the kitchen.

When we asked around, people said, "Oh, well, people always love fruit. They also love chocolate—especially when smoking, fruit and chocolate are great!" We decided to pack a cooler filled with ice, a bunch of fruit and a bunch of chocolate. This was one of those big coolers that actually needed two people for transport. We began to carry it, but we didn't fully understand the scope of what we were dealing with. We began to hike on the way up the trail, and there was a crude sign at the beginning that showed the different trails going up through the mountain. Little did we know, but that was to become an over two-hour hike.

We began to make our way. It was amazing. Everyone, everywhere, looked totally different, but they all had a distinctively Bohemian look to them. Almost everyone we walked by said, "Welcome home, brother. Welcome home, sister," and we echoed the response, "Thank you, brother. Thank you, sister. It's good to be home." We immediately got a sense of warmth on that huge mountain with thousands of people. Most people would just smile at us.

One of the things that I noticed about Rainbow was that I could always hear the drumming on the mountain; we could always hear drumming and chanting like there was this rhythm—the heartbeat—to the gathering. We made an almost immediate transition to this floral, light-hearted, soft world that almost reminded me of *Willy Wonka and the Chocolate Factory*, light spirits dancing around, everyone happy. It was one of the most unique places that I had ever visited in my whole life.

As we made our way up the long trail and the high altitude to where we would finally make camp, lugging that huge cooler (which we realized within fifteen minutes was a highly unwise thing to do), someone came up to us and said, "Hey, you guys need some help? You have a little extra ice in there?" He had a coffee, and he said, "I was just wishing that this coffee could be an ice coffee."

We said, "Sure, sure."

He opened up the cooler, grabbed some ice cubes, put them in his coffee and chugged it back, and it was as if we had given him an electric shock. He said, "Now, that hits the spot!" He downed his coffee, and said, "Let me help you with that." He grabbed Sherrie's end of the cooler and said, "Where you guys heading?"

We replied, "Turtle Soup, way up probably about another hour or so."

He said, "Alright. Hang on one second." He ran back over to a series of small tents, grabbed a little pack, and said, "Let's go." He proceeded to actually carry it for over an hour with us, helping us get it all the way up to Turtle Soup, where we were to make camp.

Bart and several of our other friends were already there waiting for us. It was awesome. As we walked through the mountains, there were literally hundreds of kitchens all over. As I mentioned, people built with the wood and the stone that was there, and they would basically bring a grate to build kitchens. One night, while walking, we came across a kitchen where they had built clay ovens and made cookies. On the mountain, no money changed hands. Everything there was free; we walked around with a cup and a spoon, asked to be fed, and people at any kitchen fed us.

People at this one kitchen made us cookies and popcorn, which felt like one of the most incredible things. At Turtle Soup, for example, they would just make huge piles of pasta, soup, or various stews. Stunning. No one was running anything, which was also interesting. One of my first thoughts about Rainbow was how it reminded me of the Borg in *Star Trek: The Next Generation*. The Borg was a cold, unified collective with no head nor leader (in the *First Contact* movie, turns out there's a Borg queen, but

I digress). The main point is that there's no sense of a central command; the group acts as one in many parts at the same time. And in the same way that circumstance can personify evil, it also defined Rainbow's goodness. There were thousands upon thousands of people interacting in that unique way, but there was no leader. We had no one running the kitchens or deciding what food to get. It was just this whole variety of people, and, somehow, magically, meals were made, and people ate, and dishes got cleaned. It was incredible.

Now, I would not want to go completely overboard into an area of unreality. I definitely noticed a stark contrast within the population there that Rainbows affectionately called "Drainbows," which were a small segment of people who didn't really participate, didn't spend any time cooking or cleaning in the kitchen. (They certainly didn't dig one of the many holes that need to be dug so that the human waste could be dealt with.) But overall, everyone was just happy and peaceful and doing what they could for each other.

One of my favorite kitchens was one that called itself Granola Funk. Literally, what they did was build a huge stage in the middle of the woods. They found a hill which leaned down so it became the natural kind of seating area for the amphitheater. There, they built a stage, and, during the entire time of Rainbow, they constantly held plays and different shows with musicians performing. It was just one of the most magical things I had ever seen.

The Rainbow Gathering's high point is what happens on the Fourth of July, and it starts with silence. On that particular morning while we were there, everything was silent. Some people were brewing coffee in the kitchen, but they were just communicating with each other with their hands or by pointing, kind of a mishmash, crude, amateur sign language that was beautiful in and of itself.

The morning continued on until what they called "Rainbow Noon." Rainbows are not terribly punctual, which meant the time could end up being around one-thirty in the afternoon. People gathered themselves from the partying of the night before and made their way to a central open area that they called the Main Meadow. In the center of the meadow, they built a giant fire pit ten-to-twenty feet in diameter. Beginning at the center of the fire pit, they sat or stood in a large ever-widening circle, expanding out away from the pit, wider and wider, until there were thousands of people.

While everyone was gathered in the Main Meadow, all of the children (there were children everywhere at Rainbow) prepared a parade. They made costumes and giant dragons like a Chinese parade. They brought drums and bells as they began their parade down the side of the mountain, all the way straight through to the fire pit in the center. As the parade reached the fire pit in the center, everyone let out a giant whooping sound and started chanting and screaming and cheering, celebrating the arrival of the children. Everything at that point went totally crazy.

All of this led up to what was to be one of the most spiritual experiences of my life. They had lit a giant fire in the center of the circle, and everyone was around and cheering and partying; eventually, they put it out by tossing a lot of dirt on the fire. What was left was a lot of red, hot embers underneath the dirt. Then, a whole series of probably twenty or thirty different drummers set up around the circle and began drumming in a massive drum circle, with this incredible beat and rhythm that I could feel, not only through the sound that they were producing but also almost through the ground itself, as so many people were dancing and bouncing back and forth. Slowly, people began to make their way into the center of the circle, dancing with their bare feet on top of the dirt. I felt that this was something that I had to do, too.

Once I reached the center, I closed my eyes because the dirt was just flying everywhere; it was as if I had gotten enveloped in a cloud. I just bowed my head and began to go back and forth with my feet and just let the beat of the drums and the rhythm of the drums move me from side to side and up and down and back and forth. I could feel the heat on my feet, but I couldn't even feel any pain, and maybe I could or couldn't even barely breathe, but I felt myself taken to this other world, and all I could feel was the beat of the drums as life swirled around me, and as embers shot up around me, I felt heat in and around, all over me, and I felt enveloped and enraptured in this sense of being in another place where the energy just coursed through my body, and, above all of it, this beat of love just penetrated me with this sense that all was okay and I had a sense of infinite love for everyone around me.

Finally, as if I was about to collapse, and I thought that cloud might take me, I felt myself fall out of the circle and through the drummers and hit the ground, gasping for breath. It was as if I was a fish out of water back in the real world, and it was harder to breathe there than it was when I was in that nirvana. That was Rainbow. That, I believe, is the experience that Rainbows like Bart try to capture in their everyday lives, when they are away from the Gathering. I wanted to do that, too.

PART II

CHAPTER 13

UNEARTHING THE SPHINX

Upon my return to school, I began to practice again. I noticed something distinctly foreign as I began to hold my violin again every day. There was the wonderful, comforting feeling that I loved, but after over four years away from it, I noticed a clear difference from those days back at Interlochen. At Interlochen, I knew I could do whatever I wanted on the violin; I could pick it up and perform almost anything, especially if I practiced. Now, I was practicing well over two hours a day, sometimes for the majority of the week, and I found myself not being able to do the things that I wanted to do. Sure, I could play through a piece, but there would be missing notes, and my intonation was intensely flawed. I'd go back and methodically dissect the passages, and practice them up, but things simply took me longer. When I came back to those spots the next day, they were not there again. My teachers passed down a basic tenet for my practicing: one should practice through something until it's perfect, then, once it's perfect, play it through three times in a row, at minimum. The likelihood of the quality being there the following day would be reasonably high. It now became exceedingly challenging for me to reach that point with the tougher parts of the pieces I was working on.

Compounding this, I was now four or five years older than everyone else in the university orchestra. It became an intense exercise in humility, rooted in embarrassment. I loved my violin, and I loved playing, but there I was, almost unable to play. By the same token, if I was practicing what should have been four hours each day, I may have worked it back. I knew that. But I simply couldn't.

I was beginning to build some friendships with some of my fellow students, which was good. But I couldn't just sit isolated in the practice room. Maybe, in the end, I didn't have the discipline or that passion for the process. I wasn't sure. Once I realized I was not going to have the soloist career I had imagined for myself, I thought about what else I could do with the violin that would have a great benefit to society. It was during this time at Michigan that I also discovered William Grant Still. Still was one of the most prolific American composers. He wrote volumes of choral and orchestral works, as well as pieces for the violin, piano, harp and other string instruments, a full opera and a string quartet. The most amazing thing was that he was African American. Perhaps more astounding was the fact that, as someone whose development as a young person was rooted in classical music, I did not know who he was until then. In fact, throughout my whole life of growing up and playing the violin, I had never even known that there were Black classical composers, let alone someone who wrote volumes and volumes of works for the stage and the screen. This discovery of some of his music led me to become so much more excited about playing! I began to play some of his music in my lessons and discovered other music by composers of color. Some of it was both challenging and unusual, but I was so excited about it that I did begin to practice more, and I loved it. For my undergraduate recital, I put together a variety of repertoire, including music I began performing on my electric violin. I also then began to blend existing genres together, taking music by Mariah Carey and Boyz II Men or En Vogue, and transcribing it for the string quartet that I had assembled. I also realized that, there at Michigan, there were other Black string musicians, which gave me a sense of belonging.

I took it upon myself to meet them and bring them together to form the first Black student quartet at the University of Michigan, and then we played on my recital. I had some wonderful fun, probably the most fun since I could remember. It was just a fresh, rejuvenating, vibrant, exciting time on my violin, though pockmarked by the fact that I was still frustrated by my more limited ability on the instrument.

One of the key friendships that I made was with LaTonya, the Black female violist of my all-African American quartet. I thought the strange thing about her was that she was from Alaska. Of course, any pictures that I had in my mind of Alaska were those of burly White fishermen. The idea that there would be a Black girl who played the violin and viola in Alaska blew my mind. She was also someone with whom I certainly didn't think that I really would become very good friends. She had a bit of a shy overtone and did not seem very outgoing. But she had been recommended to me by the cellist I had befriended. So, despite tepid beginnings, LaTonya was to become a very close friend with whom I spent a lot of time. We ended up rehearsing and collaborating musically but also just spending time around campus socially. As that year continued on, and I had my ups and downs at school, Sherrie was also taking classes and focusing on sociology coursework.

One of the things I found humorous at the time was that I would sometimes invite my new friends to come over and hang out at Bart's. For them, this was a shocking lifestyle difference; more often than not, they would find crowds of people simply spending idle time, full of love, coming and going. There was no structure, no order in things, which my college friends with big productive goals found unusual. Perhaps the influences of the school and my time with college friends began to draw me closer to them and further away from the patterns in the hippie lifestyle. Because of my return to music and my love for that, I also felt an instant connection with those who were in music and, certainly, those with whom I made music.

I also got back into cooking. At least once or twice a month, I cooked a big dinner and invited a dozen people over. We'd dine downstairs at Bart's house, at the ping-pong table covered with a giant hippie tapestry. I would cook lasagna, pasta, cakes, cookies, and brownies. We had a good time.

I spent some of my time over the summer practicing and thinking about my life. I began to think a lot about the things that I had gone through in the past year, starting up on my violin again, and the challenges that I had faced. I thought extensively about William Grant Still and the other composers whose works I had performed: there were those like Joseph Boulogne St. Georges, who was a Black Frenchman, a contemporary of Mozart, and those who were still alive and whom I actually would have the opportunity to meet in my lifetime, like David Baker. And in playing all of this music, and being excited about it made me think back to earlier times in my life, Interlochen and other places. If I had known about this music, I probably would not have taken all of that time off and would have practiced instead. I would have been so motivated and driven to discover, study and perform this music.

I would have been inspired instead of resting on my laurels, a bit bored by Mendelssohn, Mozart and Beethoven. That's not to say they aren't exciting. It's just that all classical violinists around me essentially recreated the same exact traditional works, with similar interpretations. It is like having 10 cover bands offer the same precise line-up on a daily basis. The experience becomes an exercise in assessing who's playing it better, who's playing it more technically flawless, leaving little room for discovery of new music. Especially because I had gotten such an early start tackling Bruch, Mendelssohn, Lalo and Beethoven and most of the major concertos at an early age, I had either played them or I had heard them played a thousand times. I really didn't have that much of an interest in doing what everyone else did. I think that led to part of the reason why I wasn't motivated to practice. I think something new, unfamiliar and challenging could have made all the difference.

I thought about how I felt playing with an all-Black quartet, how exciting it was. Even though we were less than a handful, it felt like something special and meaningful. This gave rise to the ultimate question: *What should I do about this?* That spirit that helped me to initially start EarthPro or Jumpstart, the homeless organization, or *The Bard*, the literary magazine, took hold of me once again. I realized that this was, indeed, what I needed to do. I needed to start a non-profit organization that would focus on diversifying the field of classical music, which would change the lives for those kids of color who were like me growing up.

When I was in the midst of a summer program at Penn State, I ended up going to Penn's Woods, a program which was merely mediocre, in my opinion. But there was definitely a hierarchy of summer programs, and this one was not at the top of that list. I also applied to one that was most coveted, Aspen. I got accepted into the top teacher's studio (Dorothy DeLay was considered to be one of the best teachers in the country). But, of course, the relationship was sour with my parents, and Aspen cost thousands of dollars. I couldn't afford the experience at the time.

The more I thought about it, the more motivated I became. *I can give young people the motivation to practice because competitiveness can bring about a sense of motivation. I can work hard to create opportunities they do not have, opportunities I did not have. We can have a big national competition that would be for Black string players. Importantly, all participants would have access to core additional resources: scholarships so that they could go to some of the top summer programs, connection to mentorship and beyond. They could get prize money and then they could get the opportunity to perform with major orchestras. I chose the competition because that could bring a lot of attention to it, but, more importantly, it will be exciting because they would have this network and be able to meet each other, collaborate musically and know that they had peers around the country. They would know they are not alone. They would feel that they belong.*

As I thought about it even more, the excitement built. It was a different kind of excitement, something beyond sitting in a practice room. I took the initial steps to file the paperwork to form what I called, at that point, Concert Competitions and Musical Development, Inc., a 501(c)(3) non-profit organization.

．　．　．

In the early fall, I went to my lesson with my violin professor, and told him what I wanted to do. My initial anticipation of his reaction was that he was going to say, "This is just an excuse for not practicing and not being fully prepared for your lesson, Aaron, and you really need to make some effort here." But he surprised me when he said, "It sounds like a fantastic and wonderful idea. I wholeheartedly support it. I think what you should do next is get the idea down on paper, and we will take it to the Dean. Let's see what he has to say. We should certainly see what kind of support the school can bring to bear."

I was thrilled. I did what my professor suggested and began trying to assemble a Board of Directors and a Board of Advisors, along with all of the structure needed for an organization. I ended up having conversations with the Dean of the School of Music, who was, immediately, very supportive. It was a wonderful development, and he offered up the School of Music with its space and facilities. In addition, I had the benefit of the incredible background and knowledge of Anthony Elliott, an African American cello professor at Michigan who had served as the coach for my chamber groups. I was also encouraged to speak with "The Fish," Ken Fischer, the long serving president of the University Musical Society (which is closely tied to the university). Ken has opened so many doors for me, and there has simply been no greater mentor or advocate for Sphinx.

I began laying out how a competition could be formulated and what we would need. I went about the hard work of trying to bring attention to the competition and how to do it. Most importantly, I worked to bring in funding, as I understood that without that, the competition would remain in its idea phase. I began to research what was available at the University, and there was, in fact, a fund for diversity through the President's Office, to which I applied. In drawing upon my experience of launching Jumpstart and what had been successful in the end for Sherrie and me personally, I organized another celebrity mailing. Along with people like Robin Williams and his wife, I sent out letters to anyone that I could think of. It was during that time that a family friend suggested that I reach out to James Wolfensohn, President of the World Bank at the time. I knew that this was one of those far shots, but why not? I sent him a personal letter describing the competition, its purpose and goals, and what we were planning on doing. The reason behind our family friend's suggestion was that the President of the World Bank was an avid cellist.

That year began to tick on, and I became energized by both this project and my upcoming undergraduate recital. I was working around the clock. The wealth of experiences offered to me while working on multiple ideas, programs and initiatives began to help me feel more comfortable. Initially, I was calling the competition the National String Competition for Young Black Musicians. In developing the idea and internalizing the need and reason behind the competition, I felt personally driven. I thought of myself and the fact that I was not only Black. I was biracial, Black and White. Throughout my life, I felt that there should not be a Black side of things, nor a White side. I used to think about magically carving myself in half to split myself apart at some points in my life, but that was certainly not feasible.

I explored where my problems lay with classical music itself. I did not think it was right that there was little Black involvement. I also realized that, simply, there was no diversity. Everybody was White in that world. There were a few Asian musicians, but, as a general snapshot, everybody was White. I began to think about other groups represented heavily in our population, but missing from classical music, such as Latino/Hispanic. This gave rise to a broadening, then refinement of the idea. Through research, I found that the two most underrepresented groups in classical music were the Black and Hispanic groups. In tying that together, I realized that what I was striving for was diversity. I didn't want to see a permanent all-Black and then an all-White orchestra in every city. I did not want to see groups of people going to the White orchestra or the Black orchestra concerts. I wanted to see orchestras that looked like our cities, concert halls that welcomed everybody. I wanted to see orchestras celebrate the history of America, as vibrant and different as I saw it to be. I wanted to see orchestras made up of people who love to play music with one another, without regard for the difference in their skin tones. I had a vision of what I needed to work on. The focus of the competition began to give way to a greater picture of inclusion.

Throughout this birthing process, I began to think about the fact that we really needed a name for the competition. The organizational name was pretty dull, but I was trying to come up with a name that sounded very formal and very professional and something that had been around for a while—Concert Competitions and Musical Development, Inc., sounded bigger than just this college student starting something while he's sitting in his room in a rented house. I began to think of "Phoenix," as I had always been fascinated with the idea of rising from the ashes. For me, that reflected not only what I felt would happen in terms of minority involvement in classical music (because we would, in fact, be rising from the ashes), but also that there had been this history that I wanted people to know. I wanted these other students to know about William Grant Still, Roque Cordero, Ulysses Kay, Florence Price, David Baker, George Walker and other great composers. *Phoenix.* I thought that this would be an exciting name for it. As I kicked this around with some of the different members that I had assembled for my board, somebody pointed out that we might be confused with the city of Phoenix. At that point, it occurred to me to think historically. As I thought back to Africa and its continental heritage, one of the great monuments to the ancient civilizations which brought a sense of greatness just in mentioning its name was, of course, the great cat/lion, the Sphinx.

And almost like a bolt of lightning, it fell on me ... The Sphinx Competition, representing excellence and greatness in terms of what a civilization was able to build, the standard for our young musicians and the level at which they must compete, and the fact that Africa is a historical reference for many minorities, not just African Americans. The Sphinx has taken a wonderful journey, bringing different civilizations and time periods together because of its timelessness. The same monolithic monument was able to mean different things to different people, and I saw it share the same course as a piece of music throughout history, that it could bring people together and bind them in a way that nothing else could, which is the true power of music. This realization gave birth to what would become the annual national Sphinx Competition for Young Black and Latino String Players.

· · ·

During the spring of that year, while preparing for my upcoming undergraduate recital, I received an interesting envelope in the mail one day. I was getting a lot of rejection letters at that point in response to the letters that I had sent out proposing funding for the Sphinx Competition. I came across a half-size letter, almost like an invitation. I looked on the back, and it said, "The World Bank," at which I grinned kind of ruefully. I thought to myself, *They don't even have enough money at the World Bank to send a rejection in a full-sized envelope. Ironic.* I opened it rather roughly, actually, as I had all of the others that I was going through with little patience. As I pulled open that small letter, I began to read, "Enclosed, please find my one-time contribution in the amount of $10,000 to the Sphinx Competition. I wish you all the best in your endeavors. Signed, James Wolfensohn, The World Bank." I couldn't believe it! It was amazing! I started screaming and immediately called for Sherrie. I yelled, "Sherrie, you won't believe this!" Then I showed her the letter and started crying. That felt surreal.

I don't think I'd ever actually seen a $10,000 check up to that point. And, beyond that, I knew that, unlike *The Bard*, unlike EarthPro, unlike Jumpstart, this was it. I would change the world with Sphinx. This led to even greater news, because I was able to utilize the fact that James Wolfensohn of the World Bank was supporting us, which certainly, I think, helped to motivate the President's Office at the University to give us a $40,000 grant from their New Century Fund for Diversity. It also helped to encourage the national home products company, MASCO (one of the major corporate citizens in southeast Michigan) and Ford Motor Company to come on board with $10,000 contributions.

With that, I cobbled together the beginnings of what was to be the inaugural Sphinx Competition to take place in the late winter of 1998.

CHAPTER 14

BECOMING STRONG

It's interesting being adopted. Throughout my life people would ask me, "How do you cope with not knowing your parentage and identity? It must be tough for you." But for me, growing up, I was always secure in who I was. First and foremost, I was Aaron, which meant a number of finite things. I was male, and that meant certain things to me. I was Black, and that defined me, as well. Then I was American, a violinist, and a host of other self-descriptors that helped to fill in the blanks in the constellation of everything I was to myself. But, despite having a focused and confident sense of identity, ever since I can remember, I found myself wanting to know the origin of my human constitution, my biological being.

The search for my birth parents began at the earliest age with what I reflect on primarily as fantasy. I have memories of seeing magazines with Phylicia Rashad and Bill Cosby and dreaming that somehow, I was their illegitimate offspring. Sometimes my fantasies went the political route and even though the math didn't quite work, I imagined that I was somehow the son of Martin Luther King, Jr., and that because he was being persecuted by the government and the FBI, I had to be hidden from the scrutiny of the government. This fantasy then followed through to its conclusion, with my mother having eventually been captured by secret forces of the government and secretly imprisoned, then giving me up for adoption. Interestingly, all of these fantasies then gave rise to the idea that I had been born to people who were celebrities or significant figures in history and my creation was the genesis of something illegitimate, possibly clandestine, but ultimately, negative. I'm sure I could spend thousands of dollars on therapy that would describe the true meaning of how this affects my psyche. In the interim, however, I'll hope that the words in this book will be therapeutic.

After years of gentle fantasy filled with celebrities and historical figures committing illicit acts that brought me into this world, I began to get more pragmatic about myself and my identity. I took it upon myself to physically search for my birth parents. Unfortunately, because of the various laws in existence at that time, it was next to impossible for an adoptee to find their birth parents, without regard to whether or not said birth parents want to be found. In essence, the laws limit either side from being able to know what is referred to as "identifying information" about the subject of a search. Initially, I went to the adoption agency itself to try to find as much information as I could. The Louise Wise agency was the Manhattan-based firm that handled my adoption. After repeated requests, I finally received a half-page letter that provided the background of my birth and adoption. Needless to say, there was not only a complete lack of identifying information such as names or addresses or my original given birth name, there was also very little information in general. The core facts that I was able to learn included that my father was Black, that my mother was White, and that they had dated sporadically against my maternal parents' wishes. In addition, the letter shared that I had been born by Cesarean section due to preeclampsia. The letter also shared the number of siblings of both my mother and my father. Outside of this core information (which confirmed I am biracial), there was very little else to help supplant the fantasies of my childhood.

Apart from this limited information, I was also plagued by the concern about whether any of the information I was being provided with was legitimate. Who was this agency? Were they telling me the truth? Why should I even believe what they said? Given the dark color of my skin, was it really believable that I was biracial? Up to that point in my life, I certainly had never encountered anyone as dark as I was who had a parent who was White. To further my concerns, one evening I was watching a *60 Minutes* episode and they ran a story about how adoption agencies could lie to adoptees about their origins. In the end, this particular story was about an adoptee that ended up developing severe mental problems that culminated in him being heavily medicated and eventually committing suicide. As the family looked back and researched the birth parents of the child it turned out that the adoption agency had lied to the adoptive family and to the child and that in fact, the mother of the child had severe mental illness and had had a lobotomy. As the segment closed, they shared that the agency that was in question was, in fact, the Louise Wise agency in Manhattan.

Fueled with skeptical thoughts in combination with fantastical childhood fantasies, I made my way through my adolescence, unsure about where Aaron actually came from. Over the next ten years I was to go through various physical and web-based searches where I was repeatedly scammed by fake private detectives and investigators who in the end just took my money and dreams without providing anything in return.

One of the most poignant times during my search was when Sherrie, immersed in the sense of how important it was for me to find my birth parents, became actively involved in this process. Since we knew that I was born in Monticello, New York, we figured that was the most likely place where my parents had gone to school. So, through Sherrie's strong persuasive skills, we convinced the secretary in the principal's office in the high school in Monticello to share their only copy of the yearbooks from the three years that we thought my parents would have been students at the high school, 1968–1970. When the yearbooks arrived, I was filled with excitement and trepidation as I anxiously flipped through the pages. Would I look down and potentially see myself staring up from the dilapidated torn pages of the book?

When I got to the second of the three years, I suddenly stopped at what seemed like a familiar face. It was Michael Strong. There was something familiar in the gaze of his portrait, but even as I looked down I asked myself if it really could be possible that for the first time in my life, I was seeing myself in someone else's eyes. I suspected I was just convincing myself that the fantasy from my childhood had finally come to fruition. I began to let my logical mind take over and looked for their siblings. Astonishingly, these siblings matched the correct number that the Louise Wise agency said that my father had. For me, this simply was too far beyond coincidence. I felt that this was it, the final culmination: I had found my father, Michael Strong. Sherrie and I began to work the phones reaching out to whoever we could at the school to identify someone who could help us to reach Michael Strong. Unfortunately, this took place in the years before Facebook and the other social media engines that could make such a search for him take only five minutes. Ultimately, we were able to connect with the librarian for that class from the school reunion. That person was incredibly helpful and shared with us that not only was there a Michael Strong but that he had sporadically dated one of the cheerleaders who was White. Given the few numbers of African Americans and that it was 1969, the chances that there were that many interracial relationships led me to conclude even more strongly that this was, in fact, my father. With every unfolding hour and every enveloping day that followed from that point, my heart would race from the moment I awoke till I was falling asleep at night with the anticipation that soon I was to encounter Michael Strong. Finally, we ended up tracking down a good friend of Michael Strong's who, at the time, was living in Australia. Then, during that conversation, calamity struck. We received the information that made it abundantly clear that Michael Strong could not be and was not my father. He had, in fact, never had any children and had not stayed in town long enough to have been my father. After having been tormented and abused financially and emotionally by hucksters on the Internet and in the Yellow Pages who used my fragile dreams of reunion to fill their own pocketbooks, I was left having created my own pain through this search, which in turn left me wishing that I had never had the high hopes of becoming Strong.

CHAPTER 15

A MIRROR FOR MY SOUL

As my first life companion from the age of seventeen to thirty, Sherrie played a pivotal role in my life. Despite her fierce atheist views, my adoptive mother shared that she thought Sherrie was an angel sent to save me. After graduating from the University of Michigan, Sherrie started a graduate program but then decided to drop out, as she really just wanted to help me build Sphinx, which she did. The work was growing, and it was a huge challenge, making our financial standing a strain once again. We were accustomed to it. A skilled editor and a person with high work ethic, Sherrie helped support us with an outside job, working for a professor at the university. While I also held a job as the general manager at Alf Studios, a wonderful local luthier based in Ann Arbor, I could not do so for very long. Sphinx consumed my life, and Sherrie helped pull us through, working outside of Sphinx, as I led all of our efforts in building it in its initial stages. During the year of the 2nd Annual Sphinx Competition, Sherrie and I had our son, Noah Still Dworkin (named in honor of William Grant Still). As Noah entered the world to the sounds of János Starker playing Bach's *Suites for Cello*, I was granted my wish of being able to gaze into the eyes of my own soul in someone else, instantly falling in love. He was beautiful. He was perfect. In the days following Noah's birth, we did experience a complication with his health: he ran a high temperature and we quickly found ourselves in the pediatric intensive care unit, anxious to do whatever we needed to in order to ensure he would be healthy and safe.

The Coming

Mute rupturing,
while eating Puerto Rican food.
Meeting by the meter
'cause the bill took too long
to pay by credit card.
Navigating,
through heavy breathing signal lights.
Parking where the permit
allows, by the wheelchairs
and automatic doors.
Mucous gushing,
car door opening too slow.
As I help her, help him.
Elevator rising,
the maternity ward.
Nurse admitting,
Never noticing she was fine.
Luxury perceptions,
mass depreciating.
Genes recalibrated.
Exercising,
now forbidden planning, damn breach.
Nine hours plus noon signaled
only the beginning
method of measurement.
Pain increasing,
six hours dilating, no progress.
Begone natural birth,
her eyes, genuflecting.
I ordered the morphine.
Five hours tasking,
fear earning five centimeters
Pride disintegrating,
frustrating the birth plan,
bidding anesthesia.

Percolating,
my wife's collecting stamina.
Ten hours contemplating,
contempt resonating
for unrepenting staff.
Undulating,
twenty-two expecting hours plus.
Repetitious pushing,
his crowning commencing,
will capitulating.
Representing,
blackness reciprocating white.
Head regurgitating,
gesticulating hands
conjugating, he comes.

We went through one of the most intensely difficult experiences of our lives. We were faced with terrible incompetence on the part of some of the staff, who were proposing aggressive treatment without a definitive diagnosis. Noah went through three unsuccessful spinal taps. Sherrie and I felt extraordinary pressure. With my adoptive dad's medical background, I turned to him for advice. Both of my parents drove to Ann Arbor to be with us: my dad was going to do whatever he could to make sure that Noah did not undergo incorrect or unnecessary treatment. For a change, his presence was an immense help and comfort to us. He had practical advice and suggestions for that team of doctors. He immediately located a good friend, a pediatrician at one of the foremost hospitals in the area and was able to help distill the enormously chaotic diagnosis to something sensible. Noah began to improve and feel better, which was a relief to Sherrie and me: we could not bear the tremendous pain and pressure of knowing that our baby wasn't well, and we couldn't help him. While at the hospital, we also shared a room with a premature baby who had been abandoned by his biological parents. He was born at the same time as Noah. The sight was unbearable. The sounds were heart-wrenching. This experience left me deeply affected, and I captured my thoughts in a poem titled "Baby Next Door."

Baby Next Door

Intravenous tentacles protruding from beneath
Sterile Muppet sheets.
Light scarce through hospital gowns reflecting IV bags
Soiled linen carts.
Preemies get their air through tubes Anne Geddes should put that
On a calendar.
No one to care that the chair becomes a make-shift cot,
Someone is to blame.
I don't often see color
but his blackness fills me, My people's madness!
Nurse Carol, his current Mom 'til her shift is over
Good for six hours.

Lungs not yet developed give a kitten's cry for milk
Lulling us to sleep.
Only his heart monitor alarm would disturb us
Before a nurse came.
What kind of Mom with no Dad leaves a fatherless son
Two months out of nine?
Curtain protecting the sight of hearing his gurgles
And lapse of breathing.
Hooked up two weeks for each day Baby Noah had us,
Still there when we left.
I wonder if Mom or Dad wherever they may be
Feel quite so alone.
I hope I would be better
if I put their shoes on, They're nothing like me.
As we left him to his plight
I felt sad yet I was glad
He wasn't mine.

The next phase of my life presented a series of greater personal struggles. As Sphinx began to gain its momentum, my personal life began to stall. Sphinx, indeed, had begun to grow into a national organization with now multiple programs, including the initially conceived competition. We've given out hundreds of thousands of dollars in prizes and scholarships, and I actually earned a half-decent salary from it. On the other hand, Sherrie and I had been separated for over a year. She no longer worked for Sphinx. As we faced the challenges of raising a young child, the obstacles that had bound us together—splits with our parents and financial woes—had been removed. We were now forced to address who we had become as adults, and why we were together. Years of dissatisfaction and unhappiness with our relationship ultimately gave way to multiple separations, then divorce. Our mutual commitment to the relationship and doing all we could do to save it, albeit unsuccessfully, created the foundation for a new relationship based upon mutual respect and care.

At the time of our separation, Noah, who was a year-and-a half, more than anything, was the true light of my life. He personified the various aspects of my own journey, from the giddy childhood innocence and times I spent with Leslie to the learning experience with Melissa to the love of Sherrie. The beat of the drums at Rainbow, the silence I now shared with God in the loneliness of my home were brought together in the presence of Noah. For a long time, I held the commitment that I made to her when I knelt down before her in the Bahamas, for I will always love her. I will always be there for her. I think that, deep inside, she knows that. That's all the happiness that I could experience at the time, and all of the happiness that I needed.

I continued to experience what seemed like the hollow success of having made a difference in the world with Sphinx and having my parents back in my life. Neither happy nor sad, I began to move on. I moved on with and for Noah.

CHAPTER 16

THERE WAS MOORE TO LIFE

On November 30, 2001, as I was sitting in front of an oversized computer monitor in the unusually large laundry room of my house on Woodland Drive in South Lyon, Michigan, its soft glow beaming on a gray Michigan day, I got an email. Sherrie (who had come back to work for Sphinx for a project) and Afa (a good friend from college, who was also working for Sphinx) were there as well. This email was special, as it was one whose time was coming since I was about twelve years old, maybe earlier. This was *the* email. I shouted in surprise.

As the tears welled up in my eyes, Sherrie and Afa immediately recoiled and jumped up, concerned that something terrible had happened to Sphinx. "What happened? Did we lose our only funding?" Afa asked, worried. Uncharacteristic of my typically verbose style, all I could say was, "It's my mom."

What they did not know was that several months prior, I had registered with a free adoption service online. I didn't think much of that act when I did it. Given the repeated disappointment I had experienced throughout my lifelong search for my birth parents, I didn't expect much from this website. In addition to not knowing that, Sherrie and Afa also didn't know that several hours earlier that morning, I had received an email from that same website. That email didn't impress me much either, nor did it distract me from my Sphinx work; it seemed like a very standard response, sharing that they thought they had found someone who could be my mother and could they pass along my email address. As with my previous experiences, I assumed it was a mere attempt to get more money out of me by forcing me to sign up for a new service. However, at least at that stage, they weren't asking for credit card information, so I provided the approval for them to share my direct email and then continued about my Sphinx work in the pressing matters of funding and program development.

So it was all the more startling when several hours later, out of the blue for me, an email opened from my inbox read: "*The birth mother I just wrote you about had a C-section because of preeclampsia . . . Her son was biracial. She was White, the father African American . . .*" As I continued to read the message, it became clear to me from the private information contained within it that there simply was no other alternative than this was, in fact, my mother. After all of my years of fruitless searching and repeated disappointments it was, in fact, the results of my smallest act and period of non-action that brought about one of the greatest moments of happiness and fulfillment in my life. What follows are actual excerpts from the initial email exchange I shared with my mother:

"Okay . . . where do I begin? Just to warn you . . . I will probably ramble here for a bit . . . After so many years, to have this kind of news. I never imagined in my wildest dreams . . . I am utterly speechless with overwhelming joy . . . What I was able to glean from my years of "investigation" is that you and my father dated sporadically in high school. By the way, what is my Dad like??? Never in my wildest dreams . . . Ok, onward.

I have had and continue to have a wonderful life . . . I am a violinist. I have played since I was five. Without going into everything right now, I ended up founding a national competition for young Black and Latino string players . . . The Sphinx Competition . . ."

Through our initial email exchanges and phone calls, I learned that my parents eventually married and had my full sister, Maddie. It was interesting to me how the details of my family history did not come out all at once but took a considerable amount of time. From the outset, I became aware that there was a difference in the level of communication between my birth parents within their family and my adoptive parents and their family. With my adoptive family, honesty was the basic tenet.

We were overly honest with each other, and we talked about everything, regardless of whether or not it was hurtful. It was honesty to the point of destruction. With my birth family, in my mother's initial message to me, she did not even mention my father. It actually took more communication in my inquiry for me just to learn that, in fact, my father was not only alive but that they were together. The history that began to unfold was relatively complex. My mother and father had dated and fallen in love when they were in high school. My mother was White and Irish Catholic. From the picture I saw, her father fulfilled every stereotype of a bruising and domineering White Irish cop (even though he wasn't one). My father was a Black Jehovah's Witness. He never really knew his father and was the son of a poor single mother on welfare. Growing up in Goshen, my father was the main sports figure there. In addition to being a football star, he was also an outspoken community activist. There were articles in local papers showing how he coordinated a sit-in at the local fire department to help desegregate its ranks. He was even quoted in the paper as saying, "We will integrate this town or we will burn it down." He was also a musician who played drums and did vocals in a mixed band that he co-founded. They played in both White and "colored" sections of town, in the hopes of keeping young kids off the streets and bringing people together. I thought it a harbinger of the life's work that I was to engage in with Sphinx.

So while in love with my father, my mother ended up pregnant with me. Needless to say, her parents were incredibly upset and forced her into an unwed mother's home. At the same time, they forbade my father from seeing my mother and in the end helped to have him arrested and ultimately drafted into the Army. While they wanted my mother to have an abortion, her religious beliefs prevented her from permitting them to go that far with their racial prejudice; instead, they forced her to spend the rest of her months until my birth at the unwed mother's home, ultimately requiring her to give me up for adoption. At the same time, my father, luckily, ended up posted in Germany for his service in the Army and was not to return to Goshen until three years later. As the hospital worked with my mother's preeclampsia, they cut open her stomach on September 11, 1970, allowing Jason (Moore), my original given name, to greet the world.

While this information about my parents and background on their history came to me in bits and pieces from my mother, I also learned more about my sister, who was fourteen years old at the time that we were reunited. If ever there was another time in my life where I instantly fell in love, this was it. As my emails and phone conversations with my mother continued, I was to learn that my sister actually knew all about me. The previous Christmas, my sister, curious about what my parents had gotten her for Christmas, snuck into my mother's purse to see if she could find the receipts for what had been bought. This act called for creativity and originality; it resonated with me for sure. The average kid would have just shaken the goods under a tree and took a wild guess. While my sister was rifling through my mother's drawer, she came across my adoption documents. A spirited personality, she immediately went to my mother and demanded to know what the papers meant and if could it be that she actually had a brother. My mother shared the truth with my sister, but for reasons still unbeknownst to me, they kept that information from my father. When we were initially reunited online, it literally took over a month before they were to share the news of my father. Because they had not shared that my sister even knew that I existed, my mother and sister had to concoct an entire scenario in which my mother and father came to tell my sister that I existed, only then sharing the fact that they were reunited with me.

Following were the words my mother wrote to me prior to our first phone conversation, which came after an initial set of emails: *"I am scared to death, but I must hear your voice. I'll take a later lunch and call at 3 p.m. I will probably cry, hope that's okay. This is still just so incredible."*

• • •

After finally having spoken with my mother (and later, my sister Maddie and my father Vaughn Moore) on the phone, the issue arose as to whether, if, and when we should meet. Initially, my father did not want to meet with me, which, of course, was a crushing blow to me. There was, however, a part of me that tried to understand. Ultimately, he did come around and we planned for a meeting. Mom wrote: *"Oh, Aaron! The most wonderful thing has happened! Your Dad just needed a little time in his 'cave.' I left him your photo from the website. I told him a little of what you said. He told me tonight he wanted to talk to me, and we did. He cried, actually, he sobbed. He said he forgives me for giving you up. He wants to see you. He wants to be a part of your life. This is all so wonderful . . . I lied. Sometimes, life is perfect. Because that is what this is . . . perfect . . . Not only have you made our dreams come true, you have strengthened the relationship between your Dad and me. I stand in awe yet again at all this."* As I thought about whether I should bring anyone to my first meeting with them, there was only one natural choice and that was Sherrie. While a romantic, intimate life partnership was not going to be possible for us, the legacy of our friendship and the role that she had played in my search up to that point dictated that her presence was required. For reasons of loyalty, for reasons of commitment, and for reasons of my sanity, we found ourselves pulling off Interstate 84 onto a small road that led to the village of Maybrook, New York. As we prepared to take the final left turn, I glanced ahead to my right and saw them. Perhaps I noticed my father first because of his height or it could've been his color or it could have been his face, or it simply could have been his presence. The things that uncoiled in my mind and my emotions in that moment are simply difficult to convey here with words. These are the things that the arts, and especially, music, I believe, were created to convey. I wish there was a way I could share some type of example to give you a sense of what I felt. *Imagine waking up one morning on an abandoned beach and before you open your eyes the smell of fresh baked bread and cooking eggs greets your nostrils as the sound of crashing waves and a cawing seagull fall upon your ears and the warmth of a rising sun slowly coats your ankles to your waist enveloping your body in a softness that turns the sand upon which you rest into a blanket of down.* That does not even remotely describe the elation I felt as we made that final turn.

My father was tall and dark and, in many ways, an older version of me. As we embraced, I felt strength along with a twinge of connection, yet it was limited by a sense of distance. I knew he had to maintain his stoicism at the moment. My mother was simply full of life. Hugging her was like hugging myself as I felt the energy that I was giving off was being returned. It was only later as we sat and spoke in their living room that I really began to take in more of her physical characteristics. She was white, heavy, and seemed to bear the weight of more than her own life on her shoulders. I was to learn very quickly that she was a heavy smoker, which immediately gave rise to concerns of the health risks she faced.

And then there was my sister. It may sound crass or in some ways limiting of my personality or character, but as I think back to the moment of meeting my sister and compare it with my interaction with any other woman in my life, I found a difference. As I greeted my sister, there was simply raw emotion made up of love and commitment, the type of relationship with another human being that I had always desired. Because of the difficulties I had with my adoptive parents and my brother, familial love was not the highest quality of love that I had experienced. For me, it was the people whom I chose to love, the people who, through the experiences that our lives shared, built a loyalty, sense of trust and commitment that were the true depths of love. Yet, here I was in the presence of someone whom I had not yet spent a moment of life with, but I felt compelled and driven to be loyal to her. This loyalty was deeper than any friendship that had come before. To this day, that feeling has not subsided.

As I fell asleep in the days, weeks, and months after our reunion, I began to ask myself what I had done to deserve this unbelievable blessing. I felt like, with other gifts that I had received in life, like my talent on the violin, I had a responsibility to fulfill a purpose in having united with my parents and sister. But I was anguished, as I could not identify what that purpose was, what role I needed to play. To this day, I still don't know. However, in the interim, I will be the best brother to my sister that I can be.

• • •

One could very well come to the conclusion that my reunion was simply the most wonderful thing, with no gray lining to that silver cloud. However, life is rarely like that. Make no mistake about it, I am blessed with two families who have helped to create me into the person that I am. With my adoptive family, the older I've gotten, the more I realize that what I initially saw through the eyes of a simple childhood rebellion did, in fact, have a truth behind it: the relationship between myself and my adoptive parents was and remains different from that between my parents and brother, their birth son. Do I believe they loved me and raised me in the same way that they raised him? Absolutely. However, I am not my brother, and the depth of their relationship and the manner in which they communicated (which came to the fore at times later in life) made it very clear that there was a breadth to that connection that simply did not exist for me. If my adoptive parents were confronted with the ultimate "Sophie's choice" of electing which child would live while the other had to perish, there would be no doubt as to who that would be. With the beauty and the magic of my reunification with my birth parents, with all of its wondrous impact on my life, for which I was and remain eternally grateful, the same underlying reality does exist. In the end, my sister is the child my parents saw grow up. The depths of their interaction and relationship with her, from graduating from diapers, and later, elementary school, to the trials and tribulations of middle and high school and then on to college, carry a very tangible breadth of connection that, while different than my brother's connection with my adoptive parents, still encompasses a wall which I will never and could never hope to traverse. And, in the end, I draw solace from my intellectual understanding that these differences are the reality, and while the emotional reality in which I must exist is not ideal, I can truly be happy and know that I am lucky for what I have been given.

May the road rise up to meet you May the wind be always at your back And may God hold you in the palm of His hand Until we meet again (An Irish blessing sent to me by my birth mom after our first meeting in person.)

CHAPTER 17

I REACH FOR OPRAH

The reunion with my birth parents was absolutely incredible and overwhelming. At the same time, the Sphinx Organization was also beginning to emerge as a credible and realistic venture with the potential to have a significant impact on society. As with any entrepreneurial venture, there is always the main startup phase, where one works eighteen hours a day, living, breathing, and sleeping the dreams one hopes to fulfill. For me, those were the early days of creating something out of nothing. Finally, there was an actual track record for us, albeit short of attaining sustainability. We had proven that we could impact the arts. We had demonstrated that there were musicians of the highest caliber who came from diverse cultural backgrounds. We had shown that we could garner resources to help fulfill the dreams of so many young aspiring Black and Latino musicians. We demonstrated that we could form an orchestra of color and have it perform at a high level on some of the greatest stages in the country and receive the highest critical reviews. However, we had not attained a position in the ecosystem where funders invested in us to ensure that we could exist long-term as an essential institution. We lacked true and solid financial footing.

Up to that point, I had secured support from key corporations like Ford Motor Company and MASCO. In addition, there were individuals like James Wolfensohn who literally made the difference early on between Sphinx having a chance to succeed or never getting off the ground. I knew that this support could falter in the following year, and I needed to bring breadth and diversity to the revenue streams of the organization that I was building. I had to look at Sphinx not only as an artistic creation but as a business.

It seemed logical to me that I should begin to reach out to the leadership in the African-American community in particular. My sense was that if I was going to identify individuals who would want to make that ultimate sacrifice of sharing their hard-earned personal wealth behind the project that was transforming a part of society, this was one of the most logical groups for me to turn to. After all, at that point in Sphinx's history, with two-thirds of our applicants and constituents being Black and one-third Latino, it made the most sense to focus on Black philanthropists as a key area from which to draw potential support.

Given my early success with outreach and, to be frank—luck—with James Wolfensohn, I certainly was approaching the things that I did with a belief that anything was possible. As I looked at the African American community, the first name that came to mind was Oprah Winfrey. From my perspective as a fan, it seemed that no one would have more concern, compassion and empathy towards the idea of empowering and enabling young people of color to be successful in classical music and in life than Oprah. In my mind, the idea of one of our laureates standing on Oprah's stage performing in front of millions of people would have taken us to a higher level. One performance by one of our laureates would have engaged hundreds of thousands of parents of color to consider exposing their children to classical music. After all, if Oprah could get people to stop eating beef, my thought was she certainly could have gotten them to start supporting classical music en masse.

I began my diligent quest to engage Oprah. This started with a standard letter, though very personalized, addressing the things that I had researched about her and her various interests. I referenced several recent shows and included in the letter examples and recordings of our Sphinx artists as well as testimonials that we had already received from leaders in the field. Like with much of my outreach, there was no response. I sent another letter and followed it up with a call. Now, a call to Oprah is not a simple thing. There was no number in the phone book. I called her show in order to reach her. I could only imagine the thousands of calls every day to her offices, so I began consistent monthly interactions with her offices. Persistence is the ultimate quality that enables success. From a very pragmatic perspective, if you are persistent, then there are simply only two ultimate outcomes. One, you will continue in your endeavor until you expire. In that effort you will always be on the journey towards success and, as you draw your last breath, you will do so with the knowledge that you literally gave your all towards the belief and the goals that you were pursuing. Or, since that outcome is certainly by no means ideal, the other outcome is simply success. The only outcome that is not possible is failure.

I began a regular monthly Oprah mailing, which meant that every month I sent Oprah something from Sphinx. It was not necessarily always the same letter or the same packet, but it was something that shared more news, provided more information and always contained a request, not for money, but for exposure for our young people on her show. In addition, I began working the phone tree within her organization. What that meant to me was that I would talk with as many people as I could, referencing the people that I had spoken with, as if they were long-time friends or colleagues. Being able to reference people in a given office immediately opens up a receptionist or other assistant to connect one with even more people. In doing this, however, I always keep things honest. In my pursuit of Oprah through the integrated phone tree, I never misstated that my conversations were direct communications with someone on her staff.

Over the course of approximately six months, I finally reached one of Oprah's producers. When I was finally able to get her on the phone, she had somewhat of a knowledge base of both Sphinx and myself. Her response to me was something along the lines of "Yes, we know all about you and appreciate your efforts and the information that you have shared with us repeatedly." This of course, made me smile, however, what followed led to one of the darkest periods that I experienced at Sphinx. She went on to advise that I should take a hiatus from my persistence and from sharing information with them, as I had achieved my goal of being able to get my information in front of Oprah. In that conversation, she assured me that she would in fact share information about Sphinx with Oprah directly, but she felt compelled to share that this simply was not the type of project that they were interested in.

It was those words that struck deep within me. From my perspective,

Oprah's show was bringing to light inspirational people and issues that were part of our society. I believed that Sphinx embodied the spirit and the heart of everything that Oprah publicly stood for.

If one of the most affluent Black women in the country who cared about the uplifting of society and empowering young people didn't find Sphinx worthy, who on earth would? I came to the conclusion that there were no other efforts I could put forth that could further the engagement of Oprah at that time. I could fill several more chapters of this book with similar stories of other leading African Americans whom I reached out to at that similar time frame to no avail. I found myself in this period of Sphinx and uncertainty with an odd sense of déjà vu from my childhood. At the core of that emotional envelope in which I found myself was ostracism. American society has mainly dealt with me as an African American only, not biracial. Yet here I was being rejected again, but this time by the leaders of the African American community. This filled me with a sense of doubt and concern for the dream I was trying to build that was more acute than any other challenge I was to face in the history of the Sphinx Organization.

• • •

Thankfully, years later, I have the benefit of the history of Sphinx and of my enduring persistence. So while I went through this very dark time, I never lessened the outreach that I made specifically to those who are affluent in the Black community. In the entire history of Sphinx, I must share that while the majority of our funding had not come from the communities of color, we have also received funds from many leaders of communities of color who have stepped up. They do it not only to honor the mission and the vision of Sphinx, but they also sacrifice their financial resources in the furtherance of our goals. Years later, that paradigm was to evolve further.

Within the Black community, philanthropy has been tied historically to the church. This stems out of the role that the church has played in the community; at the most difficult times in this country, it was the church in the Black community that saved lives and provided the hope that there could be a future for Black people in America. Classical music has not played a major role in contemporary Black America (despite the rich his-

tory that Black people and other people of color have played throughout the history of classical music), until now. I made the argument that
the focus and mission of Sphinx is not to try to compete with the church
for community dollars, but that it should be considered as an additional
aspect in addition to giving to the church.

I also continued to argue to the general public as well that classical
music positively impacts youth of color and deserves consideration for
funding. Training our young people in the arts benefits America as a
whole. Creating viable opportunities in the arts produces young people
who are well-educated, more creative and more tolerant, all special qualities we need for the betterment of society.

CHAPTER 18

A DETROIT RENAISSANCE

For a long time, Sphinx remained based out of offices in my house in Ann Arbor. I loved that arrangement because it saved Sphinx rent money and made it easy for me to work 24/7. Unfortunately, nonprofit organizations need to exist in the real world; board members and funders are not inspired by nor feel high confidence in home-based nonprofits. One of our core funders finally made me realize the importance of this issue. We had previously received a grant from a foundation, a rather sizable grant, to support some of our very important programming in Detroit. I was called into their offices and shared that they had a delicate and important matter to discuss. In essence, they shared that while they wanted to continue supporting our work, the home-based offices had to go. Needless to say, I had no choice but to address the foundation's concerns and immediately made preparations to move our offices.

It is important to note that this began an evolution of my understanding of my role with Sphinx. The process helped me understand that what I was building was, in fact, a separate entity from myself and that I needed to respect and value that independence. Eventually, what I had created would move forward without me actively involved in its day-to-day operations. If I was to be able to fulfill the dream of building a mechanism that brought classical music to the everyday lives of all young people and helped increase the representation of all corners of society in this vibrant art form, then I had to build the infrastructure of an independent, viable and sustainable organization.

Whenever possible, we tried to secure things needed for Sphinx in-kind. We approached local restaurants and asked them to provide the food for our artists. It is always easier for restaurants to give you food, for a hotel to give you hotel rooms, or an airline to give you flights rather than give direct dollars. So, when faced with the issue of Sphinx's office space, like everything else, I looked at what initially seemed like a challenge as an opportunity. In the city of Detroit, there is one central landmark that is the most visible and one of the most important addresses in the city. That is the General Motors Renaissance Center. Now, of course, I knew in this giant office structure that towers over the city, there must have been some under-utilized space, so I took this opportunity to approach General Motors and shared with them the importance of Sphinx and its mission. I also shared with them how they could align their corporate community efforts with Sphinx. Through that initial approach, we were able to build a partnership where Sphinx, literally, moved from the laundry room of the founder's residence to the 21st floor of the most respected office building overlooking the city of Detroit and its riverfront. Our partnership with General Motors continued for more than twelve years as it grew into a respectable institution.

• • •

At this point in my life, Sphinx was more than a full-time job; it was my life's work. While this was true, I was always a multi-dimensional human being, a creative and artistic personality. I actually looked at the Sphinx Organization itself as my primary artistic instrument, one that requires not just a pragmatic analytical and organizational approach, but equally, if not more importantly, a creative and artistic one. Yet, despite this focus, I also have an internal need to express myself personally through artistic means, whether through music, poetry, visual art, or otherwise. At the time of rapid evolution in the Sphinx Organization's history, I found the need to do more on my violin and did so by producing and performing on two CDs entitled "Bar Talk" and "Ebony Rhythm." With "Ebony Rhythm," I began to take existing poetry and score it with classical music (what I call "musetry"), then perform it in a very integrated way, creating a new artistic piece. This then led me to write more and more of my own poetry, and it was during this time period that I first began to pen the first words of this book. At the time, I never anticipated that I would actually generate what would become a memoir. Rather, I just felt the need to put the experiences that I had and was continuing to go through down on paper, if for no other reason than for my own edification and to help me understand the unfolding process of my life.

For a time, while carrying out the work of Sphinx from behind a window overlooking the city of Detroit and its beautiful Riverfront, I felt I had achieved a great balance in my professional life. I had successfully integrated all of my artistic talents into one powerful, multi-faced mode of expression.

CHAPTER 19

PICTURE PERFECT

In the fall of 2003, my close friend and colleague Afa and I found ourselves on a rare, brief break from our work at Sphinx. We were down in Florida, and after a series of meetings with some artistic and funding partners, we decided to take a few days off to spend time with Phil. Phil was living in Naples in a small two-bedroom, one-story house on a canal. Afa and I were staying there for a couple of days before the four of us, including Phil's girlfriend, were going to go to Discovery Cove, the exciting outdoor water experience in Orlando where you get to swim with dolphins. While there, I got a call from my adoptive mother, Sue. Since our reconciliation, my parents and I spoke on a relatively regular basis; they were far more engaged with my life and work than they had been previously. In addition, you may recall the importance of honesty not only for me but also for my parents, who had always been brutally transparent with me and demanded it of me as a child. As I sat on the beaten-up couch in Phil's living room, I spoke to my mother, who sounded different in a way that I had never heard her before. My parents were not prone to emotionality; they were the quintessential academics: methodical and analytical, not ones given to emotional outbursts or matters of the heart. In a broken, stilted voice that I simply had never heard exhibited by my mother, even with the emotionality of our reunion, she said, "I have cancer, Aaron."

· · ·

It took me several minutes to internalize what I heard. The one thing my parents always had been was absurdly healthy. My mother weighed probably about 110 pounds, my dad probably about 160. They took those long walks every evening; they biked and exercised regularly and generally ate more like creatures from the bird family than from the mammalian one. Other than their disciplined process years ago of sharing one cigarette a day, they simply did not have any of the lifestyle risks that most Americans had. That call was the last thing I would ever have expected. As I sat in stunned silence, she shared the history of how she had an enduring cough, which they hadn't gotten checked out, given the limited affinity or respect for most in the healthcare profession. This had been growing to a level of getting out of breath, where they finally got it checked out, and they had just gotten the diagnosis that, in fact, it was lung cancer; it was at a stage where there was very little doubt that it would progress and ultimately take her life. Because of my parents' honesty and their incredibly high level of medical knowledge, they knew exactly what that represented. In many ways, it was on that day that we really dealt with the death of my mother, even though her actual passing was to take place only slightly more than two months later.

Afa comforted me as I sat on the couch and cried. In retrospect, I found the depths of my sorrow intriguing. I am someone who values not only honesty but also loyalty. I felt like my adoptive mother had committed one of the greatest betrayals of loyalty when she abandoned me for those six tough college years. Despite her knowledge of the financial troubles that Sherrie and I were going through, she implicitly said that I was too much trouble and that their lives were simply better off without me. In my sense of loyalty, one doesn't have the luxury of excising the people with whom they exercise unconditional love just because they find them inconvenient or annoying. As I sat on the couch in Naples, the loss that I was viscerally experiencing was unsettling. But then I realized she was my mother, and I loved her. Even during the six years that they had abandoned me, I still knew that she was there; it's interesting that you can feel negative emotions towards someone, but just knowing that they are there, even if out of sight, can be comforting.

Afa shared the news with Phil, and we immediately canceled our plans for Discovery Cove and drove to Hershey. Over the next several weeks, we visited Mom and Dad regularly, focusing on time together. On one of our later visits towards the end of November, when my mother had difficulty walking even from one part of the house to the other without running out of breath, we had a memorable dinner, which my brother attended as well. It was at this dinner that my mother shared she was okay with her death and that she felt my brother and I were in good places. I periodically see my brother and his family in New York and have done so for years with some interruption. He graduated from Swarthmore College, did his postdoc at Harvard, and is now a Professor in Cellular Biology at Columbia University in New York. He has a wife, Courtney, a son, Solomon Ezra, and a daughter, Hope.

While I didn't fully realize the extent of it, my mother saw the emerging love between Afa and me; she conveyed a strong sense of comfort in her knowledge that I would be taken care of and had, in fact, found the person who would be my life's companion. It was also at this dinner that my mother and father shared the depths of their relationship: it was something of which they never spoke. They talked about how they had a forty-year love affair working in the same lab, just the two of them, and how they would miss each other when my mother would go grocery shopping. They also spoke about how they created a bubble around themselves and that they wouldn't let anything disturb that love affair; to me, they were speaking very specifically to my rebellion and the time when they abandoned me for six years. While they never apologized for the pain they caused, it was clear to me that they were explaining and trying to share what they had and had been trying to preserve all of those years. While it very much felt like abandonment to me, there was an acute essence to their love, which was admirable and to be respected. It was in that moment that I realized there was no way I could fully empathize or understand the loss my father was going through.

• • •

On a surprisingly sunny day on December 13th in Michigan, as I happened to be sitting on Sherrie's couch with Noah, I received a call that my mother was dead. I now know that you have to go through the experience of losing a family member or someone close to you to actually know what to say when someone close to you loses someone. The reality is that there are no words to soothe the pain. When someone dies, his/her physical presence is gone, and unlike so many other things in life that you can potentially change for the better, physical loss is something I could not comprehend.

• • •

As my father scattered her ashes in the backyard (potentially one of the only rituals I've ever seen him practice), his tear-streaked, barren face showed the complete destruction of this methodical and analytical man. This gave me the greatest fear that he would be one of the many statistics of spouses who died shortly after their long-term spouse does. However, through the combination of his sense of obligation to be present for my brother and me, which I believe was a request my mother made of my father (otherwise, they may have just jumped off a cliff together), along with his own ability to persevere, he made it through this tragedy and has rebuilt what I consider to be a new life, one which met its birth upon the death of my mother.

As I grew up, black-and-white photos of my mother filled the walls of the house in Hershey. To honor not only her memory, but the experience and trajectory of our relationship, I wrote a poem after she died about the evolution of my understanding and affection for her. One of the ensembles associated with Sphinx that my mother loved the most was an all-Latino group called the Carpentier Quartet. They arranged and performed a piece called "La Tuna" that my mother loved. I scored my poem with that piece that she loved, and I intertwined it with visual imagery and photos that my father took of my mother from the years when they were young up to a picture of them together mere weeks before she passed. As part of the words in the poem share, in many ways, I find my affection for my mother having a depth and breadth more expansive in her death than I was able to experience when she was alive. In the end, so much of who I am and what I've been able to accomplish is owed to her. One of my greatest joys was performing that poem, that artistic piece, during my wedding to my beloved wife, Afa. I titled the piece "Picture Perfect."

Picture Perfect

Picture perfect,
It took your death for me

To realize how perfect
You really are.
Violin lessons,
You took from me the hate I
had for you for making me
Do things that gave me life lessons.
You loved how much I loved another
And how you knew I needed
What I knew wasn't needed but now I do . . .
But now I do.
And it's too late to tell you
But I said enough for you to know, before you died.
Since I was a child I never lied to you I fear
I didn't try enough.
To share the truth of my life
And now I know you better than I did
When you were alive and I want to try harder
But why?
When Dad scattered your ashes
The sky in the backyard turned to music
And I heard your hair whistle
Through the evergreens and Dad's tears.
. . . and we stood there . . .
And maybe it's not right but
I'm mad at you again, I see
Ten or more years of his life without you
Looking at him and I can't bear the pain.
I've only got years of love to gain,
I'm just a child but he's taken the train.
I know you made it easy on us but
If you would have made it harder, it'd be easier now.
And Dad loves you more than I do
Which is more than I did before
So I weep for him
Because it's easier.
But I don't want things easier
Because I need to earn the pain of your loss

And you are in most things of my day
So I move on.
And make them mine again
And then I see you
And you'll be there . . .
Today . . . in May.
You will be there and all that I am
That is owed to you is finally a part of me with you
So you're in the backyard and in my violin
And in my son's eyes and Dad's tears.
And, I love the things I do
Everyday
With you
Still.
Picture perfect . . .

CHAPTER 20

A NEW PLACE FOR MY HEART

Sherrie and I had gone through a difficult separation and, ultimately, a divorce. As that process unfolded, however, we ended up with respect for each other born out of the years of our relationship. We were committed to making a relationship work. After several years of separation and, ultimately, divorce, I spent about a year sporadically dating with no great connections. At this point, my friendship with Afa began to morph into something different.

I first met Afa Sadykhly in studio class at the University of Michigan, where we both studied with the same violin professor. While I was going through all of my issues as a slightly older student getting back into my music from my four years off after Penn State, I initially found her to be a very interesting, yet obscure, person. She would keep herself very much under the radar and physically almost seemed to hide herself by creating a veil of her own hair, behind which she quietly existed. However, when she would begin to play her violin in class, it was as if she was a flower opening up. She would truly blossom and begin to move her body in ways beyond the music itself with a rocking back and forth. She was fully immersed in the music as she shared it with others. She had a deep love and passion both for the music and for the instrument through which we were all trying to develop our craft. We became friends through our interactions in studio class and other musical projects on which we collaborated. As a student, she not only was engaged with things of the University but also played as a full-time member of the Ann Arbor Symphony at the time. The more I got to know her, the more I liked her. She was a fascinating person who was not only brought up in a varied background with interesting diversity but also conveyed a deep knowledge of music that I respected to the highest degree. Afa was born in Moscow and then, soon after, lived in Baku, Azerbaijan, where she spent the majority of her childhood. When she was seventeen, she moved to Michigan with her father, who was doing some work in the oil business. She spoke four languages and brought a breadth of worldly experience that her minimalist appearance and attire belied.

As our friendship began to deepen over music and food and her deep care and affection for Noah, Afa also seemed to evolve. At one point, she cut the waist-length hair that served as her biological burka, veiling herself from all others. It was in the midst of this deepening friendship that Afa came to know about Sphinx. Initially, she was just aware of me up late nights working on this project for a competition for students of color, but her real first immersion was during the inaugural Sphinx Competition itself. At that point, I didn't even realize that I could assemble an orchestra of color, such as the Sphinx Symphony, and so for the inaugural year, I engaged the Ann Arbor Symphony as the orchestra to play with the final Laureates of the competition. Afa came up backstage after playing with the orchestra in that concert and shared that this was one of the most tremendous experiences of her life. As a result, she became the first intern at Sphinx and brought a wealth of musical experience to the task as she began to build the programs, ultimately fulfilling a number of senior roles. When our relationship started to bloom, there was the physical attraction, of course, which seemed relatively minor at the time. Of greater importance was the depth of friendship that we had built over the years. In addition, there were times when I found myself in great need and very alone as I came to terms with the reality of my divorce. Afa was that friend who was by my side during the toughest of those times. Friendship gave way to sporadic expressions of physical attraction. Interestingly enough, both of us—I, from the context of my divorce, and Afa, from the context of her prior engagement—were both adamantly opposed to defining our relationship.

We just chalked it up as the understandable attraction between two people who worked so closely together. After about a year, though, the question of what our relationship was and had become could no longer be ignored. So, on a hot day in early July, just prior to the beginning of our summer program, which was currently held in Boston, we took a long walk (something that we love to do in cities when we travel). That time, we walked from the East Village in New York to the West Village and then up to midtown. For those four or five hours, we had, in fact, reached a point where we were sharing life together. Through the erratic-chaotic-yet-ultimately-seemingly-planned course of the universe, our lives had somehow settled onto a path of one instead of two.

The Music of You

Ringing in my head
Composers living closer than Beethoven
Sitting in studio class
I listened to your love.
Of music I knew
Nothing of the dead men who colored the mask
You wore protecting strangers
From knowing you within.
The imperfect hair
Interlocking, cascading, encircling,
The truth was I did not yet
Love you in that way.
In the way that words
Can ring true to those who wander in heather
But the key in Ysaÿe
Changes like butterflies.
Then I was alone,
For long enough for people but not enough
To know that on bended knee
Left skinned, scabbed and bleeding.
The cacophony of Ysaÿe,
I wanted sonority
Melody to shower me
Replace delicacy.
I threw the symbol

Of what I knew I needed but did not need
Because melody does not
Suit me one little bit.
The music of you
Dresses me every day in a way that draws
My mother's breath through Dad's tears
And wilted evergreens.
The ringing did stop
Once my finger felt the ring whose time was wrong
But wasn't and I know
Now what I knew then.
You are in my life
My violin carries your soul through Noah's voice
Your dress colors the backyard
In Asian Spring tears
I shed tears for your
Tears you shed for me for the tears my Dad fails
To shed for me once before
Or now from afar.
And Sue was right,
The ring brings the music of my life through
Reviving the truth that I
Love that I love you.

I always saw myself as the black sheep of my family; this doesn't just relate to race and other aspects of difference between me and my adoptive family, but it had to do with my character. They always seemed analytical, unemotional, pragmatic and methodical; I, on the other hand, was passionate, artistic, creative, spontaneous and, unfortunately, too impatient. Very, very impatient. In some ways, this impatience helped me build Sphinx but at other times in my life, it's certainly caused me great frustration with others and caused me to act recklessly. So, it wasn't even a mere eight or nine months after Afa and I formally began our relationship that I began to ask myself what was I waiting for. In reality, I knew I was in love with her. I knew that I loved our everyday work together. I knew that I loved our intimacy. I knew that I loved every moment we spent together. I started thinking about asking her to marry me. When I ended my relationship with Sherrie I had sworn that I would never get married again. I felt like there was no way that my body or my mind could go through the loss and change of expectations that I experienced at the ending of that relationship. Yet the everyday intensity, passion and love for Afa led me to abandon those fears.

For me, the act of marriage doesn't change something but rather symbolizes something that already exists. I sought the appropriate symbol that could capture what it is that I felt for her. One of our passions at the time was islands. We loved thinking about them, we loved picking up magazines to read about them, we loved the shorelines and beaches. I got in my mind that if I was going to ask her to marry me, it needed to be on an island. Though this was going to be a bit difficult because while I was finally receiving a regular paycheck from my work at Sphinx, it certainly did not bring about the resources for me to rent a private island. However, being true to my level of persistence, I figured that there must be a way.

I began to research a number of the islands that were available for rent and came upon a phenomenal island called Emerald Isle, or Money Key, in the middle part of the Florida Keys. It was simply perfection, a gorgeous island with one centrally located 5,000 square-foot home. Needless to say, its price range was too high for me. By that time, I had gotten the imagery in my mind and had already relived asking her, multiple times, to marry me on the island.

I did some research and found out that the lead singer from the band 311, Nick Hexum, owned the island. Employing some additional creative skills I was able to track down his contact information and reached out to him. I felt it was important to not simply just ask for him to give me use of the island, which, to me, seemed silly and could most likely garner a negative response. I shared a detailed letter outlining the work that I did in music and specifically with engaging young people in classical music education, which I thought would resonate with Nick, and shared that while I earned a nice income, it was not at the level that would enable me to afford the standard rate for his island. In that process, I then asked whether I could pay a rate for the island that would be the equivalent for an expensive hotel and waited for his feedback.

Surprisingly enough, the work that I did in the nature of my request resonated with Nick and he readily agreed to let me rent the island for three days at the rate of just a slightly expensive hotel. I was incredibly grateful and went about all the plans to surprise Afa as we drove down from Miami for a supposed break in the Keys. Ironically enough, the only days that the island was actually available, and we could take a couple of days' break from Sphinx, ended up being on March 11 or 3–11, which was of course very humorous to both Nick and me. And so it was on the widow's walk on the roof of the house on an island in the middle of the Florida Keys at exactly 6:20 as the sun set over the ocean that I knelt down on one knee and asked Afa to marry me. Unfortunately, I was on my knee for longer than I anticipated, as it did take her a little while to recover from the shock of me asking her as well as considering my request; however, I am pleased to share that the answer was in the affirmative.

While we basked in the excitement of symbolizing the experience that we felt every day and began to lay out plans for our wedding, we were faced with the unfortunate reality of her family. Afa's mother is Azeri (Muslim), and her father was Jewish. Despite that, they fell in love and lived for most of their lives in a country just north of Iran and south of Russian Federation. You would think that they would have been relatively tolerant for people getting married who have differences. Unfortunately, this was not to be the case here, for reasons related to my race as well as the fact that I was previously married and the fact that I was American. Her parents strongly objected to our relationship and getting married. They refused to attend our wedding or accept me into the family. While this was a huge annoyance and disappointment to me, what was far more acute was the deep pain that this caused Afa. Over time, though, her mom finally chose to come visit us and after just one evening in our home sharing dinner and breaking bread together, her mother and I developed a deep sense of mutual respect and affection, which has endured to this day. After her mother came around, her father slowly began to change his approach and finally agreed one day to come see us in our home. When he arrived, it was clear that he had changed his mind and he accepted me into the family. Even though he never apologized, he brought several key heirlooms from the family that he shared with Afa and me that we could share in our home. In addition, her father was a smoker, and he invited me to have a cigarette with him. Since we didn't smoke, we went into the garage of our house, and her father and I shared some of the Meukow Cognac that he had brought along with the cigarette; I shared with him my love for his daughter and plans for our life together.

After causing so much pain from the lack of acceptance they had for our relationship, both mother and father came to love and respect our marriage and our family, which led to numerous wonderful times and experiences shared together. Those times made it all the more tragic when two and a half years later, we learned that Afa's father was ill with advanced cancer and that it had metastasized. In an odd circle of life, Afa and I were there close with him, along with her mom Rosa during his final months. He often looked to me for guidance and insight into his care. Afa called me from his bedside in their home a moment after he took his last breath saying her name. I was there twenty minutes later and held her and Rosa as they took him away. The depths and the nature of those relationships and the paths which they took inform me every day and give me insight and hope. Even in my darkest of interactions with other humans, I know that there is always the potential for light and the truth and a genuine love that you can share and give to those who sometimes have caused you the greatest pain.

Garage Cigarette

Smoke fills the openness and tool shelf
Around cars sitting cold
Coldness fills the distance
Of cultures and geography
Icicles of disdain for Americana and divorce
Serving as a true love's resistance
Maybe even color played a part
But did it really matter?
A cognac cat smoothed our breath
As we spoke of the love I had to impart
To a woman from a nation I thought
Treated her as a daughter but she was a daughter
So respect was due to parents responsible

For such an incredible creation
We breathed the same air of cognac smoke and casino players
I came to know the man who was smart enough
To doubt that my love would endure but smarter still
To see the loyalty that lay beneath layers
Of Americana and divorce and still glimpses
Of the face of family that would be near
And share the humor of shallow care
And countrymen with empty promises.
Filling the fear of the inevitable
But knowing the legacy would be revered
And Alexander would carry the memory
Through casinos and mockeries of society
I am comforted by the infrequency
Of the rose petal voice that brings a decency
A decorum to his tragedy with a loyalty
That inspires me to follow her legacy
And love her daughter not as I would have
Or as my mother loved me but as she loved he
For Rosa's love personifies an integrity
That only death can truly define
I knew him as he smoked in the garage but didn't know
What he already knew
That family trumped all else and in the end
I was to be part of what he had determined
And would make sure that of all the fears
That a father might have for his daughter
Could be lifted from him
and be carried away by the wind
The sense of who he was
How he met life's lessons
How he filled the lifetimes of those who carry on
Will be treasured still, forever more
By those who loved his presence

CHAPTER 21

UNCOMMON GENIUS

September 5th, 2005, started off pretty much like any average day. Sphinx was still progressing, and my work schedule was still 24/7.

The work we had done was garnering a significant amount of national attention. I remember being excited because I had an interview scheduled for late that morning with a Chicago reporter who was interested in doing an article on diversity in classical music and wanted my feedback for the story that would be running in the local paper. A little after eleven a.m., the phone rang, and I closed the door to my office so I could take the interview call. However, I was to be quite surprised because the voice on the other end started off the conversation by saying, "I have both good news and bad news to share with you today." Needless to say, all of my alarm bells immediately went off, and I began to prepare for what I thought was either a prank call or some type of strange sales scam that had made it through. He followed up with, "The bad news is that you are not going to be having the interview call you thought you would today. The good news is that I'm pleased to share with you that I am Dan Socolow, and you have been selected as one of our 2005 MacArthur Fellows."

What followed was a stunned silence as my mind reeled and tried to connect the dots and make sense of the news he had just delivered. I was, of course, aware of what MacArthur fellowships were. These were the famed genius grants, as many in the media call them, that were unrestricted $500,000 awards provided to people who have made great strides in their particular field. To me, the idea that the work that I was doing earned me such an honor bordered on the ridiculous. Also, up until that moment, my perception of MacArthur Fellows was that they were mostly found in the fields of science; my awareness of the award really came more from my interaction with my parents and brother, all of whom are steeped in the fields of science. So, after recovering from what seemed like a very long and awkward period of silence, I immediately began doing a quick Google search for Dan Socolow to make sure, in fact, that this wasn't a call from a friend of mine who had decided to play a terrible joke on me. When I ended up on their website and found his name and bio, I realized the call was legitimate and that my life, literally, had changed in a moment. I really don't remember much more of our call, although I'm sure we spoke about some logistics and aspects of the award, but in the interim, my mind simply had done something it rarely does—it ceased analyzing and planning and strategizing about a situation and just focused on coming to terms with the incredible news. After the call was finished, I walked to my door and called out to Afa; I tried to choke back the tears so that no one on staff would see them. She came up and we shared a hug as we talked about the impact of what the award meant for both of us, as well as for me.

The interesting thing about MacArthur fellowships is that they are intended to recognize creativity, and in my particular case, creativity within the field of education. I took seriously the idea that this award was recognizing that and specifically the impact that I was having on arts education through the Sphinx Organization. As a result, although Sherrie had, at that point, not worked for Sphinx for years, I reflected on the role that she played in its initial birth and founding. To me, the fact that she was part of that initial genesis needed to be reflected and respected. I arranged to meet with her to share that I felt that ten percent of the award, or $125,000, should go to her for the role that she played in the early days of the Sphinx Organization and the resulting impact that it continues to have to this day. Because I didn't want this issue to be clouded in any way by our personal interactions or potential disagreements, I shared with her that this was a commitment I was making to her regardless of whether or not we were getting along personally. While we had our obvious disagreements, we were friends, and I believe that she recognized and understood why that was important to me. Over the next five years, I kept that commitment to her, knowing that she made an impact with her part of that award for her ongoing role in education as an amazing elementary school teacher and a strong advocate for diversity.

Unfortunately for me, this did mean that the reality of the award—which is spread out over five years and unfortunately subject to federal and state taxes—left me with quite a different allocation of resources than what was thought after the announcement of a half-million-dollar award. However, over the five years of the grant, I was able to bring about a substantial impact in the field as well as launch other additional non-profit projects furthering my mission, including "The Catalyst," a social entrepreneurship reality TV show.

What was most interesting about the award was not the financial component but the change it brought about for Sphinx and, in particular, my access to major foundations. The reality is that, prior to the MacArthur announcement, it was difficult and sometimes impossible for me to even get a sit-down meeting with many national foundations. After the announcement, I found that the percentage of instances in which I could at least get an in-person meeting with the major foundation increased multifold. It was around that time that I learned that often the media or other awarding mechanisms focused on me as the founder of the organization rather than the organization itself. I realized that it would be critical for me to connect them immediately to the organization as a whole so that there would always be the sense that the work our entire team was doing would be recognized. I consciously worked to steer the media away from simply fixating on the founder as an individual, hoping to further the image of Sphinx as an institution.

While it's nice to be honored and know that my hard work is recognized by others, I am also a very pragmatic person. To me, the overriding importance with any award or visibility was tied to an assessment of whether it will help further our mission. I implemented a policy of referring to myself less by my given name but by the name of "Sphinx Founder." This enabled us to associate the name of Sphinx with the honors as opposed to my personal name, or at the very least, in addition to my name. I strongly believe that it was this policy and approach from a very early point that helped to build the awareness, visibility, and respect for Sphinx as an organization and enabled me to have the organization move beyond me.

What soon followed were national Governors Awards, the coverage in *Newsweek*, *People*, CNN, Fox News, and the long list of other media. They have almost without exception all been attributed and associated with Sphinx founder and hence the Sphinx Organization. In the end, I was aiming to create a stage upon which the future of the Sphinx Organization would endure beyond my own or any single person's leadership.

CHAPTER 22

(FUND)RAISING THE DREAM

With any nonprofit venture, fundraising never ends. The simple reality is that even the greatest idea in the world addressing the greatest need in society fails without a sustainable funding mechanism. Since the inception of Sphinx, I have always made fundraising a priority.

When building an organization (as I was while still a student), one has to fight, scrap, and pull funds from wherever one can and do everything on a shoestring budget. This was true not just for some of the core basics (such as the fact that I did not have the luxury of paying myself a salary early on) but also that I had to be able to convince others to work either for free or at the very least, at significantly reduced rates. In addition, I had to look at literally every single cost item and explore whether there is a way that you can get someone to provide it in-kind or find some way to create and build what we had to in a way that is consistently cost-effective. As a student, I would spend late nights at the computer lab printing out as many sheets as I was allowed through my student account. I would spend late nights at the copy shop key-lining our program ads, pasting each one up myself and lining it up with a ruler because we didn't have the money for design people or software. And the list goes on and on. But while all of that is necessary at the early stages of building an organization, no worthwhile initiative will have long-term sustainability without a major funder. I started focusing on foundations and corporations. The reason for this was that the potential for an individual to provide Sphinx with a major grant would take a significant amount of cultivation with no definitive ways to predict or assure the outcome.

Likewise, corporations and foundations also require cultivation, but one can easily access and research their interest and priority areas, saving lots of precious time. I also knew that it was very important to have a detailed targeted approach to a small number of corporations and foundations while combining that with a more shotgun approach that at least got the information about the Sphinx Organization out to a wider group of foundations and corporations.

I will share one example of how we engaged one of Sphinx's largest corporate partners. In the year 2000, Sphinx was really continuing to just get off the ground, even though we had at least two competitions behind us. Our top laureates were performing with major orchestras around the country, including with the National Symphony Orchestra in Washington, D.C. However, while we did have a few very generous corporate sponsors, we had not yet secured a major six-figure leadership grant that would really enable Sphinx to move to the next level. I, along with everyone in the national arts community, was aware of the Texaco Foundation. It had one of the longest and strongest histories of giving in the arts, especially to the Metropolitan Opera. It supported national broadcasts and a variety of other programs. In addition, (unfortunately for the corporation), it had experienced a recent scandal related to race and how some of its employees of color were being treated. So, with this awareness, I identified a major arts funder who understood the arts and needed to repair its image in terms of diversity. It felt that there could have been no better convergence of timing and opportunity. One of my most beloved quotes is, "Luck is when preparation meets opportunity." Needless to say, I saw a unique and momentary opportunity for Sphinx with said foundation, one that I knew was time-bound.

I went about preparing myself and the Sphinx Organization as best I could for that opportunity. We forwarded our most recent packets of information, which, compared to today's standards, were incredibly antiquated but at the time, I thought were miraculously effective. I then began my persistent yet calculated approach of calling regularly to connect with the right program officer. And so it was on one of those calls where the program officer for music for the foundation happened to overhear my discussion with the receptionist I had befriended. Preparation met opportunity, and in a matter of minutes, I found myself speaking with the President of the foundation for an extended period of time.

Interestingly enough, she used to be the executive director of an orchestra and, in addition, had heard from other third-party sources about the Sphinx Organization and our work. I shared that I would be in the area (not fully knowing what that area actually was at the time) and would be more than happy to stop by and meet with them to share with them the work of Sphinx and a proposed outline for partnership. She let me know that while it wasn't totally necessary, they would be happy to meet, and we agreed and set a date and time. That process then prompted me to develop the first PowerPoint presentation that Sphinx ever had. It prompted me to develop and go through all of our existing materials and, in any possible way, subject them to other third-party criticism so that I could bring them to the highest level possible.

It was on a slightly grey day in early December of 1999 that I arrived at the headquarters in White Plains, New York. Sherrie and I had actually driven together with Noah, who at the time was only one year old, and Sherrie dropped me off in the front of the office building. She then went to a local mall to spend time playing with Noah while I was in the meeting. After checking in with the receptionist, I sat in what was simply the largest lobby that I had ever seen in my entire life. The couches seemed out of sync with the space; to fit, they must have been made for giants. As I sat there fully suited up going through my PowerPoint in my mind repeatedly (having prepared for it more than I had for my graduate recital at the University of Michigan), I felt like I was in a situation completely and utterly beyond my capability. Eventually, I was taken upstairs and began my well-planned and thought-out presentation in front of several top executives. Unfortunately, I could not have gotten more than five minutes into my presentation before they began peppering me with various questions, some of which I was not ready to address.

While I felt and still believe to this day that I prepared to the highest level possible, the reality was that I simply did not have the experience of meeting with top-level foundations up until that point and had not been interrogated or questioned to the level that was currently occurring. In the end, I held my ground and had the benefit of clarity of purpose with what I was doing. I articulated the need for the impact for what we were trying to do, a sense of integrity which I was bringing to the process, and the sense in my own ability to effectively bring about change. In the end, I requested of them $150,000 a year for three years for a total grant of $450,000.

After the usual polite farewells, I made my way out of the lobby and into the waiting car and arms of Sherrie and Little Noah. I told Sherrie that I felt I did my best and we should feel good about that. I did not, however, share my fear that the meeting did not go well.

In the ensuing several weeks, I continued to follow-up as I did with the fifty-plus corporations and foundations that we were currently approaching at the time. So, it was all the more such a huge surprise when on December 20th, I received a call that it was unfortunate that they could not approve our proposal as submitted; however, they had decided to approve a $100,000-a-year grant for three years for a total of $300,000! This represented the largest grant in Sphinx's history and the stamp of approval of one of the most respected arts funders in the country. To this day, I am absolutely convinced that without the encouragement of the foundation executives—combined with the unique moment in time in which our paths crossed—the Sphinx Organization might not exist today.

It is through the resulting ripples of this partnership that we have been able to build the long-standing relationships that Sphinx has built over the years with countless other corporations and foundations. I no longer felt the same level of nervousness or doubt when I sat in the corridors of the most powerful corporations and foundations in the country, yet I keep the memory of that couch and the great hall in my mind as a reminder that without the resources that these critical partners bring to bear, none of the important work that Sphinx does would be possible.

CHAPTER 23

GETTING TO CARNEGIE HALL

There's an age-old question: "How do you get to Carnegie Hall?" The answer, of course, is *practice, practice, practice*. When I was eight years old and heard Isaac Stern perform on the stage of Carnegie Hall, I don't think I ever thought my life would take the path that would bring me to that very stage. As a child, I always dreamed that I would one day be a world-renowned soloist and that, as a violinist I would win the famed Tchaikovsky Violin Competition. As a result of that victory, not only as an American (who rarely ever wins the competition) but also an African American, my music would transform the world and bring together the Soviet Union and the United States in peace and bring the world's diverse populations together through the power of my music, breaking down cultural barriers, centuries of man-formed walls and ending all prejudice. As a kid who grew up in the 1980s, I saw this as a peace mission to end the Cold War through the power of music. I saw music as a common language, shared and understood by all humankind, irrespective of geography, politics, race, or culture: a force that is not governed by artificial laws. Yes, I may have had some grand plans and was a bit egomaniacal about my musical prowess, but that dream of standing on the stage at Carnegie Hall and being able to share a part of myself with those sitting in the audience was very real to me. As our programs began to develop, not only in Detroit but nationally, and the network of musicians of color and communities that we had been engaging grew around the country, we found several key geographic areas that emerged as dominant. The largest and most significant centralized area that we found our programming developing was in and around New York City, one of the grand cultural meccas of the world. On one of my trips to the city to meet with our various partners schools, and funders, the question was posed to me by more than one person about why Sphinx did not have a base in New York.

I took their critical feedback to heart and thus began to develop a plan of how Sphinx could build its presence not only in New York but in a more visible national arena. For a musician in me, there was only one obvious choice: the famed, legendary, one-and-only stage of Carnegie Hall. I also felt as though Sphinx already had almost a spiritual connection to Carnegie Hall through Isaac Stern. He had played a pivotal role in the early days of the competition by attending the inaugural competition in Ann Arbor and spending significant time with the number of our semifinalists, offering them private coaching at his own expense in his studio in New York until he passed away. He was also the savior of Carnegie Hall. If not for the efforts of Isaac Stern, Carnegie Hall would most likely not exist today. We decided that if we were going to build something in New York, why not do it in a manner that affords our artists a venue of the highest profile; arguably, on one of the greatest stages in the world. We did our due diligence in researching the costs associated with assembling such an event, and then I went about the hard work of identifying a partner who could help make it happen. After multiple attempts of trying to build a partnership to no avail, I was finally granted a meeting at the national headquarters of JP Morgan Chase, which had a strong commitment to the arts. Afa and I thoroughly prepared for the meeting, developing a strategy and a plan of how to persuade them of not only the importance of Sphinx's mission, but also inspire them to step up and support an unprecedented project: Sphinx Artists Series at Carnegie Hall. We met with Janet Rodriguez and felt an instant rapport, as she clearly saw value and the likely impact of such a project. I shared the history and the legacy of people of color in classical music and the hard statistics of the lack of diversity that currently existed. We discussed the impact that Sphinx had over the years and the level to which that impact could be increased if we could bring our mission and our work and our artists to the stage of Carnegie Hall. As we discussed this dream, Afa and I walked away determined to do everything we could to make this a reality. In those days, we often teamed up at meetings and would combine our efforts to actually produce the grants themselves. As Afa worked on the initial draft, I was able to construct the budget and formulate a final copy. We knew that this would take courage on behalf of JP Morgan Chase to take on a relatively young organization that had a compelling dream, but young in years. I remember receiving an email from Janet, letting us know that the Senior Team was prepared to partner with us and that our grant was approved.

In an instant, I shared the news with Afa, and we could both feel that this would, likely, become one of the most powerful statements not only to the industry, but also to the public as a whole . . . a dazzling showcase of artists of color, representing the new face of classical music. We focused on carefully shaping the repertoire to combine the well-loved master-pieces of traditional chamber music with seldom-performed works by composers of color. Coleridge-Taylor Perkinson was showcased along-side Mozart and Vivaldi. We also kept the format dynamic, tempering the length of the concert and showcasing select soloists next to the orches-tra playing works by themselves. The orchestra was comprised of top alumni and laureates of the competition, who represented excellence, hope, and a future of music reflecting the richness and diversity inherent in our society. The image was compelling. The meaning was even more augmented for Afa and me, as we engaged two wonderful conductors, Kay George Roberts, an African American woman who became a men-tor and role model to us both, along with Anthony Elliott. Tony Elliott is a remarkable cellist, conductor, and a selfless educator. Both of them were true pioneers in the field and incredible examples to each one of the musicians in the Sphinx Chamber Orchestra. Beyond that, Tony taught chamber music to Afa and me at the University of Michigan, and his advi-sory role was one we both treasured. Having him lead the alumni ensem-ble was a true gift.

• • •

The first Carnegie performance also carried the unforgettable detail of having the honor and pleasure of Sanford Allen's presence. Sanford is the first permanent Black member of the New York Philharmonic. A concert violinist and life-long artist, he has served as one of my key mentors. I have relied upon his expertise and advice since the early years of Sphinx.

Sanford was able to hear the program and, in particular, share in the joy of listening to a work by Coleridge-Taylor Perkinson, one of the greatest American composers, who was also an African American. Sanford and "Perk" as many referred to him, were close personal friends, and I knew that the pride that I felt looking at Sanford at that moment was one I would treasure for the rest of my life. We had lost Coleridge-Taylor Perkinson to cancer in recent years, and for Afa and myself, it was important to honor him and his terrific work, which absolutely deserved recognition. I knew that Perk would have been pleased to see his iconic yet seldom-heard work performed so well by this new generation of artists of color.

It was all the more momentous, when, after that debut at Carnegie Hall, our artists got a rave review in the *New York Times*. The piece praised the artistic excellence, mission, and quality of Sphinx and its programming. It was a moment of pride, tears, joy, and hope for a future filled with possibilities and meaning.

JP Morgan Chase opted to continue our partnership, which eventually led to the ongoing Sphinx Artists Series at Carnegie Hall, which continues to this day. This historic commitment also translated into a $1 million dollar grant on the part of the foundation to enable this legendary series to sustain itself over the past six years. As a result, not only have dozens of our artists graced this stage, generating rave reviews every single performance in a sold-out magnificent venue, we have changed the face of the audience. One of the remarkable aspects of the Carnegie Series is that its audience could not simply be described as a traditional classical music audience, nor an audience that one would term Black or Latino; rather, it was an audience that one could truly say represents New York City, New York state and the country as a whole. This is an audience that reflected Black, White, Asian, Latino, mature and young from all corners of society and from every class. Students from all boroughs and their families with no resources come together with those who have the ability to make five- or six-figure commitments to the Sphinx Organization. Through venues such as this, Sphinx has been able to take a vision of what otherwise would have seemed impossible, to become something that occurs regularly. This program has enabled Sphinx Organization to further its mission of bringing about social change. It has helped us create a better reflection and representation of our society in a vital art form that is necessary to express one's culture, national identity and pure being.

• • •

Remarkably, several years later, we have been able to take the track record of the Sphinx Chamber Orchestra and its artistry to the next level by securing the resources and partnership to launch an annual tour. Since 2008, the tour has replicated the magic of Carnegie in countless communities nationwide and internationally, showcasing our remarkable artists, now known widely as Sphinx Virtuosi. The group has undergone an artistic evolution to become the nation's most diverse and dynamic group, which performs as a self-conducted ensemble. The programming has grown to challenge listeners even further, continuing to share the overarching mission of Sphinx and the message of diversity and excellence.

One of the most important things we share with all of the young people we work with is that they should not spend any of their time worrying about whether they might be discriminated against because of the color of their skin. We share with them that they should let us worry about those challenges, and what is most important is the commitment to the work and the dedication they bring to their art form and craft.

CHAPTER 24

BUILDING BEYOND ONESELF

When Sphinx approached its most significant milestone to date, our 15th anniversary, I reflected on our first competition, first jury panel, first guest artists, and my early vision of what I could offer to those who looked like me, who had similar dreams and challenges and sought success in music. With 30,000 youth reached through educational efforts, some of the most revered icons of the field serving on our national jury panel and Honorary and Advisory Board, and satellite offices in Chicago, New York, and London, I look back with pride and look forward with excitement. Most importantly, however, I felt an enormous sense of gratitude for the present, for that is what's most important.

At that moment, Sphinx was placing quarter-sized violins in the hands of hundreds of young people in Detroit and Flint, Michigan, sharing the talents of the professional all-Black and Latino Sphinx Symphony and competition Laureates with over two million in broadcast audiences, creating educational residencies in South Africa, Belgium and the UK. Our premiere ensembles were reaching thousands on their annual national tour. I could not be more proud in recognizing that Sphinx has become something far beyond and above me and my dreams. It was becoming a creative vehicle, an avenue through which hundreds of artists channel their talents, give back to the community, hone their skills and realize the dreams. Hundreds of our alumni created a familial circle, a connection I could have only dreamt of as a young undergraduate student at the University of Michigan.

As I looked at all of the challenges presented to me on the path of launching and building the Sphinx Organization, I could say that I took every obstacle and turned them into new opportunities. One of the core values I have worked to instill in my team has been the ability to adapt. We crafted proposals. We told the Sphinx story. We programmed works by little-known Black and Latino composers who deserved to be studied and performed. We kept our beginning students from single-parent households from quitting the violin due to social and economic pressures. We challenged negative perceptions and broke down boundaries. Sphinx was and today continues to change the face of classical music and the world for the better, one note at a time.

It has been a long journey from my early days on the violin in Manhattan to the days of my rebellion and Interlochen, my resurrection phase at the University of Michigan, and all the way to the current day, when I humbly reflect on having been honored as President Obama's first nominee to the National Council of the Arts. I had been confirmed by the U.S. Senate and was looking forward to serving in this unique national capacity. I hoped to have even greater impact on how the arts are infused into our diverse society.

I was indeed living a dream, combining my affinity for young people, the arts, and social entrepreneurship. During that phase of my life, I also devoted more time to my performance art, my multi-media spoken word concerts (presented by the University Musical Society, my alma mater, University of Michigan School of Music, Theatre & Dance), as well as the Galapagos Art Space in New York. Finding my own voice as an artist was becoming an increasingly greater part of my life. While I gained unbelievable satisfaction and a sense of helping to impact the world through my work at Sphinx and other professional organizational roles that I play, in the end, no other sense prevails over what I feel toward my sons, Noah and Amani, and my wife, Afa. This intimate feeling resonates to this day with what I experience when practicing an art form for others. More recently, I have come to terms with my whole self as an individual, artist, social entrepreneur, and author. At that time, I began to more intensely and intentionally reflect on the body of work which I have been able to build throughout my life. As I looked forward to—hopefully—numerous decades of impact that my efforts will carry forward, I found myself with a growing sense that what brings me that ultimate joy every morning is not, as I once thought, my work at Sphinx. I still regularly shared with people that I never truly work because I love what I do. Every morning, I'm thankful my day will be filled with things that bring me happiness. More and more, though, I knew that the source of that joy that I felt every day also came from my love for my family. When I opened my eyes every morning, the first thing that I saw was the two sets of eyes of my sons Noah and Amani looking back at me. The feeling of looking into their eyes and recognizing myself is a source of unmatched happiness. The boys would announce my mornings with "Wake up, Daddy!" the immediate gaze of my loving wife, Afa, followed with a smile. Each day, I concluded with a "Night-night, Sweetie" to both of my sons as they lay back on their pillows while laying down to rest my knee over the leg of my life companion. That nightly saying and awareness of unconditional love that greeted me every morning and enveloped me every night creates a cocoon which I still continue to walk through every day. While I do employ the skill sets of persistence, a constant quest for excellence, logic, and efficiency to impact the world around me positively, what really gets me through all of the greatest challenges I've faced is my family. If the worst calamity were to befall the Sphinx Organization, I know I would derive solace from moving forward with those whom I love the most. I would remain happy, for I know that if I were to experience any loss related to my family, even the greatest worldwide impact of Sphinx would be unable to bring a happy note to my soul. I hoped that as I moved forward, something I felt would be imminent, I would be able to honor and live up to the unconditional love that they gave me. They are truly the heartbeat—the rhythm—of my uncommon life.

PART III

PART III

CHAPTER 25

A CHANGE IN DIRECTION

By 2014, the Sphinx Organization had reached a point of maturation. As an institution, it was broadening its embrace of the communities we were so committed to serve. Having launched as a single initiative—the inaugural Sphinx Competition for Young Black and Latino String Players in 1998—our effort was becoming an institution, a movement, with a compelling mission and impact for our artists, our art form, and the greater society. Sphinx was also gaining ground with the philanthropic community, ensuring a future for itself and for those who have been steering the ship alongside myself and Afa.

Our journey was not always smooth, nor was our future secure. In the beginning, the organization worked out of my house, mostly with volunteers who shared my hope that music could bridge the chasms of color, poverty, and opportunity. I believed then and now that diversity is the strength of a society. Each person is responsible for continuing or breaking down the walls that fan stereotypes, prejudice, and discrimination.

I have always been aware of the relationship between cause and effect, whether instilled by my adoptive family, gained by personal experience, or, as in most things in life, an intricate blending of the two. I am a consummate planner. I constantly develop alternative scenarios of future events, projecting their impact on my objectives and weighing the best strategies to reach my goals. When considering a new programmatic expansion for Sphinx, I was most concerned about its likely impact on our intended beneficiaries. Would the project deliver on its promise? How will our intended beneficiaries—young Black and Latino classical musicians—benefit? What could go wrong? How can we reduce the risk of a poor result, which may set us back rather than propel the cause forward? How does the project fit our overall mission? Some business leaders call this practice "anticipation"; some theorists incorporate an aspect of this process into modern-day "theories of change" and "consequentialism." On an instinctive level, my goals were always driven by a combination of intense empathy and a determination to maximize their beneficial impact.

To ensure that Sphinx would continue to build on its accomplishments, I knew we needed to ensure that the values and practices underlying our success continued. I also recognized that the only constant in life was change. We had to become an "autopoietic organization," an institution that functions in an unstructured, horizontal fashion and maximizes flexibility, learning, and an openness to the environment to change. In short, Sphinx needed a mission to inspire and the ability to adapt to its environment to thrive continually.

My experience as a serial entrepreneur was instructive in my vision of what Sphinx was to become. My path before Sphinx was rooted in innovation due to necessity, whether the consequence of my will to survive or the fulfillment of a dream emerging from my aptitudes and passions.

During this time, my life with Afa had flourished on a personal and professional level. She was my wife and the mother of my children, as well as primary counsel, friend, and confidante. The term "soulmate" has become a hackneyed cliché, but I can think of no other description that better describes our relationship. After a long workday, we usually shared the events of the day over glasses of wine, the two of us in sync. It is a ritual we treasure to this day . . . though our preference for wine has evolved over time.

We had our challenges like most couples, especially navigating the lines between "I," "you," and "us." Almost separate from contemplating our future as a romantic couple, we shared a beautiful vision for Sphinx, each passionate about opportunities for aspiring musicians of color and expanding diversity in classical music. Sphinx—for both of us—was a labor of love, a calling. We spent hours in private conversations about Sphinx and what steps we needed to take to protect its continuity.

The donors' tendency to consider the organization and me as one and the same troubled me because its accomplishments were only possible due to the contributions of many—our employees, volunteers, advisers, and the classical music community. In addition, the link was a significant vulnerability of Sphinx. If I had been hit by a truck, the organization's progress might have been affected, and its objectives questioned.

With Afa's advice and consent, I decided to open the organization's leadership, allowing our capable people to operate more independently, though no less coordinated. One of my first actions was to use the title "Sphinx Founder" in lieu of or appended to my personal name, thus bolstering the organization's brand, rather than my own. I believe that leaders, especially social entrepreneurs, should recognize that the impact of their work cannot simply be attributed to them as an individual.

Afa's willingness to take on extra duties, including sharing public speaking engagements and meeting with potential and active donors, along with her other Sphinx responsibilities, super-charged the organization's activities. From a personal viewpoint, her extended role gave me the time to do what I do best—think and function as a mentor, a macro thinker. We were a team, a yin and yang combination feeding off the other's energy to grow the organization and its impact.

Sphinx's success to that point was personally gratifying, especially the strides we were making in breaking barriers for children of color in classical music. The MacArthur award opened doors for funding that had been closed previously and we had justified the donors' faith in the Sphinx mission by expanding our outreach across the nation and the world. As the founder of the Sphinx Organization, my professional and personal contacts with influential people in business, academia, music, and philanthropy broadened and deepened, raising the bar for what might be achieved by the Sphinx Organization.

I always viewed Sphinx as my life's work. I thought I would do it my whole life. There are few callings as compelling as helping other people to realize their dreams. Due to the increased visibility of the organization and its founder, I became the target of headhunters hoping to tempt me to leave Sphinx and run another organization. I was flattered, but extremely satisfied with my work at Sphinx.

The work was challenging. Even with our accomplishments, there was so much more left to do. I don't believe that hierarchical structures or command-and-control leadership produce superior results or the agility to adjust to changing circumstances. My team was extraordinarily dynamic, and everyone was sincerely committed to the organizational mission. Our culture of cooperation, mutual respect, and personal responsibility had developed over a decade of working together. We were not afraid to "push the envelope," knowing that great accomplishments rarely occur easily. When we had a setback, we diagnosed, pivoted, and forged ahead undeterred.

Perhaps the greatest source of my happiness was the family relationship that Afa and I developed outside our professional life. Many adopted children struggle to build reciprocal trust in a relationship, despite their adoptive parents' best intentions and efforts. The feelings of not belonging, of being different are inevitable, especially in biracial children. I believe the need for unconditional love is universal, though many never experience it.

It is at around that time I began to review my journey up to that point, taking pride in my accomplishments and revisiting my priorities. While totally committed to Sphinx, I had changed. There were other elements of my life at least as important as the organization—my sons, Noah and Amani, and Afa, my wife and life partner.

I loved our work and the challenge of advocating for one's dream to others, the thrill of philanthropic success, whether producing a sold-out performance of the Sphinx Symphony Orchestra or receiving a transformative gift from an inspired donor. But I had missed the time to explore my personal creativity, my writing and the very process of ideating and innovating. Afa's business acumen, her readiness to step up in a new role, and her ability to seamlessly mesh the responsibilities of family and Sphinx freed me for some of those pursuits. She created a safe place for us that nourished, sheltered, and blessed us.

In early 2015, I answered a phone call from a headhunter. Such calls were not unusual, as many people used me as a reference. After a few moments of perfunctory conversation, the headhunter asked, "Mr. Dworkin, you have been recommended as a candidate for the Dean of the University of Michigan's School of Music, Theatre & Dance. Could we arrange a meeting to discuss the opportunity?"

Stunned, I did not reply for a moment. Unlike other calls offering academic employment, this position was at my alma mater, the place that I credited with resurrecting my life and my home when I initially began the forerunner of the Sphinx Organization. Afa was another alum of the school and each of us had maintained contacts within the music department.

"I'm flattered, of course, but I have a full-time role here. I love the school, but we still have work to do here. I like to finish what I start, and I would never leave Sphinx in a bad position," I finally responded.

"Mr. Dworkin, the powers that be at the University know all about your work with Sphinx. In fact, your success in turning it into an international organization is one of the reasons they want to consider you. I am sure that they are willing to make allowances so that your contribution to Sphinx can be continued. I really hope we can meet and I can give you some details about the position. May we have dinner one night and discuss this further?"

"I don't know," I replied, recognizing his skill at keeping the door open. "I'll have to talk it over with my wife and see what she thinks. Unless she were willing, I would not consider it."

"I understand. I would like to meet her, too. If she is agreeable, she could join us for dinner. I'll call you tomorrow to set up a meeting," he said.

"No, give me a week for us to think about it. If she has any reservations, there is no need to meet. I appreciate the consideration. Would you pass on my thanks to the responsible parties?" I asked.

That evening after dinner and the boys busy doing their homework, we sat in the den as usual to discuss the events of the day.

"I got a surprise call today from a headhunter that I need to tell you about," I began. Afa, holding her wine glass in the hand resting on her knee, looked at me without expression, not saying anything. "It was about the Dean of Michigan's School of Music, Theatre & Dance. Apparently, they want to consider me for the job."

She reached to put her glass on the end table between us, then asked, "Well, what did you tell them? Are you interested?"

Shaking my head, I said, "I don't know. Maybe. It would depend on many things, including how you felt about it. I told the recruiter that I was happy in my job at Sphinx, and I wouldn't consider it without your blessing."

One of Afa's best attributes was staying quiet until she considered the situation. She picked up her wine glass and took a sip.

"I told him that I wouldn't leave the organization or you in a lurch. He said the University knew that and they were willing to make some accommodations." I continued.

"What accommodations?" she asked, her forehead wrinkling in doubt.

"I don't know," I admitted. "He wants to have a dinner with the two of us and tell us more about the position. What do you think? Would you go?"

"I don't know why not, especially if there is a chance you're interested. I'll need time to arrange my schedule and get a sitter for the boys." The tone in her voice told me that the matter was decided, and it was time to move to another topic.

"Okay. I'll set it up," I said. The next morning, I called the recruiter and arranged a dinner meeting the following week. Several evenings later, Afa brought up the subject of the Deanship.

"I've been thinking about the possibility of you taking the Michigan job and what it might mean for Sphinx, you, me, and our family. The last few years have been really good, and I don't know how a change might affect what we have," she said.

"I know and I . . . ," I began, but she interrupted me.

"Even so, I would never want to stand in your way or be the reason you did not pursue an opportunity you wanted. I will support whatever decision you make," she said.

My eyes filled with tears. Her words showed me that my wife, an incredibly able and strong woman, had complete trust in me to make the decision. Afa is not the type of person to make intemperate decisions nor react without careful consideration of the circumstances. She means what she says, not just in the moment but whatever the future holds.

I stood up and pulled her to me, embracing her in a fierce hug, my face buried in the nook of her shoulder and neck. "Dear Lord," I thought. "What have I ever done to deserve a woman like this?"

As we stepped apart, I said, "Let's not get the cart before the horse. I don't know for sure that I'm interested in the job or, after learning more about me if the school will consider me their best candidate. I truly appreciate your support, but both of us will need to understand how a move would affect the organization. And I'm not sure I want the job or what they expect from me."

Our first meeting was the start of a months-long wooing process as I tried to decide the best outcome for me, my family, and the school. I have long suffered from anticipatory anxiety, probably stemming from my childhood desire to be accepted and experience unconditional love. I could spend hours going down proverbial rabbit holes before upcoming events, carefully developing all kinds of scenarios and my optimum reaction to each.

While anxiety can be a limiting trait for some, I believe it was a strength in my entrepreneurial endeavors. I always meticulously prepared for scheduled meetings with potential donors, considering everything from the way I dressed, the points to be made, the donor's possible reactions as I made the presentation, and my best responses to any comments or questions. The upside of my anxiety was the determination to be totally prepared. A decision to initiate a new program at Sphinx was preceded by hours of research and introspection to leave as little to chance.

I had no doubts that I could excel as the Dean, having spent years in undergraduate and graduate schools at the university. I was not worried that the school might find another candidate more attractive. I felt the outcome was solely dependent on my decision and that depended on the answers to three simple questions:

1. **Would the change adversely affect the Sphinx Organization?** The Sphinx Organization was my baby, birthed with critical help from Sherrie (my first wife) and Afa (my present wife). I had sacrificed sweat, blood, and tears to bring it to life. More importantly, it had made a positive difference in the lives of thousands of young musicians. I know that I could not leave the organization without being certain of its continued progress.

2. **What difference could I make at UM's School of Music, Theatre & Dance?** The school, established in 1880, is considered one of the best in the nation with more than 170 resident faculty members with a growing list of distinguished graduates. Were the Regents and Provost seeking a non-controversial leader who played nice

and didn't rock the boat or someone that could make a good music school better? I was not ready for green pastures and gold watches, believing that I had much more to give to promote diversity and young musicians.

3. **Did I want to change careers?** To me, the ideal job is the one that provides meaningful benefits to individuals and society *and* is fun. By fun, I don't mean easy or frivolous. Fun is continually learning and using your talents to make a difference. It is the satisfaction of meeting a challenge, not unlike an Olympian standing on the platform to receive the Gold Medal or solving a problem that seems unsolvable. For many people, the trials and tribulations I experienced when growing Sphinx might be debilitating, but I relished the moments. I expected to find similar satisfaction in whatever I chose to do.

I wrestled with the questions for weeks, regularly seeking counsel from my two oldest mentors, Ken Fischer and Ron Crutcher. Ron had been a dean at several music schools, a provost, then president of the University of Richmond. He was a phenomenal cellist and lifelong chamber musician. He had experienced extraordinary challenges and obstacles yet carried himself with equal measures of reverence, calm, and dignity. I drew heavily on his insight and experience in making my decision.

Ken was the long-serving president of the University Musical Society of the University of Michigan. In addition to his long tenure with the Society (1987–2017), he was a Trustee of the Interlochen Center for the Arts, the school I credit for saving my life. He was one of the first people I talked to when thinking about Sphinx. Ken had not been a dean, but he was an extraordinary arts leader and led a very dynamic arts institution. Both men were incredible assets during the interview process; sources of stability and knowledge in academic matters I did not have.

The input I valued most came from Afa. Early in our discussions with the search committee, they agreed that I would step away from an official position with the Sphinx Organization but would continue to serve in a formal advisory role. In our private conversations, Afa pointed out that having an office at the school would have little impact on our working together.

"It would be as if you moved your office home. I'll still see you every day, talk to you over the phone and email. We'll talk together each night like we do now. I really don't see much difference than how we work together today," she said.

Though I wasn't as confident as Afa that our communication would remain unchanged, I realized that Sphinx under her leadership could continue and absolutely thrive without me. I knew that the entire team Sphinx would be in phenomenal hands. With that knowledge, I knew my taking the Dean's position would not endanger Sphinx or the fulfillment of its mission.

The question about the difference I could make at the school was much more difficult to resolve. Though I loved the school and was grateful for the education and experience I gained as a student, I was frustrated about how it approached certain things. I knew it could serve its students better, serve its faculty better, teach the arts better, and, most importantly, prepare young people better for the real world of the arts.

The elephant in the room at all arts and music schools is the lack of preparation for real life after graduation, a life that the majority will never achieve. Students in the music schools, especially in elite institutions like Michigan, expect to find orchestra jobs waiting or to become college teachers, but the number of those jobs available are miniscule compared to the number of annual graduates. At the same time, there are amazing opportunities in the arts one can lead, but our institutions aren't exposing or preparing our students to exploit those opportunities.

At my core, I am an entrepreneur and Sphinx is an entrepreneurial organization. We live in a fast-moving ecosystem where decisions and implementation are often indistinct. The Sphinx Organization had a $5 million annual budget and a full-time staff of ten complemented with 40 to 50 part-time workers and volunteers. The relationship between leaders and employees is direct and personal.

Universities are large, lumbering organizations, restricted by levels of hierarchy and bureaucratic processes. The Music School had 180 faculty members with 90 administrative staffers and served more than 1200 students. Objectives are often fussy and interpreted as "Be safe, protect the status quo." Academic tenure—the system of job protections that guarantees lifetime employment except in the most egregious situations—

fosters independence, if not rebellion, by professors enmeshed in office politics.

I did not want to be a caretaker of the school, someone who comes in, acts nice, and avoids controversy. I'm passionate about everything I do, and I know friction creates heat and, sometimes, fire. Good leaders know how to control and direct that intensity.

I am a change agent, but I wasn't sure that the search committee and the school realized the consequences of change. I made it clear that, if chosen as the Dean, I would bring change and disruption. I expected it to be good, thoughtful disruption, not chaos. I am not the one to drive safely down the middle of the road. I knew the core components of greatness—talent, experience, creativity—were already in existence, just waiting for a spark to set them off.

The educational committee was familiar (and comfortable) with other candidates that had followed a traditional career trajectory, progressing through a cycle of associate professor, professor, assistant dean at a smaller institution, dean of a smaller institution, dean at a large university like Michigan. My background as the founder of Sphinx, partnering with the top music conservatories and music schools across the country and associations with the giants of classical music and philanthropy was unique. I brought skills to the table other candidates lacked.

University departments always need funds, so fundraising is a key success factor of a dean's success. I knew I would open purse strings for millions of dollars to have more resources to do more and better work. But I also knew that issues of diversity confronted every music school in the country. Michigan had the diversity issues in faculty, students, and staff. Initially, I considered my appeal to the school might be my color, not my skills, experience, or abilities. I had no interest in being a "token" hire or being limited to diversity matters.

Fortunately, my concerns were unfounded. Over weeks of meetings, I was convinced that they wanted me to help them become a better school, a better place to prepare young people for the arts and the lives they would have after school. I planned to improve diversity—an objective I've had since my first days in Hershey—but I knew that allowing the perception that the progress of Black and Brown students was my primary goal would detract from my ability to make things better for everyone.

A CHANGE IN DIRECTION   211

While academic deans have considerable autonomy to manage their responsibilities, they too have a superior, the provost of the university. I decided that I would not consider the job unless I had a meeting and an understanding with the Provost of the University of Michigan. When we met, I made a similar presentation to her as I had done previously to the search committee. She listened, asked a few questions, and said, "I think you are exactly what we need. I look forward to working with you if you decide to come on board."

Following our meeting, I realized that the possibility of becoming dean was very real. I was excited about the challenge and the assets I could bring to the position. But one question remained: Did I want the job?

That question became the most difficult to resolve. Only six months before the Michigan contact, I had considered my life to be the best anyone could have. I had created an organization that positively affected millions of people, one note at a time. I had met and become friends with the idols of my youth, men and women equally committed to a future of opportunity and equality like United States President Barack Obama. I worked, ate, and slept with one of the most extraordinary women in the world, as beautiful as she was smart, a rare combination of toughness and compassion. My two boys, Noah and Amani, reassured me every day that life is more than possessions or accomplishment, but love, pride, gratitude, and hope.

Would accepting the position at Michigan change any of that? Could I be as happy as Dean as I was at Sphinx? What ifs flooded my thoughts, the anxieties of the unknown were hidden terrors behind the door and under my bed.

"Are you sure that leaving Sphinx is the right thing to do now? You've worked hard to get Sphinx going. Can you just step away?" Afa asked.

"I don't know. I think so. I want Sphinx to exist long after I am gone until diversity in music is not an issue. Maybe different skills are needed to keep it growing. You have more impact on it today than I. Are you ready to replace me?" I responded.

"Look, I haven't thought about it. I can't imagine Sphinx without you. You know I am determined that Sphinx will continue. But I want you to be happy. I don't think this is a question of replacing rather than succeeding. And I don't want to lose what we have together," she said, reaching across the table to grasp my hand.

"I know," I answered, squeezing her hand. "I don't want to lose it either. The most important thing in the world to me is you and the boys. I'll never let something mess that up, but I have a nagging feeling that it's time to try something different, that I can do more to change the future for Noah and Amani."

After more soul-searching and heart-to-heart talks with Afa, I realized that accepting the Dean position provided a more visible platform to direct change than my role with Sphinx. I could influence the influencers, geometrically spread the message of inclusion through music. I had no guarantees that my efforts would bear fruit since universities are invested in the past and skeptical that change is always good. In hindsight, my decision to accept the offer may have been motivated as much by my determination to prove naysayers wrong as any personal benefits.

My last responsibility with Sphinx was informing the organization's board of my decision. When the likelihood of an offer from the University became clear, I had notified the board of the possibility that I might leave. I also noted my expectation that Afa would succeed me as president. At that time, she was the organization's Executive Director and its Artistic Director. To my surprise and disappointment, the board insisted on a formal search and review process, a decision I later agreed was proper, prudent, and beneficial to Afa.

The Board of Directors for a 501(c)(3) organization have legal responsibilities as fiduciaries. Afa's position as my wife could be viewed as nepotism, rubber-stamped by the board. While untrue, the perception might have affected her position as CEO with affiliates, donors, and the public.

The subsequent review excluded me in every detail. They implemented complete due diligence, including multiple interviews with her, staff members, representatives of organizations working with Sphinx, and donors. I think the process gave Sphinx a higher level of stability, signaling that the mission was greater than any individual, including its founder. It confirmed that Afa was truly the best person to succeed me and her accomplishments since then are a testament to her capabilities.

CHAPTER 26

DEAN OF THE BIG BLUE

The culmination of the talks with Michigan's search committee ended with a five-year contract to serve as Dean, starting two months after signing. The position, excluding its focus on music, was unlike any of my previous work experience. Since beginning the Sphinx Organization, I have pursued a single goal—diversity through classical music—with the ultimate authority to decide strategy and direct operations, albeit with thoughtful guidance from the board, advisors, and our mighty team. The Dean's position encompassed a much larger organization with a long-established culture of employee independence (faculty tenure). While I had never managed Sphinx as an autocrat, I was used to fulfilling my role as the final decision-maker, with the associated accountability and ultimate sense of duty to our community.

From observing the culture as an outsider, I knew that academic independence is a hallowed feature of university management, insulating professors from external pressure to conform to a specific doctrine of thought. I agreed with the sentiment but recognized that managing in a university environment would be similar to herding cats, each feline believing that they knew best and determined to follow their own instincts. Successfully managing an academic structure requires as much public relations and persuasion skills as possession and exercise of logic and authority.

Nevertheless, I accepted the job and was chosen to bring change to the school and the traditional ways of serving its constituents. I knew the core components—talent, experience, innovation—were there to make a significant difference in the practice of musical education that would benefit each of the university's stakeholders. My challenge was to redirect the organization's culture and trajectory with new objectives and systems necessary to succeed in the rapidly changing music industry. In other words, my intent was "disruption without chaos," effecting change while avoiding its classic danger of throwing out the baby with the bathwater.

Before beginning my Deanship, I had some remaining responsibilities at Sphinx, principally transitioning my leadership role to Afa. Monetary donations and gifts from institutions and patrons are the lifeblood of non-profit organizations, and Sphinx was no exception. The relationships with our sponsors had been built and cultivated through years of personal contact. I did not want my taking a new position outside the organization to jeopardize those relationships.

I knew (and the Sphinx Board agreed) Afa could take my place in operations without difficulty. She had developed connections over the years, though many of her contacts with significant donors had lived in my portfolio. Though unfounded, to avoid any concerns about her leadership, I determined to clarify my faith in her ability to lead Sphinx personally. For over a month, the two of us met each significant contributor to confirm their commitments were in good hands and Sphinx would continue to thrive in my absence.

In hindsight, I may have had an inflated view of my contribution. Not a single contributor jumped ship, and Afa has delivered superior results in the months and years following.

My Sphinx responsibilities were complete, and I began preparing for my new role at the School of Music, Theatre & Dance. The school, opened in 1880, consists of 17 Departments housed in eight buildings with four large performance and eight small performance halls on two campuses in Ann Arbor, Michigan. It offers more than 40 undergraduate and 25 graduate degrees. Students participate in more than 600 performances annually, ranging from small string quartets to Symphony and Philharmonic orchestras. The Department of Theatre & Drama presents four to five main stage shows each year. By any measure, Michigan's School of Music is a large, world-class unit that influences the direction of music on a national scale.

The challenge facing me was immense, much more significant in scale than anything I had attempted in the past. Even so, I was not worried about whether I could succeed. I understood my capabilities and my weaknesses. I believe that preparation is the key to any accomplishment, and I was determined to know as much as humanly possible about the University's and the School's operation, culture, and systems. At Sphinx, I had the opportunity to work with music schools across the country. Concerned that I had been optimistic in assessing the situation, the objectives I hoped to achieve, or the obstacles confronting me, I spent the interval between accepting and starting the University job in continuous research.

Since I had no experience as an executive of an academic organization, I reached out to others with that experience. I talked to former and current Deans of other music schools across the continent, openly asking for input about the position. What should I expect? What should I avoid, if possible? How do I prepare for this situation or that circumstance? Their information was invaluable and much appreciated. I subsequently established a personal, though informal, board of directors consisting of five working Deans that I regularly consulted in my tenure. I also relied on Ron Crutcher and Ken Fischer as sounding boards. Their knowledge of the job and my understanding of my personality helped me avoid mistakes arising from my naturally assertive personality.

A cultural difference that surprised me was university operations' unhurried, placid pace. The contrast between activity at the Sphinx headquarters and the Dean's office was stunning. While the disparity in staff size may account for a portion of the difference, I suspect the primary cause is the sense of urgency between academic and programmatically driven operational pursuits. Academicians tend to think that they are above the rough and tumble business world where time is money and competitors battle for every advantage.

Tradition is more cherished than progress in the ivy-covered halls of learning. The guardians of the past are incredibly proud of their disdain and distance from actual world events. Adjusting to the sluggish pace was one of my more difficult and frustrating accommodations to the academic environment. In hindsight, I underestimated the faculty's resistance to my ideas, especially from tenured professors with a stake in the status quo. From the faculty's perspective, I was an outsider. My credentials were established beyond academic halls and distinct from the typical path to becoming Dean. My prior relationships with the School had been as a student years before or incidental to my work at Sphinx.

In meetings with the faculty about a new program or outreach, I learned to expect the first question would be "Why?" followed with the declaration of "We've always done it this way." Perhaps 25%–30% of the faculty were tenured, a group that can impose significant obstacles to change to any degree. Learning how to work with . . . or go around them . . . took months before I felt I was in a state of relative control.

After one of our nightly conversations centered on my difficulty with the group, Afa aptly christened them the "kindergarten squad." She could tell how my day went by the expression on my face and my hurry to pour a glass of wine. She began our nightly purge of the day's events by asking, "How were the kids today?" I subsequently learned from other Deans that my situation was not unique. Everyone had one or more tenured curmudgeons that reveled in arguments, delay, and one-upmanship.

One of my first initiatives was to offer classes relating to popular music in the curriculum. I polled the faculty and installed a committee to study its impact and potential challenges, a standard process for introducing new programs when working in academia. Discovering the majority were in favor, we began by sponsoring several symposia on the subject, including "Teaching and Learning Popular Music," ultimately creating a minor study program (Popular Music Studies) that remains exceptionally popular with students today.

Despite the consensus, about one-third of the faculty, primarily from the tenured professors, vehemently resisted the addition, raging against the concept and me in apoplectic tirades. I recognized that there would be people who would disagree with my objectives or approach but assumed that disagreements would be resolved dispassionately between two reasonable people or in a faculty meeting. But the opposition was neither thoughtful nor academic, proffering no substantive, rational, pedagogical arguments for their position. Instead, their justifications were "It seems beneath us," "This may dilute our brand," and "We don't do this, you know, this kind of thing." I suppose I should have expected the pushback. Many classical musicians feel that popular music is unsophisticated, repetitive, and intended to entertain rather than inspire and challenge.

My efforts to have a conversation, understand their concerns, and possibly reach a middle ground were spurned. Instead, they resorted to pettiness and personal attacks to undermine my capability and authority. Accepting that some of them disliked me for various reasons was difficult. I do not like hostility or attempts to gain an advantage through your position; it reminds me of the schoolyard bullies in Hershey. In the past, I would have angrily confronted them. However, I realized that retaliation would not solve my problem.

I learned to play the academic bureaucracy game, anticipating when and where my opponents would arise. Sometimes, I would approach the potential recreant with the benefits for them in the program I intended to propose, hoping that they would not try to torpedo the effort. Other times, I relied on allies I had developed in the faculty to carry my message. If challenged, a tenured peer had no reservations about using a fireball when a spitball would suffice. Slowly but surely, I learned to manage the complex chess game to accomplish my agenda.

Fortunately, most of the school's faculty and staff agreed that change was needed. Like me, they believed that we could better serve our students by updating our curriculum to reflect the present-day environment. Without their support—overtly and covertly—I would have been unable to accomplish many of the goals I had established when accepting the position.

The first six months in a new position are often referred to as the "honeymoon" phase—a period that is exciting, hectic, and sometimes bewildering. Time moves quickly when you're trying to get your bearings. My change in commutes from downtown Detroit to Ann Arbor required adjustments, as did my attendance at innumerable staff and faculty meetings, some of which had little purpose or relation to actual events or problems.

Afa, engaged in her new position as CEO of Sphinx, experienced a similar adjustment, euphoric but slightly disquieting. We had always served as the other's consigliere, devoted to the other but always offering truth and an independent perspective. Knowing that our work focus would be separated for the first time in our relationship, we worried about the effect on us as a married couple. Would the difference lead to our own separation? We had no experience as a normal working couple—each party spending most of their time apart while trying to maintain a life together.

We intentionally established a time each evening to be together and share the details of our respective workdays where we could gloat, blow off steam, be petty, or feel sorry for ourselves in a safe place. On some occasions, our role was to give advice; on others, to be a sympathetic listener. In hindsight, working apart deepened our personal connection. I remained invested in the success of Sphinx, but seeing it from Afa's perspective opened a new awareness and added dimensions about the organization and her. I believe that Afa had a similar epiphany about me as a person in my capacity as Dean, distinct from my former role at Sphinx.

With a 5-year contract, I intended to spend the first two years instituting the changes I believed necessary to reach the School's potential as an institution and a leader in diversity. After the changes were implemented, my objectives were to build the essential systems and reinforce the culture to ensure their continuance.

Organizations are like people. They tend to repeat routines (processes) that produce satisfactory work with the least effort. Repetition becomes automatic, i.e., habits that, in turn, create and mold culture. I believed that a culture focused externally on all the school's stakeholders rather than internally on the academic community was imperative if the school was to be relevant in the future. With that goal in mind, I initiated new projects, reinvigorated the better existing programs, and deemphasized policies and courses that were stale or irrelevant to the modern music environment.

During my tenure (2015–2017), the music school created numerous groundbreaking programs and initiatives, including

- Entrepreneurial and leadership training in the new Excellence in Entrepreneurship, Career Empowerment & Leadership (EXCEL) program providing the most direct support for student entrepreneurial projects of all performing arts schools nationally,
- A new Department of Chamber Music with Matt Albert as chair.

Matt is internationally renowned as a violinist, a founding member of Eighth Blackbird, and formerly directed Chamber Music at Meadows School of the Arts at Southern Methodist University,

- Expansion of UM's MPulse program to include Center Stage Strings (CSS), one of the country's leading summer training programs for young string musicians, ages 12 to 24,
- Collaborative partnerships with Detroit Public Television and Michigan Radio, and
- Development of the Michigan Artist Citizen program with Ann Arbor Public Schools system, doubling the music school's community engagement activities.

We also created the M-Prize Competition to identify and showcase the highest caliber of chamber music ensembles globally. In our first year, we received 172 applications from 17 states and 3 countries, officially making it the largest chamber music competition in the nation and world in terms of prize money and the number of applications. The prize and cost of the Competition were covered by private donors.

External fundraising is critical to the future of higher education, particularly schools of Arts and Fine Arts with the increased emphasis on STEM education. I arrived on campus in its first year of raising $90 million in the University of Michigan's multi-billion-dollar Victors for Michigan campaign. When I stepped down as Dean, we had exceeded the goal by $4 million.

I am most proud of my accomplishments in opening the school to students of color. One of my first acts as Dean was establishing the chief inclusion officer role. In two years, applications from underrepresented communities increased 30%, the largest increase in the school's history. Matriculation (attendance) increased 20%.

Not everyone agreed with my diversity activities. A White, tenured faculty member came to me about an impending appointment of an African American to a director position in the school. He was a short man well past his prime physically. His unkempt gray hair and ferocious eyebrows warned of his pugnacious nature honed by years of internecine warfare protecting his turf. He marched into my office, sat down, and, without a preamble, began speaking.

"Aaron," he said. "Are you sure that _____ is the best for this role? I have some doubts and I believe others might share my concern."

Taken aback, I did not respond immediately. After a moment of silence, I answered, the two of us staring at each other across my desk.

"Well, I appreciate your concern, but I have no doubts about his qualifications or the job he will do. As you know, he was the product of a search committee and vetted by members of the department he will be joining. They recommended him, and I agree with their recommendation."

The professor's face hardened as he turned his head and stared at the floor. I waited, not knowing what might come next.

"Have you thought about the fallout that might come from this appointment? You are a Black dean appointing another Black person in the department. Some might say that the only reason he got the position was his color, that you overlooked his qualifications to satisfy your own need for diversity." He straightened in his chair, raising his eyes to glare at me, his chin jutting forward and the mottled skin of his hands throbbing as he squeezed the arms of the chair in agitation.

"Here it is," I thought. While I knew some faculty members disliked me and doubted my leadership, I had hoped it was not due to my color. People are generally judged by their competence and artistry in the music field. Overt racism, where it exists, is usually hidden in academic circles and boardrooms, even by the most virulent bigots. Had my visitor crossed that invisible line that triggered an angry response in Black people in retaliation?

To be honest, I do not know. Nothing in our previous encounters had suggested an underlying prejudice. His dislike was apparent, but I thought it was due to our different ages and backgrounds. He was envious of my position and the future I represented, not my color but the emergence of a new view of music and how it was to be appreciated and taught.

Whatever his true motives, I realized that an angry retort would only escalate the situation and harden his opposition to my ideas. Moreover, retaliation was more likely to create sympathy for him among our colleagues since he was at least twenty years older and respected for his long association with the school.

I took a deep breath and replied, "Thank you for your thoughts. To answer your question, I do not have any worries that his appointment will be considered for anything other than merit. I chose him, with the advice of others in the department, because I believe he is the best choice for the position. I know you will respect my decision and do everything to help him be successful."

I picked up a pen and began reading some notes on my desk, clearly signaling that our discussion and meeting were over. My visitor got up and left the room without another word. I don't know about his relationship with the new director, but neither man brought up the issue to me. As I hoped for, the appointee was an excellent selection and continues to occupy the position today.

By the end of 2016, I was comfortable in my role as Dean, satisfied with the changes I had initiated or encouraged, and looking forward to the remaining years of my contract. Afa had surpassed every expectation I had of her as the CEO of Sphinx Organization, and it was in great shape. Our family life was even better than I had hoped. I was the epitome of "fat, dumb, and happy" when the greatest challenge of my life erupted.

CHAPTER 27

A NOAH CRISIS

On December 17th, Afa and I were amidst last-minute preparations for a holiday celebration at our home, welcoming several dozens of faculty and staff from the School of Music, Theatre & Dance. We both noticed that Noah's arrival home was somewhat delayed. When my cell phone dinged, I was shocked to get an email from Sherrie, my ex-wife, and Noah's birth mother, that he would no longer live with us or have any contact with me.

"Noah is distraught and has shared that he has had thoughts about hurting himself while at your house . . . After Noah returned from your house this week, he is expressing that he will not go on the trip with you next week or return to your house."

The first sentence shook me to my core. As I steadied myself, I looked over to Afa, asking her to read the email. I immediately called Noah for an explanation but got no answer. I then called Sherrie, incensed that she had emailed rather than called me.

When she answered the phone in her rather impassive tone, as if nothing unusual had occurred, I said, "I need to talk to Noah."

"He doesn't want to talk to you or go to your house anymore," she responded.

"What on earth do you mean? I'll come get him now so that we can talk," I angrily replied, immediately regretting my tone, knowing how she would react.

"No, no, you won't. He doesn't want to live with you anymore, and I won't make him," she declared in a loud voice. "He is my son, too, and you can't take him out of my house if he doesn't want to go."

"Look, I don't want to fight with you. I just want to understand what's going on. We literally have spent an evening laughing for hours together, watching a TV show. My parents are looking forward to seeing him next week." I tried to keep the anger out of my voice, knowing that hearing me upset would only add to her satisfaction.

"You'll have to go without him." She hung up.

Afa was staring at me, listening to my side of the conversation. My throat was dry, my heart racing as I turned away and fell into a chair by the kitchen table. I caught my breath, trying to control my anger. We knew that people were about to begin arriving for the holiday celebration. I had to find a way to my son while managing the appearances. It seemed impossible.

The entire reception was a blur. Afa and I maintained decorum while attempting to plan our next steps for as soon as guests departed. The very moment I could, I wrote Sherrie back. "I am completely shocked and worried by your message. Noah has made no indications such as this in any way. On the contrary, he has commented how he has appreciated some of our very long conversations including the last night he was here. He has not responded to my texts today (first time he has ever done that which I completely do not understand and am worried that I cannot reach him). Given what you have stated about him hurting himself, I am requesting that we have him evaluated immediately by a medical professional and, I would want to attend with you."

Her response, even while reliving the whole situation today, was on a basic level, cold, detached. My retrospective analysis, albeit theoretical, led me to suspect that it was coached, which would suggest that the entire process was planned, premeditated, and executed. I was in raw agony and felt that the pain was greater than any I had previously imagined. So much greater than any distance imposed upon me by either set of my parents or any external occurrence. My firstborn, my son, the human being who, upon his arrival on this earth, for the very first time in my life afforded me the feeling of belonging and recognition in his eyes was gone from my life. Upon his own desire and choosing, to the best of my interpretation.

"It's not my responsibility to make him go or explain to you why he doesn't want to talk to you. Maybe he got tired of you always telling him what to do. I don't know, but there is nothing more to say. I won't answer if you call back." Sherrie hung up. I tried calling her several times, then Noah. Neither answered.

Noah's implicit declaration occurred the week prior to Christmas Eve, which is when we were scheduled to visit my birth parents. There was no way to resolve the issue with Noah before leaving for the visit. I wrestled with what to do—cancel the visit and try to reconcile with Noah or continue with our plans and amend our relationship when we returned. There was not a good answer. My parents and sister had looked forward to our visit for months, especially seeing the kids. At the same time, I didn't know how Noah would interpret our going without him. We made the trip, but my heart remained with Noah. This may have been the most difficult Christmas of my life. I felt numb and the world around me seemed distant, unaware of my pain and incapable of soothing it. Even those whomI regarded as closest to me. I tried to talk to him on Christmas Day, but he refused.

I was devastated, uncertain of his reasons or how to fix our relationship. As a biracial child, I experienced the loneliness of being different and trying to find my way in a society that characterizes the color of one's skin with their capability. I remember the sense of hopeI felt when imagining that someone would wrap their arms around me and whisper, "I love you. You will be all right." Unconditional love and acceptance should be the birthright of every child, but, sadly, it is not.

My relationship with my adoptive family was one of contingency and consequence—if you do this, we will do that—and often interrupted by periods of non-contact. During my first wife's pregnancy, thoughts of my pending parenthood were always present. I did not wonder about the father I would be, or one I had often dreamed of as a child, for I knew that given my experience, I would choose a different path. Even today, the miracle of birth still awes me, an unimaginable gift of pride, hope, obligation and responsibility.

For several years before my first son's birth, Sherrie and I had been growing apart. Having met at seventeen, we were unusually close, each of us estranged from our parents. As we transitioned from naive teenagers to adults, our once shared ambitions and expectations developed, and we grew apart. Personal idiosyncrasies, once overlooked, became irritations, then arguments and fundamental differences. We separated several times, repeatedly reconciling in hopes we could recapture the magic that we once shared. As we grew apart, Sherrie's professional passions and pursuits led her elsewhere. She applied to and was accepted into a graduate degree in education, a path she pursued with passion and determination. It was also a path that concluded her journey at Sphinx. Sherrie began her degree, weakening the link of working together. When Noah was about a year old, we realized that being together was not something either of us desired.

For those who have never experienced it, divorce can be a dispassionate, painless legal exercise about splitting any accumulated assets and finding a new place to reside. For me, it was incredibly sad, the death of a deep relationship forged by years of shared memories and mutual dependence. Even as my head told me that it was right for both our sakes, my heart wondered how I could survive the trauma or ever find real happiness again. Most of all, I worried how Noah would be affected. Would he think I had abandoned him? As he grew up, would he worry that his arrival was the reason for the divorce?

Our divorce was handled by the University of Michigan's Student Legal Services. Despite our differences, Sherrie and I agreed that our problems would not be visited on our son. She did not complain when the judge ruled that we would share custody of Noah. For the next fifteen years, he would spend Wednesday through Friday and every other weekend with me and Mondays through Tuesdays with the remaining weekends with Sherrie. The schedule persisted after Afa and I married. Noah adjusted to the arrangement as well as could be, especially since the atmosphere in each home was decidedly different. Sherrie had her rules and way of doing things unlike the rules in our home. Even the food was different, each favoring the foods of childhood and acquired tastes. I think the arrangement worked because Afa didn't try to be Noah's mother, nor a friend (though she could be strict when necessary). She was certainly a parental figure, but one who retained a healthy respect for Noah's mother and her place in his life.

When we learned of Afa's pregnancy, I remembered my own experiences with my adoptive brother. My worst nightmare was that Noah would feel separated from the three of us, especially if Afa favored

Amani. I wanted my two boys, even though years apart in age, to be close. I didn't know how to discuss my concern with Afa since the new baby was her flesh and blood and Noah was from another mother. Fortunately, Afa's maternal instincts, developed with Noah long before Amani was a thought, along with her heart being big enough to love both boys, eased my fears. I would watch Afa and Noah together during the later stages of the pregnancy, Afa sitting uncomfortably erect in a chair, her slender body bulging with the miracle inside her, while Noah gently rubbed her belly, mystified by the tiny movements of the growing Amani.

Sherrie and I had been divorced for most of Noah's life. Our world had witnessed so much during that period, including a tremendous growth of the Sphinx organization, my marriage to Afa, and the birth of Amani. The years went by quickly and they were good years. My responsibilities at Sphinx allowed me to spend time with both boys and the two of them had a true brotherly relationship, Noah looking after Amani and Amani tried to copy everything Noah did. That infatuation from Amani with his older brother is something I continued to notice for so many years.

What had happened to the little boy who seemed so happy, I wondered. Was it me? Had I been so wrapped up in myself and my ambitions that I failed my son? Hoping to find a reason for his rejection of me and our family, I tried to remember any incident over the years that might have festered beneath the surface of our relationship until it burst into total rejection.

I remembered Sherrie's comment that I was too authoritarian, too strict for a teenage boy coping with finding his own identity. My first reaction was denial, remembering the beatings I had received during my own childhood. I certainly was not the demanding, critical parent of Sherrie's accusations! Afa was as much in the dark as I was about how to resolve the issue. We had no clue to the cause of Noah's decision and little information on how to proceed due to Noah's silence.

As he entered the teenage years, he had become moody and withdrawn at times. I knew that most teens experience periods of the blues or feeling down in the dumps; feelings brought on by the physical, psychological, and social stresses of that age. In addition to the normal teenage angst, Noah was dealing with the realities of biracialism and split families. On weekends, he sometimes sat alone in his darkened room for hours, the door closed, and the window shades pulled down.

I worried that his isolation might lead to spiraling depression or worse if it continued. When I noticed his absence on the weekends I was at home, I would go into his room, raise the shades, and ask, "Are you okay?"

His response was usually a grunt or a slight nod of his head, avoiding my eyes.

"Is something bothering you? Do you want to talk?" I continued, getting the same response.

"Well, you can't hide in this cave all day. It's not good for you. Amani is worried about you and wants to play. Come out with the rest of the family."

"I don't want to," Noah complained.

"Nope, that is not going to happen. You're part of this family, so act like it. Staying in here is not an option," I insisted.

After a few minutes, he would appear in the den, sullen and clearly resentful. Afa and I did not acknowledge the sentiment, figuring his presence, no matter his mood, was better than remaining alone. Amani, too young to recognize the mood of his older brother and happy to finally be with him, always greeted Noah enthusiastically, pummeling him with questions or jokes picked up in the schoolyard. Eventually, despite Noah's determination to remain aloof, he usually broke down laughing and hugged or picked up his younger brother. Even so, the incidents of rebellion and withdrawals became more frequent, I assumed due to typical teenage angst associated with the onslaught of puberty and self-discovery.

Over the years, the difference in parenting style by Sherrie and me had become apparent, especially the importance of learning self-discipline. As a boy, I had resented my adoptive parents' insistence on practicing my violin every day. As an adult, I am thankful that they refused to relent or relax the rules to make me happy. In addition to improving my musical proficiency and opening doors for me as an adult, I gained the power to overcome procrastination and laziness. Self-discipline is self-control and the realization that accepting the status quo is a choice, not a condition.

The most loving parent cannot protect a child at age 16 or 26 from the dangers and temptations of the world. Shielding children from reality does them no favors. Good parenting isn't always being "nice," but preparing a child to live in an impersonal, even cold world. Too many parents, I think, seek to be friends, not parents.

Sherrie's parenting style was more relaxed, less demanding, perhaps in response to my "strictness." She shared she didn't believe in consequences, while I thought that teaching a child the consequences of their actions is critically important. I am sure that, like me, she carried a burden of guilt about our divorce which had deprived Noah of a conventional home with two present parents. After a divorce, many couples unintentionally compete to be the "favorite" parent, operating as if the situation was "I win, you lose" in the child's mind. Whether she ever insisted that Noah take on or complete a task he disliked, I don't know.

Even so, I had to consider whether I had been too demanding, unintentionally acting in the manner of my adoptive father. As I remembered my conflicts with Noah, I questioned if I had been a good parent. I did not know, an unresolved mystery that confronts most fathers and mothers. There is no book to read or guide to show how to parent. You do the best you can and hope that your mistakes are minimal and will be forgiven. After hours of introspection, I decided that the problem with Noah was not caused by harsh treatment on our part, yet, I had to find a way back to him.

Had Sherrie precipitated the breakup in some way, knowingly or unknowingly? Had she poisoned my son's mind against me? I had no way of knowing, but I suspected an underlying hostility toward myself and Afa. I didn't know why the relationship had fractured. We had shared joint custody for years without major issues and only a few inconveniences. I thought Sherrie was a good mother and believed she felt me to be a good father. Sherrie had begun dating after our divorce before me and I believed the relationship between Sherrie and Afa to be friendly. There was nothing on the surface to explain her coldness to me.

Whatever the state of my relationship before that fateful Christmas, I cannot forgive, nor forget Sherrie's role in the schism between Noah and me. I considered it a personal betrayal. She knew that a loving family was beyond important to me. It was a dream that I had chased my entire life, the feeling that comes from unequivocal acceptance of who you are, warts and all. Sherrie knew the distress and hurt of a child disconnected from those expected to love them most. She had suffered a similar pain during the years she was separated from her family due to our relationship. Yet, she was simply standing by, allowing the same heartache to afflict Noah.

I think, had the situation been reversed, I would have insisted that he postpone any decision, to talk to his mother and work things out. No sixteen-year-old considers the effects of his actions, responding emotionally to the stresses they might be feeling at the time. Had Noah announced that he wished to drop out of school, would Sherrie have given him the same passive assent? I don't know.

In the weeks and months that followed, Sherrie and I continued to communicate exclusively on email, as I tried to understand what had triggered the situation. Noah continued to avoid me, not returning my phone calls or emails. I would leave messages, "I love you. I'm always here for you, no matter what you do. I will always love you. You are my son, and I am proud of you." Eventually, Afa, Amani and I chose to send Noah a weekly email, just updating him about our lives and hoping that he may wish to reconnect. In part, this was a suggestion of mine, as Amani, for many months and on an almost daily basis, would break into tears randomly. As we tried to comfort him, he always said "I miss my brother: is he coming home?"

Sherrie was of little help, giving me no information and urging me to accept Noah's decision to step out of his life. Several weeks into the ordeal, she asked that I increase the child support I had always paid since she would be bearing all his living expenses in the future. I realized that I could go to court and enforce the joint custody agreement since he was underage. That step meant forcing him to live with a person he had already rejected, even possibly criticizing his mother in public. Noah was much like me, I knew, and that action was more likely to drive us further apart than facilitate a reconciliation. As much as I hated not seeing and talking to him, I rejected taking legal action.

Without any help from Sherrie and being unable to talk to Noah, I considered any possibility that might have provoked our separation. I knew my ex had a new man in her life from the comments Noah made. Sometime after our separation and long before the divorce, Sherrie had begun dating. As far as I knew, none of the relationships were serious, her major priorities being Noah and the progress of her teaching career. Possibly her new relationship had abused Noah and threatened him if he told me. When I floated the possibility of abuse to Sherrie, she reacted angrily, vowing it was not possible.

Her subsequent email communications retained the dispassionate, coached language, which in my mind, dishonored the legacy of our relationship and our commitment to Noah. She insisted that the mediator of her choice needed to get involved, and at a mere suggestion from me that a formal psych evaluation was in order, she sent a carefully phrased email suggesting the impracticality of such an approach and how going with her idea had to be the way. Essentially, anything that came from me was rejected, ignored or countered. She quickly back-pedaled, suggesting pretty immediately that Noah was not in "any imminent danger" and that she was able to talk to him and reason with him, which meant that idea of a formal psych evaluation seemed off-place.

"I don't believe that" I exploded. "Something is wrong, and I am worried about it getting worse. I think he should see a therapist to be sure that he is not in any danger from others or himself. I might learn to live with our separation, but I need to be sure he is safe." I held my breath, waiting for her answer. If she wouldn't agree that he should see a professional, I had no choice except the court.

"You're over-reacting," she retorted, "just like you always do. I don't think he needs to see anyone. He just wants you to leave him alone."

"Look, I'm very worried about him and I want to be sure he will be okay. That is more important than anything, he and me, or you and me."

That final call ended in an impasse; she was against a therapist in place of a mediator, while I was determined that Noah have help. After several weeks of butting heads, she finally agreed if the therapist was not someone I recommended. I think she thought I would somehow influence the outcome to my benefit. I agreed to consider her choice provided I had the chance to check their credentials and reputation.

While he was not willing to talk to me, Noah began going to therapy. I hoped that I might learn what had caused his rejection of me and the family, but the therapist was careful to keep their discussions confidential. However, the therapist did report that no abuse had occurred, and that self-harm was unlikely. His diagnosis was a relief even though our estrangement continued.

Being apart from Noah affected everyone in the family. I wavered between moments of desperation, despair, anger, and reluctant acknowledgment that the rift might not be bridged. Amani was particularly distraught, missing the big brother who had suddenly disappeared without a word. Afa and I were unable to console him or promise that things would return to normal in the future. I suspect Noah missed Amani too but didn't know how to contact him without talking to us. If Noah ever mentioned to Sherrie that he missed Amani, she never told us.

The therapy session continued for weeks even as I hoped that I would finally learn something that I could fix between us. I begged to attend one of the sessions, promising to listen, not to find fault or justify what ever I might have done. Not knowing why my son had turned against me was the heaviest, most painful burden I've ever carried. Every day, my mind filled with "what if" and how I might turn back the calendar. Our family was in a crisis that might never end, I thought, maybe the cosmic retribution for the good things I had experienced.

I suspected that Sherrie's involvement in Noah's decision had not been passive but added to the fire of his unhappiness. During one of our communications, she insinuated that Noah didn't like to eat at our house because we "had weird food." Noah had never complained about meals to us, and they were not abnormal or exotic. If he felt that way, his dislike stemmed from his mother's Machiavellian denigration, not the taste or amount of food on our table. I concluded that Sherrie must have sabotaged the connection between Noah and me deliberately. I detested the consequence of her anger on the relationship between Noah and Afa. Sherrie effectively destroyed it, requiring months to rebuild the trust and affection that previously existed.

About two months into the therapy, I was invited to observe a session. That was a huge step for me, since it could only happen with Noah's permission. When I arrived at the therapist office, I was the only one in the waiting room, a small, almost cell-like space with several armchairs around the room and prints of pastoral scenes on three of the four walls.

As I sat there, I thought about seeing Noah for the first time since that Christmas. Would he greet me with a hug? Should I reach out to him? What should I do if he ignored me?

In the few minutes before the door opened into the therapist office, my thoughts raced from one scenario to the next, ranging from an exuberant union and a return to our previous family rapport to Noah's total rejection and my loss of him forever. When the therapist opened the door and invited me to join the two of them, I stood up, wiping my perspiring palms on my pants, as nervous as the night he had been born, and followed him into the office.

Noah was sitting stiffly erect on one of two chairs facing each other in the corner of the room, his back to me. He didn't turn to see me or acknowledge my presence in any way. The therapist gestured to a chair behind him saying, "Mr. Dworkin, you are here as a guest only because Noah agreed you could attend. That does not mean you are a participant. Do you understand?"

I nodded, then mumbled, "Yes."

I subsequently attended several sessions, listening to Noah as he talked. The subjects of the sessions were private, and I intend that they remain so. However, despite my efforts to remain impassive, there were times I could not stop the tears as I witnessed the anger and agonies of my flesh and blood and knowing I was the cause. My guilt for failing to recognize his pleas for help was especially pernicious because I, more than anyone, knew the terrible hopelessness of feeling forsaken by those who love you. How could I have been so oblivious to his pain, so wrapped up in my personal good fortune to miss the warning signs?

I had never considered his difficulty of living in two different worlds, moving back and forth between two homes that were very different from each other. He was forced to live on the schedules of others, to adapt seamlessly between the rules and values of different families. In many ways, his life was more confusing and isolated than mine had been. At least with my adoptive parents, my life had been consistent day to day. I knew what to expect, even if I hated it. Noah's efforts to appease parents in two households was, I realized, extremely complex and sometimes impossible. And I never realized the toll it took on him. In just a few months, he had gained over fifty pounds, becoming morbidly obese.

I had experienced a similar gain at his age dealing with the trauma of puberty and living in Hershey.

Family crises strip away the pretenses, excuses, and games people play to satisfy their egos. Some wounds are so deep that the only cure is total cauterization by the truth. Over several months, initially with the therapist, then in meetings with just the two of us, we reached a renewed, though different understanding of each other, one I hope will persist for the rest of my life.

I realized that he was no longer a child, but a capable young man able to reason and make his own decisions. More importantly, he recognized that actions have consequences for him and others, some of which can't be ignored. On the other hand, Noah understood that, as his father who loved him, I had a responsibility to protect and nourish him, regardless of his age or circumstances. Whether my comments might anger or amuse him, it was my duty to make his travel through life easier and less dangerous, no matter the path he might take.

Even as we worked to rebuild the trust and affection between us, I struggled to understand how I had missed the signs of Noah's growing disaffection. Had there been a single instance that precipitated his leaving? I didn't think so and he had not mentioned one during our many talks afterward. I tried to remember what had changed during his adolescence before deciding that I had taken the Deanship two years previously. The decision had been made without talking to either Noah or Amani since neither Afa nor I believed that the new job would affect either one of the boys.

We were wrong. The new position meant that the two of us were away from home more often, leaving the boys alone. When we worked together at Sphinx, we had total control over our agendas. Plus, working together, we could accomplish the work more quickly than each of us alone.

I had not realized the time commitments associated with a dean of a major university. It is a 24/7 responsibility, attending faculty meetings, directing staff, romancing potential donors individually and at fundraisers. Getting things done required personal influence—the outcome of building relationships and being visible in the academic culture. Michigan football is a big deal, so attending games when the team played at home on Saturdays was important. Suddenly, I was away from home and family dinners three to four times a week and away on most Saturdays. While I tried to be home with the boys as before, fulfilling my responsibilities at the University made it impossible.

Afa's schedule became more complicated too as I was no longer at Sphinx to share the workload. We blithely assumed the truth of the aphorism that all parents with busy schedules take comfort: "It's not the quantity of time spent with family that matters, but the quality." That "truth" was a fiction, at least in my case. People absorbed in a job are rarely able to compartmentalize it. When you are not at the office, you think of the tasks needed to be done, in effect, "being here, but not present." Looking back at those days, I had become an absentee parent, delegating many of my paternal duties to Afa or rationalizing that I would make up for my absence in the indeterminable future.

Until I lost Noah, I had forgotten that moments missed are never found, especially in the lives of a child. There is no makeup, just loss. In that moment, I realized nothing was more important to me than my children, not the public awards, not the Deanship, not even the future of Sphinx. That same evening, I sat down with Afa and Amani.

"You know, Amani, that I have to be gone a lot in the evenings to do my job, so I'm not here before you go to bed. But you know I love you. Right?" I asked.

"Yeah, I guess," Amani answered, not looking at me.

"I mean you could hardly miss me, doing your homework and all. We wouldn't be talking if I was here," I ventured, hoping he might agree.

He looked up at me, his brown eyes shimmering with disappointment. "Dad, it matters to me if you're in the house even if we're not doing something. I can always talk to you if I need to. When you're gone, you're gone. Right?"

I got up and walked to the kitchen, my eyes brimming with tears. "Out of the mouth of babes," I thought.

Later that evening after Amani went to bed, Afa and I talked.

"It's clear he wants me home. My presence is needed." Afa nodded in agreement. "But how can I do my job at the university and be here? I can't be the dean that I know I need to be and that the school needs. And be at home every weekend, weekday night, you know. Or not do the football game when a big donor comes in. It's just not possible. You understand that, right?"

She didn't say anything, recognizing the battle that was going on inside my head. I continued.

"These two things are incompatible. I cannot be the father that I clearly needed to be, especially to rescue the relationship with Noah. I'm worried about him and how his loss affects Amani." I paused, trying to get my thoughts together. "But what if I step down? What will the school do? No one ever resigns a deanship, especially in the middle of a contract. Will I destroy my professional career?"

I knew what I wanted to do, had to do, but the decision to step down affected others, too. The blowback could damage Sphinx and Afa, too. I knew some among the faculty would be glad to see me gone, but I was concerned of the rumors they might spread for the reason. People naturally assume in resignations like mine, a scandal is the cause, usually something sexual. The classical music crowd is relatively small, including academics, artists, and those who support the arts. A stain on my reputation, even unjustified, would invariably affect Afa. I wanted her to know that I was considering all the consequences, not just those that affected me.

"Look, you know what you must do for the sake of the family. That is the most important consideration. I'm not worried about academic consequences. I didn't marry a dean, but a man I knew would love and protect the family. No matter what happens, I'm behind you." She smiled and I began crying again.

At that time Noah and I had begun meeting to talk, just the two of us. I shared with him that I was thinking of stepping down to have more time at home.

"That's probably a good thing for Amani," he mentioned.

Hearing him, I knew it meant something to him, too, but he didn't want to say so directly. I believe that he knew giving up my dream job was my way of showing him that our relationship and the relationship with Amani were more important than my work. If there were any doubts in my mind about resigning, that conversation with Noah clinched my decision.

Even so, the meeting with the president and the provost of the university was the toughest professional meeting that I've ever had. I was incredibly grateful for their confidence in me, especially their willingness to risk their own credibility by going outside normal channels to hire me. None of us expected that my tenure would be so short or unexpected. I explained that my decision was made and the explanation of the situation leading to it was important to me. Being the people I had believed them to be, they were extraordinarily understanding and sympathetic. We agreed to make a formal announcement of my resignation "for personal reasons" to the school and developed a plan of transition to minimize any difficulties that might arise.

As a tenured professor, I intended to remain with the school and teach new classes in arts entrepreneurship and leadership in the arts, two subjects I felt strongly to be missing from most arts education. I felt my life experiences—combining entrepreneurship and classical music—had uniquely prepared me for the task and I looked forward to returning to the classroom.

Ironically, the reaction from the school's faculty was not what I expected. Many had disagreed with the changes I had instituted, and some actively disliked me. To a person, the faculty members were wonderful. Many shared personal stories of difficulties with their children. I heard different versions of "I wish I would have made a decision like this when...". People who had never shared their stories opened up, becoming an emotional catharsis of regrets kept secret that so many people have. Some of my dearest friendships started with that sharing of mutual loss.

The decision to resign as Dean of School of Music at the University of Michigan is the most momentous of my family life. Oddly enough, other than founding Sphinx, stepping down has been the most profound professional decision I've ever made.

CHAPTER 28

THE SPIRIT ENDURES

The decision to step down as Dean was momentous, affecting the relationships with each of my sons and triggering a renaissance in my approach to life, self-fulfillment, and the arts. I've always been driven, always seeking new creative outlets. It's a thirst that can't be quenched, an emptiness that is filled for a time to make way for new endeavors.

My adoptive parents triggered, then reinforced, my hunger to excel in whatever I attempted. In my adoptive family, the dispensing of love and affection was directly correlated to accomplishment: Get an A on a report card, play a great violin recital, or practice for hours every day to precipitate acceptance. Failure or rebellion caused withdrawal and punishment. That style of parenting, whether well-meant or rendered as a consequence of imitation of their own respective childhoods, has produced mostly doubt and estrangement. My drive, however, was only strengthened as a by-product of said approach.

My relinquishment of the Deanship occurred at the end of a dozen years of constant planning, progressing, confronting immovable objects (or so they seemed at the time), and restarting to create, establish, and stand up the Sphinx Organization. Sphinx was my ultimate creative outlet, which became my legacy, as I always strove to make it into a sustainable enterprise, an institution. Today, its stature is one of a movement rather than one organization. While I had the help of incredible people, there were times when I had to pick up the organization and carry it forward by sheer will. That commitment to attain excellence in serving and empowering others kept me going.

My charge as Dean of the University of Michigan's School of Music, Theatre & Dance was also demanding, though in a rather different way. Changing an entrenched culture of the past to explore new avenues and possibilities meant overcoming the resistance of tenured professors wedded to tradition, the "way we've always done things." It was a 24/7 job that consumed my thoughts and my time, ultimately to the detriment of my family. Despite my decision to step down—a decision I would repeat today—I believe I made a positive difference for the school and its future.

Once relieved of the administrative responsibilities, I focused on two objectives—being (1) the best father and (2) the best teacher I could be. Even as I developed my curricula and presentation skills, I still felt a need to do more, especially for artists and leaders of color. I realized that new definitions, shapes, and scopes of art were emerging by artisans of all types across the country and world. Many will not endure without encouragement and mentorship.

I sometimes wonder if the world would ever know of and benefit from the legacy of great artists, composers, and musicians without their patrons and champions who either enabled or empowered them to develop and refine their gifts. Countless artistic geniuses or musical prodigies of yesteryear and today either never made it into musical history or gave up, rejecting their talents because they did not know how to create while sustaining themselves.

"Art for Art's sake" is a justifiable argument for a society to support artistic endeavors. While artistic expression is often controversial, even disturbing, it also enlightens, comforts, and inspires us. According to the Metropolitan Museum of Art in New York City, "Looking at art from the past contributes to who we are as people. By looking at what has been done before, we gather knowledge and inspiration that contribute to how we speak, feel, and view the world around us."

Part of my quest as a dean and now as a professor was to help young creatives to move past the starving artist mentality and toward practical empowerment. While painters like Gauguin and Van Gogh are often exemplars of young creatives willing to sacrifice comfort and security for the sake of their art, in our day and age, many avenues exist to help us build sustainable portfolio careers. I also presume that sacrifice and poverty are not necessary nor practical for true genius to emerge. I wanted to ignite the hunger and curiosity within my students to develop new sets of skills that will empower them to succeed in the real world and sustain themselves through their primary art form.

Students arrive at schools like the University of Michigan's School of Music, Theatre & Dance expecting that they will teach at the college level, join an orchestra, or start a solo career after graduation. But the majority find that time, effort, and the financial penalty required of an artist are too great. At best, their art becomes an avocation, a hobby to pursue in their spare time by playing in a local orchestra, teaching part-time, or joining a chamber group. Who knows the talent that goes to waste, the great works that will never appear?

When I founded the Sphinx Organization, I had limited business experience. I did have an entrepreneurial mindset, which developed out of the necessity to survive. Even so, I realized that pursuing the mission of the organization—to increase the participation of Black and Latino individuals in music schools, as professional musicians, and as classical music audiences—required that I develop, organize, and manage an organization not dissimilar to other businesses.

Businesses sustain themselves by generating revenue and profits through sales of a product or service. To sustain itself, Sphinx needed to secure consistent revenue by delivering concrete objective progress on its mission. In each case, founders must be willing to take a risk, have an inspiring vision, solve problems, and be flexible in a continually evolving ecosystem. In other words, the challenges and tasks of creating a viable non-profit organization are parallel to those of a new software company or a manufacturer of gadgets. I was, for most of my adult life, a serial entrepreneur though I didn't necessarily realize it at the time. Prior to and after Sphinx, I continued to innovate and try various initiatives to better either an aspect of the same industry or something entirely unrelated.

In 1996, the venture capital frenzy for technology startups was in its nascent stage. Institutional investors, venture capital firms, and wealthy individuals, realizing the potential profits to be made, were beginning to promote entrepreneurship by establishing professional staffing and systems to solicit, analyze, and financially support founders of companies with new products or services with the potential to be successful.

Many educators in 1996 believed the necessary skills to start and sustain a business could not be taught, only learned through experience. Nevertheless, some universities such as Duke, MIT, and the University of Chicago initiated new studies to promote entrepreneurship alongside STEM courses. At best, those in the non-profit world could attend classes about completing grant applications or responding to government bids.

With my experience at Sphinx, one of my goals as Dean of the school for the performing arts, was to create and promote entrepreneurial studies for those in the Arts. I knew that our students needed to think strategically about their careers, specifically how to build a sustainable enterprise around their art form. The entrepreneurial skill set is not just helpful but critically important to our graduates' career paths.

According to the Strategic National Arts Alumni Project data for 2015–17, about half of arts graduates are self-employed. And eighty percent report having been self-employed at some point. Nine of ten arts alumni feel that entrepreneurial skills and critical thinking are important to their current work. As Dean and a musician, I know that all artists share a need to expose their work to others. The successful ones build a business to accomplish their goal.

The entrepreneurial infrastructure to support new technologies significantly matured after the turn of the century, no doubt driven by the obvious profit potential in a successful technology company. A 2022 Bloomberg Business article chronicled the emergence of more than 1,000 unicorns—startups with market values greater than $1 billion in 2022. There are over 20,000 venture capital funds investing more than $132 billion in 2020 in the US. alone. Almost every college and business school offer courses in entrepreneurial studies today, including the University of Michigan. The process of creation, scaling, and funding for a potentially profitable technology enterprise is developed, documented, and in place.

Entrepreneurship for an artist is necessarily different from a technology-based, profit-seeking business. Creativity is the product of the artist, and its value is subjective. The worth of a painting or a musical composition is not the cost of materials or the production time of the artist, but its resonance with individual viewers or listeners. While there are ways to leverage created art, i.e., mass replication in print or digital, their use can also lower the value of the product by over-supply and limited demand.

The obstacles facing a performance artist, or a musician are especially complex since their performance is finite, occurring at a specific time in a particular space. In most cases, the artist is indirectly connected with the consumer, delivering the art through the agency of a producer or director. In other words, actors and musicians sell their creativity like carpenters sell their skill and experience. A successful arts entrepreneurial program must meet the needs of all artists. For successful careers (however they might define it), students need to learn how to differentiate themselves from others in the market, control their expenses, raise funds, and find a market for what they create. In the current vernacular this process is often referred to as "branding."

Though I successfully birthed and scaled a non-profit organization blending music and social justice, I elected to move away from trying to build a career as a professional violinist. I recognize that gaining the actual experience as a solo artist to expand my skillset enough to stand out on the market was not my passion. I innovated, pivoted, and evolved my capacity while channeling my artistic creativity for and through others.

My decision was also inspired by exposure to new technology and its application in the arts world, which always excited and reignited my creative juices. As part of my portfolio career, I published a poetry collection (*They Said I Wasn't Really Black*), authored a children's book (*The 1st Adventure of Chilli Pepperz*), developed a spoken word performance arts series and had a successful critically reviewed digital art exhibit and much more. I had also written a published autobiography and more recently developed two internet shows that are impacting the world of performing arts and their intersection with science.

As a teacher and student, I know humans typically learn from the experiences of others. Sir Isaac Newton, the 17th-century physicist and mathematician credited with the discovery of gravity, acknowledged the contribution of others in his success: "If I have seen further, it is by standing on the shoulders of giants." "How great it would be," I thought, "if my students knew the experiences of other past and current artists developing a successful career?"

That inspiration led to the publication of *The Entrepreneurial Artist* in late 2019. The book was a compendium of life journeys of thirteen artists ranging from Shakespeare to jazz legend Wynton Marsalis and country singer Lee Greenwood and their success turning their talent into a sustainable business career. The book illustrated the business aspects that are necessarily required of creative types in building a career.

A commercial startup typically progresses through defined stages from beginning to sustainability, including business concept, the creation of the Minimum Viable Product (MVP) to test the market and scaling to reach financial success. Artists, since their product is their creativity, pursue a different, though similar path to career success:

- **Creativity.** Before an artist can create tangible expressions of their art—a painting, composition, poem, book, or performance—they must initially master the necessary technical skills. This mastery requires hours of study and practice to reach proficiency; Malcolm Gladwell, in his book *Outliers*, claims at least 10,000 hours is needed to become an expert in any skill. Only after mastery can the artist create something unique that is their own. The combination of mastery and creativity is the distinction between Jimi Hendrix and competent studio musicians, the listener's emotions during a Yo-Yo Ma's performance versus other cellists, or the paintings of Michelangelo to those of long forgotten Renaissance artists.
- **Monetization.** Everyone seeking to make a career of their art must identify an audience for their work, those willing to employ them, buy their physical output, or attend their performances. In other words, every successful artist is an entrepreneur, using the same business skills as a software CEO to exploit a market. As such, they must identify the needs and wants of potential customers, the prices they are willing to pay, when and how often. A successful artist needs to understand traditional distribution channels for their work and the possibilities of online opportunities.
- **Sustainability.** Unlike a manufacturer who replicates a product over and over to meet a growing demand, the artist typically deals with custom products created uniquely in a single time and space. Consequently, the product or service is the artist's capacity and capability to produce a series of output, each at least as desirable as the previous offering. Each creative field is populated with one-

hit wonders, a painting, song, book, or performance that captures an audience for a single moment never to be repeated. Even so, a competent entrepreneur can "milk the moment for all it is worth," extending an income stream as long as possible expecting that inspiration will return.

I believe that teachers in the performing arts must prepare their students for the inevitable ebbs and flows of a professional career, giving them the tools and examples to overcome the difficulties that they are likely to face in their artistic pursuits. The preparation includes their recognition that hard work and persistence is required and stepping out of one's comfort zone may be necessary.

I determined to use my experiences as an example to my students, testing the boundaries of my creativity and skills. The experience of writing *The Entrepreneurial Artist*, working with an agent, editor, and publisher, opened new avenues for me to pursue as an artist and teacher.

In addition to my affinity for music, I have long sought to expand the opportunities for people of color in arts and the community at large. Years before while working with Sphinx, I realized that leaders of color needed exposure to the community at large. Like many, I had been a long-time listener and supporter of public television and WTVS, Detroit's PBS station. I imagined a regular interview show where arts leaders, especially those of color could be seen and share their thoughts, ideas, and the initiatives they were working on with the community. The time presented itself in 2020 amid the COVID pandemic and the isolation measures that kept people in their homes. At the same time, Zoom, a technology software provider allowing multiple people to communicate simultaneously online, had replaced the need of an expensive studio setup for interviews. In connecting with the station, we decided to explore the idea of bringing the voices of top administrative leaders in the arts world to the forefront of the field.

Consequently, *Arts Engines*, the only arts show of its kind with an African-American host, went over the air on July 3, 2020, with my interview of Toni-Marie Montgomery, dean of the Bienen School of Music at Northwestern University. Today, the series is produced in partnership with and distributed by Detroit Public Television, Ovation TV, The Violin

Channel, and American Public Media and reaches two million viewers each week.

In the beginning, the station's participation was limited to airing the show. In effect, I had to learn how to produce a series of shows while building what would be a sustainable enterprise around it. At this stage in my career, I was fortunate to create a robust circle of creative partners, making the show for, by and with the field itself. Of course, I continued to raise institutional funding to ensure the show's future, as well. At that time, early in COVID, everyone was starting audio and video blogs competing online with television. I knew that many would sunset, so it was up to me to stand out and create an enduring product.

To build something to last, I had to solve different problems: How can I build a revenue model? How can I build partnerships and sustainable collaborations? How can I build distribution partners and build an audience? I am proud to say the program has been a greater success than I imagined and is now a case study for my students.

That fall, just a few months after the launch of *Arts Engines*, I began designing a similar program for science. *Artful Science* debuted on Detroit PBS on December 11, 2020. The basis of the program was to put art into science, i.e., make the sciences, technology, engineering, and math (STEM) more relevant, exciting, accessible, and entertaining through the prism of an artist. Every episode of *Artful Science* invites a leading scientist, technologist, engineer, or mathematician to delve into a relevant topic of interest to our audiences.

The first guest on the program, Mae Jemison, an engineer, physician, and the first Black woman to travel into space, succinctly explained the purpose of the show: "Sciences provide an understanding of a universal experience, Arts are a universal understanding of a personal experience ... they are both a part of us and a manifestation of the same thing ... the arts and sciences are avatars of human creativity."

The technological advances during the past twenty years offer new opportunities for artists to control their career. For centuries, painters depended on patrons then galleries to connect their work to the public. Poets and writers had commercial success only if they successfully convinced a publisher to print and promote their works. Event promoters, radio disc jockeys, and record producers limited musicians' access to the public. For years, the whims, prejudices, and politics of the gatekeepers determined the value of art and its creators' ability to survive.

The Internet and the development of social media shattered the walls between artists and their audiences. Anyone can establish a personal website and connect directly to potential patrons, customers, and fans. My personal website—https://www.aarondworkin.com—showcases multiple aspects of my life and art.

A plethora of independent sites provide multiple channels to advertise and sell artistic output—fine arts, music, literature—worldwide. The technical skills to exploit online audiences are not excessively complex, with instructions for specific tools readily available to anyone with an Internet connection.

For those who prefer to leave the technical details to others, websites like Fiverr, Freelancer, and Upwork access professional help on a global scale, ranging from website design and ghostwriting to songwriting and session musicians. Amazon, through its Kindle program, guides writers through the formatting for an eBook or print and then offers it to a worldwide audience for purchase.

Technology also offers new ways to explore one's artistic talents. The possibilities of digital art intrigued me, especially creating abstract visions combining symbols of music, history, people of color, and my family experiences. My creations are available through Saatchi Art, a leading online gallery.

To my delight, I discovered that my creative instincts, once awake and allowed to explore, took me in new directions, specifically marrying classical music, multimedia, and the spoken word to create dramatic expositions of contemporary subjects. The YouTube channel was a perfect low-cost media where video artists and new filmmakers could show their work.

In 2020, prior to the COVID shutdown, I wrote, scored, and narrated *The American Rhapsody*, a spoken-word piece that combined the words of America's first President, George Washington, and my own commentary. I performed the work with multiple major orchestras and greatly enjoyed the process. The work is set to Samuel Coleridge-Taylor's *Symphonic Variations on an African Air*. During that year, the extent of the tragedies wreaked by COVID overwhelmed me. The bravery and personal sacrifices of healthcare workers inspired me and kindled an obsession to tell their stories. That led to another project, which reanimated my attraction to the film medium. *An American Prophecy*, an hour-long film, which received an Emmy and multiple film festival distinctions, featured a cast of six real-life health workers across the US. Each cast member recites chapters from Khalil Gibran's *The Prophet* infused with the struggles and triumphs of their modern lives intertwined with pictures and a soundtrack that conveys the emotions of the moment. As the writer, director, and co-producer of the film, I tried to reflect the connection that all people share through time and culture.

My experiences as an entrepreneurial artist helps me communicate to my students that the limitations of tradition and custom in the art world, if not extinct, are transformed. With talent and effort, they can successfully pursue an artistic career without accepting the hardships of the "starving artist."

Over the past several years, I have been taking my spoken word and poetry journey into a new period of evolution. I originated the term *poet-journalism*, which I define as "the research, creation, and distribution of writing that evokes an emotional connection to news-related subjects or other relevant ideas utilizing elements of sound, meter, rhythm, and/or creative illustration." This has led to my latest collection of poetry entitled, "The Poetjournalist" and roles as the Poetjournalist-in-Residence of the City of Ann Arbor's Bicentennial, the Rodham Institute at George Washington University, Max and Marjorie Fisher Foundation, Charles H. Wright Museum of African-American History, Complexions Contemporary Ballet, Grantmakers in the Arts, Ovation TV, and Shar Music. Following in the entrepreneurial spirit that fueled the Sphinx Organization, I have founded The Institute for Poetjournalism to further this new discipline, which is designed to evoke a profound emotional connection to current events and relevant ideas, making the news experience informative, enlightening, and deeply human. I seek to revolutionize the way stories are told by infusing the time-honored tradition of storytelling with the urgency and veracity of modern journalism. Ultimately, through the Institute, I want to deliver news and ideas that resonate on a deeper emotional level, making consuming information a more impactful and memorable experience. I hope all of you, as readers, will consider joining

me on this newest adventure in the landscape of my evolving existence.
Following is the poem that started this movement.

Poetjournalist

I am the multi-colored tubes looping down the wall
Darting around outlets colored red and yellow
Snaking into veins of the elderly woman
Gasping from within the sheets of her COVID bed
Anchored by technology to the protocols of strangers
Dedicated to prolong the life she faces
Without the grip on her lover's wrist.

I am the passive man in straight black pants
With my untucked white shirt
Facing the column of tanks as their turrets salute my defiance
In Tiananmen Square before my movement falters
Showcasing my human right to exist
My freedom to persist.

I am the failed bank filled
With the empty paper and promises of people's dreams
Chosen for their inability to pay like the stray gazelle
On the Savanna as the lion poaches their prey
In the early morning mist.

I am the twin towers twisted metal
Exploding into crimson blossoms
Fading into black entrails and futures lost
Shading the horizon of our lives like
The passions of lovers before they fall into disarray
And forget what sparked their rise and hatred of their demise
And events regretted yet still reminisced.

I am the 9 minutes and 29 seconds
That a black man donning a black tank top
Felt the knee of dispassionate authority on his full-throated neck

Before his life with voice was ground into silence that was heard
And shook the sugar maple trees of Richmond Virginia
And broke the blue wall more than any afro pick with fist.

I am the grist for bottled water office talk
I assist the memory to feel the moments lost
I am the emotion of every story missed
I am the words the newsprint failed to list
I am our soul we must enlist.

I am the Poetjournalist.

CHAPTER 29

FAMILY AND MY BOYS

My reunion with my birth parents in 2001 was one of the most eventful moments of my life. I suspect only those who have experienced something similar can understand the emotional complexity accompanying such events. I realize that I was extremely fortunate to find my natural parents. I was luckier still in that they had subsequently married after my birth and adoption.

Many adoptees never learn of their roots, blocked by arcane privacy rules and hidden in insensitive bureaucracies. Fortunately, as science has discovered that genetics play a decisive role in our health, more information is now available to those seeking to connect with their natural families. Even so, reunions can be emotional, often traumatic, and sometimes disappointing.

My connection with my natural mother and younger sister (fourteen at the time) came with more ease. Despite the lack of a past between us, love and trust were more organic. Initially wary about meeting me, my father was more reserved and less willing to talk about his past and feelings. Dad was a regular drinker and marijuana user. I always felt those were ways in which his past and its burden allowed him to cope. In the evenings, his reluctance to communicate about personal issues was weakened. I learned what little I knew of his family and childhood, his experiences as a soldier, and his work as a hospital orderly in bits and pieces over the years.

Reconnecting with my birth parents was the end of a years-long quest to understand myself and the meaning of family. No matter how loving adoptive parents might be, an adopted child knows the relationship is different for children with their natural parents. They (and I) eventually deal with "why" they live with someone other than their biological father and mother. Probably like more adopted children, I rationalized why my birth parents were missing and fantasized about the circumstances leading to my being given up.

My adoptive parents—the nurture side of the genes versus environment debate—unquestionably influenced the person I am today. Though I resented and rebelled against their rules, my drive for achievement was birthed in my homes in New York City and Hershey. On the other hand, when I looked at my birth father, I saw and heard myself in the ways he moved and held his head, his voice, and his aloofness with strangers. I could imagine his parents, grandparents, and a long line of ancestors continuing in me and, subsequently, my children. They anchor my identity and gratify and content me in ways my adoptive family cannot. They are my family and the family inherited by my sons, Noah and Amani.

My birth father enjoyed connecting with his first grandson, Noah, who was barely two at the time, and called him "Poppy." He was naturally guarded in his words and actions with me, possibly due to his guilt for having to give me up and worries that I might blame him as an adult. I suspect, in some ways, he saw me in Noah, and being with his grandson somehow made up for the time we had lost as father and son. In the years between our first meeting and his death, the two of them spent hours watching and talking about sports, especially football. He had been a high school football star in Goshen, New York, in the late 1960s, and Noah always liked sports better than music. The three of them—Dad, Noah, and Amani—would watch games sitting together on the couch, laughing and talking with a certain sense of familial ease.

Having a real multi-generational family was something I had always dreamed about but never thought I would get. Reuniting with my birth parents closed the circle, and I was determined to instill in my sons the importance of family and the personal sense of stability and permanence it brings.

I had given up the Dean's position at the University of Michigan to rebuild my relationship with Noah, a teenager at the time, and to ensure that I would be there for Amani. Noah's mother and I had divorced when he was less than two years old, the beginning of a shared arrangement where he spent separate times living with his mother and me. For the most part, the format worked well, at least for Sherrie, his mother, and me.

In my memory, I don't recall any rebellion or complaints from Noah about the inconveniences and difficulties of fitting in two different households with different rules and expectations. At the time, I was absorbed in Sphinx and avoided thinking about the effect of the arrangement on Noah. In retrospect, I was naïve in not realizing the custody arrangement might cause him tremendous anxiety and resentment as he grew older.

I suppose the curse of driven people is that they are often oblivious to the events occurring around them. While focus is a necessary trait of an entrepreneur, it isolates them from others. Anything outside their immediate attention fades into the background, forgotten, not gone. My pursuit of professional goals, rewarded with occasional wins and recognition, dominated my attention, thoughts, and time. Whenever I felt guilt for missing dinner, attending a recital, or simply being with my boys, I quickly justified my absence by telling myself, "It's all for them. They will understand and appreciate my sacrifices when they're older."

My fantasy world crashed and burned when Noah announced that he did not want to talk with me or stay in our house any longer. I was stunned, hurt, and angry, a gamut of emotions that raced from one to another. I couldn't imagine what might have happened or anything that I had done leading to his rejection. As I reported, the two of us subsequently engaged in a long and painful process to recover the trust and love between us. I am determined that we will never go through a similar estrangement again. To avoid a similar disconnect with Amani, I've challenged how I parent, hopefully strengthening the link between us.

Having built an international organization and collected awards and recognition for my work, I know the difficulty and sacrifices necessary for professional success. I also know such achievements are pale imitations of genuine success—being a father who protects, nurtures and encourages his children in their life journeys.

Good parenting is simultaneously the most rewarding and challenging role anyone can undertake.

There are no rulebooks to follow, no tried-and-true methods to ensure a child matures into a competent, confident adult ready to take their place in the world. To become the father I wanted, needed to be, I spent hours of recollection and analysis of what I had said and done in the past with Noah, some of which was obvious, others not so much.

Absence in a child's life does the greatest harm. While physical absence is sometimes unavoidable, the more damaging impact is being there in person and somewhere else mentally or emotionally. "How many times," I wondered, "did I listen without hearing or look without seeing?"

Sometimes when we listen, we don't understand. Most of us do not realize the subtle changes that occur over time in our lives. We falsely assume that our children experience life as we did at their age. We don't recognize the broad societal changes from one generation to the next or the differences in the circumstances of our childhood. While my sons are biracial like me, our childhood circumstances and perspectives differ.

When Noah was seven or eight years old, he asked, "Daddy, am I Black?"

Taken by surprise, I didn't immediately answer. I recalled my questions as a Black child raised by two White parents. Due to his mother's genes of White skin, blond hair, and blue eyes, Noah is light-skinned, so visible racial characteristics are muted. I should have expected the question would arise for him as it did for me, especially since he split his time between a Black father and a White mother.

"What do you think?" I replied, knowing that an easy answer was not possible.

"I don't know. I'm not as dark as you or Poppy or as White as Mom. Most of my friends are White, but I look different from them. I don't know what I am," Noah said, a frown on his face.

"That is true," I said. "Your skin color is different from me and your mom's. That's because everyone inherits some things from their father and some things from their mother. You are part of both of us and our parents and grandparents. When you grow up and get married, your children will be part you and part your wife. I guess the best answer is that you are both black and White like me. We're like President Obama who has a black father and a White mother."

He looked at me, and I realized my answer did not satisfy him. I decided to try again.

"People around the world have different skin colors today, but all humans come from Africa, thousands of years ago, and they were black skinned. Dark skin acts like a sunscreen and protects the body from the harmful effects of ultraviolet radiation in sunshine. As they moved to other regions away from the equator and sun exposure was less, their skin colors gradually lightened. Today, there are people of all skin colors and shades around the world—black, brown, yellow, red."

"Poppy and Grammy are like your mother and me. I'm not as dark as Poppy because I'm part of him and part of Grammy. You aren't as dark as me because you are part me and part your mother. If you want to tell your friends that you are part Black, that's okay. However you want to describe yourself won't matter to your real friends."

I'm not sure whether Noah understood much of my explanation at the time, but it seemed to satisfy him. Our conversation morphed into stories about dinosaurs and troglodytes, which interested him much more than skin color. However, as he grew older, I knew further discussions about race and the Black experience would undoubtedly arise.

The rift between us was possibly due to his struggle for self-identification as much as rebellion over my parental restraints. The onset of puberty triggers psychological, emotional, and physical change. Social pressure is intense for those entering their teens. Everyone wants to be accepted by their peers, to feel an identity with a group. As I well knew, being different was an invitation to be bullied psychologically and physically. My responses to being an outsider in my family and the Hershey community ended with my adoptive parents sending me away to boarding school and a new start.

Noah's questions about race forced me to consider my feelings about race and what being Black meant. Though I struggled with being different, I never felt less than other kids due to my color. My adoptive parents never acted in any way or suggested that they considered me inferior to their natural son, my brother. They expected him to excel in academics and me to be a great musician, believing that I had a unique gift.

While neither was religious, they knew the historical Jewish persecution, especially the Holocaust. I am sure they had heard the unfair stereotypes that persisted for generations. Knowing that Blacks in America suffered the same ugliness and discrimination might have been a factor in their decision to adopt a biracial child. We never talked about it, preferring to ignore bias as if it did not exist. My cloistered childhood on the upper East side of New York City, the imposed long hours of music practice, and the lack of a television sheltered me from racial considerations for the most part.

My first experience with overt prejudice was in Hershey. Even then, I consider the harassment was due as much to my small size, glasses, a big Afro, and violin player as my blackness. In college, the overt racism from Sherrie's family enraged me, but I considered it to be a failing in them, not due to anything I did or didn't do.

That is not to say that I am a pacifist when I experience prejudice in real time. If I experience discrimination of any sort, I sometimes react in kind, either verbally or physically. No one familiar with American history can deny the injustices and persecution that Black people have suffered and continue to experience since the founding of the colonies.

The exploitation of enslaved Black people is a stain on the fabric of the country that may never be excised. While we may no longer be required to enter through the back door of cafes and restaurants for service, step off the sidewalk to let a White person pass, or ride in the back of the bus, a Black shopper is more likely to be followed and watched by a store clerk than given assistance. The fact that Black parents must counsel their children how to act when around police officers to be safe is abominable.

Dating across racial lines remains a taboo, something my natural father and I experienced. My birth father and mother fell in love during high school, hiding the relationship from her parents. When she became pregnant, her parents forced her to give me up for adoption. My father was forced into the Army to keep them apart. Even after their marriage, my mother and her family remained estranged. I had similar experiences with the parents of each of my wives' families, though we eventually reconciled to a degree.

While the memories of those days have faded over time, I will never understand or forgive them for the pain they caused their daughter. I still struggle with my guilt for having been its cause. How a parent can purposely send a child away is a question I cannot answer. I can't imagine any circumstance that might cause me to stop loving and supporting one of my children.

To me, racism is ignorance and evil. The idea of judging me or any group of people by skin color, the way we speak, or how much money we make is crazy and should never be tolerated. At the same time, my natural mother is White, as were my adoptive parents. Some of my best friends over my career are White. I know that most White people are not racist and feel, as I do, that each person deserves to be valued as an individual, not as a member of any group. I also have Black friends with prejudices against White people; in some cases, their feelings are more than justified. All races are guilty of subconscious stereotyping that underlies misunderstanding and permits irrational prejudices to thrive.

Our innate tendency to seek out those who look and act like us perpetuates and emphasizes the perceived differences between "us" and "them." The artificial barriers between races are only breached when good people of all colors recognize our similarities, not superficial differences.

As a father, I want the best for my children, the freedom to be whatever they dream and be judged on their merits. However, as a father of color, I recognize that their paths are more dangerous, more demanding than those in the majority. My biggest challenge is to prepare them to succeed in their lives and avoid the poisons of the past.

My oldest son is light-complected with curly brown hair. People meeting him might suspect that he might not be White but are unsure of his ancestry. When Noah was born, Tiger Woods was rewriting professional golf record books. Later in his life, Barack Obama was the President. Both men are biracial, the sons of Black men and lighter complected women. Tiger's mother is of Vietnamese ancestry, and Obama's mother is White. Their examples as biracial people make it easier for other mixed-race individuals to accept their heritage.

Even so, the whiter you are, the less likely you are to experience discrimination. Eight years younger and darker skinned than his brother, Amani also deals with his biracial identity. Their difference in color affects the way people treat them. While Noah is more likely to be considered "White," Amani is seen more "of color," though not necessarily Black. The circumstances in Amani's life have made him comfortable to embrace his Blackness. The distinction affects their choice of social groups, although both have friends of all races.

I am unsure whether anyone has the perfect solution to teach chil-

dren how to react to racial incidents. Cases like Trayvon Martin and
George Floyd disturb everyone, not just the Black community. Even so,
they are constant reminders of how far society needs to come for everyone to realize the American Dream. I'm glad that incidents of racism are
no longer swept under the rug as they were in the past. However, I'm also
sure to talk with my sons about what it means for them and their behavior to avoid a similar experience.

The intimacy of relationships between fathers and sons is a gift. In a
world as divisive and complex as ours, I have felt it a gift and a privilege
to help my sons process the complexities of life. Finding my birth parents
and subsequently losing my birth father brought up incredibly complex
feelings. My natural father passed in 2021, giving us a short time to make
up for the years we missed due to my adoption.

My father was a good, though complicated, man. Abandoned by his
father before birth, he was an only child raised by a single mother. By all
accounts, she gave him a safe and happy childhood by working a series of
minimum-wage jobs. As a teenager, he was a popular high school football
star in his hometown of Goshen, New York, an athlete whose accomplishments on the gridiron are still remembered by football fans in the area.

He intended to marry my mother when she became pregnant in high
school, but her parents had him arrested on a drummed-up charge and
sent my mother to an out-of-town Catholic unwed mothers' home. I
understood from my mother that he had desperately wanted custody of
his baby, whom he intended to raise with his mother's help. However,
fathers had little parental rights. My mom told me that he forgave her for
giving me up just before he and I met the first time. I think his guilt for
losing me stayed with him for years afterward.

At that time, local authorities offered young offenders the choice
between a criminal trial or joining the Armed Services. Either way, those
branded as "troublemakers" were exiled from the town. Dad joined the
Army and served his tour in Germany, luckily avoiding the jungles of
Vietnam with nearly 60,000 killed-in-action and more than 150,000
wounded in an unpopular and senseless war. Mom said he was changed,
more reserved, and less hopeful when he returned to the States.

Learning Dad's history through Mom's stories helped me understand him. I had struggled from my teenage years, estranged from my parents and trying to fit in at college. At that age, the world had taken everything from my father—his love, his child, his liberty. He lost his future and was helpless to change anything, no different than a slave on a cotton plantation seeing his wife and children sold. I sometimes wonder how anyone survives such loss.

The personal relationship between my father and me would have been described as "evolving." Knowing very little about either of my parents when we met, I was anxious to learn as much as possible, hoping that the information would finally salve the ache for acceptance I felt for so many years. At the time, I didn't realize how uncomfortable and intrusive my questions must have seemed to him, opening old wounds that had long since scarred over.

I believe his initial reluctance to meet me was his fear of being rejected and losing me a second time. In his mind, the pain of a second loss was too much to bear. Consequently, he was always guarded in our conversations, providing just a peek of his true feelings from time to time and only after his consumption of alcohol and marijuana. I am unsure whether he realized I did not blame him or my mother for my adoption. In truth, I was proud of him for returning to my mother and raising my sister. His honor and responsibility gave me the family I had always wanted.

When Dad returned from the Army, he found work as an orderly in the local hospital, a job he held for thirty years. My mother worked as a secretary with a local emergency management agency and also authored stories for the community newspapers. The two incomes provided a modest and comfortable lifestyle in the small town of Maybrook, New York, where they have lived.

Over the years, the relationship between my father and me deepened through regular family phone calls and visits during Christmases and the Fourths of July. Dad had his peculiarities, one being an addiction to the Jeopardy television show. If I happened to call when it was on, he was quick to complain, "My show is on," and hang up. Another was his aversion to physicians; he did not trust them and refused to get checkups. Dad ignored symptoms that sent other people to their doctors.

My dad had acute or closed-angle glaucoma, a condition where the pressure in the eye rises almost to bursting point. The disease destroys the cones and rods of the eye, eventually leading to blindness and disability. The disease is easily treatable with drops if caught early, but he ignored his worsening condition until too late. I realized later that the drinking and smoking marijuana might have been self-medication triggered by the severe eye pain and headaches caused by the disease. I can only imagine the daily pain he endured at work until he could get home with a drink and a joint.

My adoptive parents erred by always insisting on honesty in all cases, sometimes causing unnecessary hurt and anger over unimportant issues. My natural parents were the other extreme. I realized that my biological parents did not talk to each other about distressful things. My father's stubbornness and the lack of honesty between the two contributed to his disability and early death. His helplessness meant my mother and sister became full-time caretakers, a burden no one wants to place on their loved ones. But we never talked about it.

I suspected his health had become a problem when he began calling me that summer during the day to talk, something that never happened earlier. We had visited them earlier, and he seemed well, at least as well as one could be in his condition. Several weeks later, at the end of August, my mother called to say she thought he was dying. She was distraught and uncertain what to do since her attempts to take him to the hospital ended in vicious arguments. He refused to consider help of any kind.

He was finally admitted to the hospital against his will. He fell and was unable to rise. He lay on the floor, refusing any assistance from my mother or sister. Not knowing what else she might do, she called for an ambulance. He continued to fight the doctors and nurses, who finally sedated him for his own protection.

Afa and I immediately drove to New York to be with my natural family. We were there for several days as the doctors ran tests. Dad remained semi-conscious, unaware, I believe, of the frenzy around him and the presence of his loved ones. The diagnosis was multiple organ failure with a prognosis of impending death. He was moved to palliative care on September 9 for his final days, the end predicted in a week or so.

Before the emergency with my father, Afa and I needed to go to Florida and attend to some business matters. Believing he was stable, we left the same day intending to return several days later. Unfortunately, Dad died the following day on my birthday, September 11. We immediately returned to Maybrook to comfort my mother and sister.

Death affects people in different ways. My parents were married more than thirty-seven years, a length of time sufficient to rub away the rough edges of youth. Over the years, I think both parties in a long-term relationship have learned how to get along and accept the other party's peculiarities. Marriage is a life of compromise, but the important issues in the early years become trivial over time.

My mother was devastated by my father's death, but her sorrow was secondary to comforting my sister and me. In some ways, his passing had to come with some sense of relief from serving as his primary caretaker. A religious person, she was thankful that his long years of suffering were over. She knew the helplessness that made him dependent on her during the last years infuriated and embarrassed him.

The loss naturally affected my mother and sister, Maddie, more intensely than me. My mother and father shared a lifetime of memories, good and bad. My father's absence was felt in a thousand ways, from his empty chair in front of the television to cooking for one instead of two. The physical relief of no longer being a caretaker cannot overcome the feelings of being alone.

Maddie lost the father she knew and had lived with from birth. When Dad died, Maddie had to deal with her own loss and console her mother as best she could. Seeing the two of them—mother and daughter—together, each focusing on the other's needs, revealed the essence of the family to me. If nurtured from an early age, the bonds between family members are unique. Though I had not known my natural parents and sibling until I was a father, I felt the same connection to the two of them, a visceral link that emerges unbidden from the soul. Blood ties run deep because they wed us to the past and the future in ways associations do not.

My father was buried in Goshen with full military honors on September 15, 2021. The skies were clear with a light wind. Summer temperatures still lingered, getting to almost 100° in the afternoon. The funeral was intentionally small, limited to family and a few close friends. While the casket was closed for the funeral, Afa, Noah, Amani, and I had viewed the body during visitation the evening before.

I have mixed feelings about viewing the remains of loved ones before their burial. I know many believe that a final viewing helps them reconcile the loss, what psychologists call "closure." At the same time, a body lying in a casket bears little resemblance to the vibrant, breathing person I've known and loved. I sometimes struggle with the finality of death, at least for those remaining behind. Is there a heaven, another dimension where the deceased continue to exist? I don't know. I hope so, as it makes losing someone easier to bear.

Before the funeral, I worried about my boys' reaction. Poppy had been close to each boy, watching sports and sharing stories of past gridiron glories. He was also the first death of someone close either had experienced. I believed that I was prepared for the final chapter of his life. Meeting as adults for the first time, I did not share my mother and sister's emotional bonds or memories of my father. As we waited for the service to begin, my thoughts centered on my need to support them, especially Maddie, who was barely a teenager when we met the first time. As her "big brother," I intended to give her any support she might need.

As the service began, I was unprepared for the overwhelming sense of loss that engulfed me. My father, the genesis of my being, was gone. The finality of such moments is intense and indescribable. I blinked and drew a deep breath, struggling to keep my composure.

"There are so many questions I wanted to ask you, dad," I thought. "So many stories that will never be told. I waited so long to meet you, and now you're gone."

Afa, seeing my pain, leaned against me and covered my clenched hands with her own. My boys reached to touch my shoulder as silent sobs wracked my body. I raised both arms to surround them, the four of us clinging together amidst the tragedy of death. I don't think I've ever felt the reality of love as fiercely as that moment.

The military escort presented the American flag to my mother at the gravesite. She subsequently passed it to me as his only son. Today, it is one of my dearest possessions, and will someday pass it to one of my sons.

In retrospect, I believe my father's death deepened my relationship with my sons. While society expects women to be emotional, men learn to be stoic, to hide their emotions in a false impression of strength. The role-playing complicates the connection between fathers and sons. My grief and emotional display at my father's funeral revealed that men could hurt, cry, or be afraid without being weak or lesser. In turn, they can express their feelings to me without concerns that I might think less of them. In our vulnerability, we hold our authentic selves, to and for one another. In that space, I continue to find strength, true love, and gratitude.

ABOUT THE AUTHOR

Named a 2005 MacArthur Fellow, President Obama's first appointment to the National Council on the Arts and member of President Biden's Arts Policy Committee, Aaron P. Dworkin is former dean and current Professor of Arts Leadership & Entrepreneurship at the University of Michigan's School of Music, Theatre & Dance. Aaron is a best-selling writer and poetjournalist having authored his poetry collections, *The Poetjournalist* and *They Said I Wasn't Really Black*, along with other books including two memoirs, a children's book, a science-fiction novel, and *The Entrepreneurial Artist: Lessons from Highly Successful Creatives*. Aaron founded the Institute for Poetjournalism and originated the term *poetjournalism*, which is defined as "the research, creation, and distribution of writing that evokes an emotional connection to news-related subjects or other relevant ideas utilizing elements of sound, meter, rhythm, and/or creative illustration." He serves as Poetjournalist-in-Residence of the City of Ann Arbor's Bicentennial, the Rodham Institute, Fisher Foundation, Wright Museum of African-American History, Complexions Contemporary Ballet, Grantmakers in the Arts, Ovation TV, and Shar Music. Hailed by critics as "powerful," "stirring," "passionate and heroic," and "a tour de force," Aaron has performed his poetry as a prominent spoken-word artist, including at Carnegie Hall, Galapagos Theater in New York, Harvard University, Chautauqua, University of Michigan, Minneapolis Orchestra Hall, NJPAC, and the Wright Museum and Orchestra Hall in Detroit, among others, and is a member of the Academy of American Poets. He has been featured on The Today Show, NBC Nightly News, CNN, *Jet* magazine, and was named one of *Newsweek's* "15 People Who Make America Great." His Emmy award-winning film *An American Prophecy* was honored by numerous festivals, while his digital art project, *Fractured History*, has exhibited to rave reviews.

Aaron is also a leading social entrepreneur, having founded the globally-recognized Sphinx Organization, the leading arts organization with the mission of transforming lives through the power of diversity in the arts. He also serves as host of the nationally-broadcast Arts Engines show with a weekly viewership of over 100,000. Aaron is a member of the prestigious American Academy of Arts and Sciences and is the recipient of honors including the National Governors Association Distinguished Service to State Government Award, BET's History Makers in the Making Award, and Detroit Symphony Orchestra's Lifetime Achievement Award, and has been named *Detroit News*'s Michiganian of the Year and the National Black MBA's Entrepreneur of the Year.

A sought-after global thought leader and passionate advocate for diversity and inclusion, excellence in arts education, entrepreneurship, and leadership, as well as inclusion in the performing arts, Aaron is a frequent keynote speaker and lecturer at numerous universities and global arts, creativity, and technology conferences and is on the roster of the prestigious APB speakers bureau. He is a member of the Recording Academy (GRAMMYs) and has served on the Board of Directors or Advisory Boards for numerous influential arts organizations including the National Council on the Arts, Knight Foundation, National Association of Performing Arts Professionals, Avery Fisher Artist Program, Independent Sector, League of American Orchestras, Ann Arbor Area Foundation, and Michigan Theater and Chamber Music America. Having raised over $50 million for philanthropic causes, Aaron personifies creative leadership, entrepreneurship, and community service with an unwavering passion for the arts, diversity, and their role in society.

Aaron has a myriad of life interests including innovation, creativity, and human pair bonding, and is passionate about social impact, having founded a homeless organization and a literary magazine. He is an avid kayaker, poker aficionado, and boater, having captained multiple crossings of the Gulfstream. He is an explorer of the culinary arts and a consummate movie enthusiast, watching over 150 films every year. He is married to Afa Sadykhly Dworkin, a prominent international arts leader who serves as President and Artistic Director of the Sphinx Organization, and has two awesome sons, Noah Still and Amani Jaise.

INDEX

Note: "AD" is Aaron Dworkin.